River of Awareness

River of Awareness

Seeking the Wisdom of Love

Stephen Sims

NOVALIS

© 2009 Novalis Publishing Inc.

Cover: Blair Turner
Layout: Christiane Lemire

Business Offices:

Novalis Publishing Inc.
10 Lower Spadina Avenue, Suite 400
Toronto, Ontario, Canada
M5V 2Z2

Novalis Publishing Inc.
4475 Frontenac Street
Montréal, Québec, Canada
H2H 2S2

Phone: 1-800-387-7164
Fax: 1-800-204-4140
E-mail: books@novalis.ca
www.novalis.ca

A catalogue record for this book is available from Library
and Archives Canada.

ISBN: 978-2-89646-122-6

Printed in Canada.

Scripture quotations are from the Jerusalem Bible (Garden City, NY: Doubleday
and Company, Inc., 1966), except where noted otherwise.

We acknowledge the financial support of the Government of Canada through
the Book Publishing Industry Development Program (BPIDP) for our publishing activities.

5 4 3 2   12 11 10 09

To all those following the call of the river.

Contents

Part 4: Sacred Fire: Compassion

Prologue

I would like to live
Like a river flows
Carried by the surprise
Of its own unfolding.
John O'Donohue

the river

Somewhere inside me, a river seems to flow, inviting a journey into the deep unknown. The mysterious river images that dance through my mind issue a call to an epic adventure of self-discovery. Those images are of winding waters cutting through life's rugged terrain, of blissful waters encountering beauty, of black waters twisting through despair and the dark passages of time, of roaring waters crossing tumultuous thresholds of transformation, and of still waters calling on the deep. A river's flow may be tranquil or rushing, but there is no arresting the push of the current. Similarly, my life knows a momentum of change; it is a story that wants to keep moving forward all the time. The compelling summons from deep within is to find a truth of love that will set me free. I know the river journey itself to be my deep happiness.

River of Awareness asks the guiding question of how the heart is taught to love. It is a journal of spiritual themes, the offspring of a personal quest initiated when I first began to ponder what it means to live an authentic life. As you read through these pages, you will catch glimpses of the riverscape of my individual journey. My real goal, though, is to relate not the events of my outward life, but rather the challenges of an inner adventure of meaning.

Everywhere under the sun an intense longing for love beats inside human hearts. It is the common thread that weaves together all genders and generations, all cultures and creeds. Each of us desires to know joy, to be a source of delight for others, and to enjoy others delighting in us. Is it not gentle kindness that engenders such exuberance? In times of dark affliction, even a single exchange of compassion and gratitude bestows precious freedom. As the wisdom of unbounded love breaks into human consciousness, the sacred beauty of life awakens. Each of us is called to discover that beauty, and only a love that knows no limits responds to the cry of humankind for a light to dispel the growing global gloom.

As I have negotiated the labyrinth of my own fears, I have enjoyed the bliss of many wonderful river companions whose wisdom and gentle goodness have steadied my spirit. In our common quest for the good life, we have witnessed one another's learning, borne sorrow together, and, in a spirit of play, known much delight. I hold in my heart a boundless gratitude for the many breakthroughs and blessings of love we have shared.

I invite you, the reader, to journey with me along this *River of Awareness*, gleaning whatever wisdom is to be found. The themes of this book weave in circles, and the ideas and images are mixed and many. I trust that as you interact with the text, questions will arise: questions your own life wants to ask, questions to spark your own creative insight and meanings, questions to be thought about, sometimes over years. As we river together in a dialogue that celebrates awareness and compassion, may we learn to open our hearts to that love that leads us into the true rapture of being.

a river map

River of Awareness is divided into four parts. The elements of water, air, earth, and fire depict the broad motifs within the human adventure: journey, integrity, darkness, and compassion.

Our central focus is the quest for that wisdom that empowers true transformation.

We first reflect on the movement of life, from becoming to becoming, and the challenges of negotiating "Live Water" (part 1). We are beckoned to identify and give expression to our unique talents, but often resist our own heroism – courage is begged that we might dive into deep uncharted waters. How do we educate spiritual imagination to shape the stories our lives want to write? The river bends, and we turn to explore ways by which we appropriate genuine awareness. Our journey of wholeness describes an "Inspired Quest" (part 2) that relies on keen self-presence, critical insight, and decisive action to awaken the power of our own determination. Emotional literacy works in tandem with our physical and spiritual well-being. There are many perilous trials to face along the "Mud Path" (part 3) of ethical disintegration and physical decay. This section calls upon us to ponder how we are freed from the grip of darkness and enabled to embrace the promise of a new dawn. Through renouncing violence and expanding our horizons of moral meaning, we realize the truth of love in our own hearts, allowing us to bring light to a sorrowful world. As we become more ecoliterate, we experience a wider harmony – an abiding friendship with all life. Once the "Sacred Fire" (part 4) of compassion and gratitude is ignited, we find a deep generosity of spirit within ourselves, authentic identity, and our true belonging.

Part 1

Live Water: Journey

1
The Pure River ...
Path of Awareness and Love

Friend, wake up! Why do you go on sleeping?
The night is over – do you want to lose the day the same way?
... O friend, I love you, think this over carefully!
If you are in love, then why are you asleep?
    Kabir

Every blade of grass has an angel that bends over it and whispers: grow, grow.
    The Talmud

The world may be finite or infinite, round or square, this way
or that way,
but we must love it.
It suffers and we must seek to relieve its suffering,
through ourselves and through others,
teaching it to love and to be happy in the love it learns.
Our bodies and our whole being flow towards death;
but matter flows towards life, and life towards consciousness,
and consciousness towards love and rapture.
    Petru Dumitru, *Incognito*

awakenings

A strong, hot summer wind was blowing in from the southeast, and huge waves pounded the Lake Simcoe shoreline. The full moon made the wet pebbles at the water's edge sparkle in the night. I was set to leave my homeland in a matter of days, and a horrible dread of the unknown arose within me. I felt like I was falling into an abyss. "Why are you going away?" I asked myself over and over. I had more doubts than ever about my decision to travel. On this night in late July, as I paced barefoot along the beach, there seemed to be no answer to the question, no resolution to my uncomfortable inner angst.

A year earlier, when my days as a university student came to a close, I became aware of a growing sense of displacement. I had graduated with awards and the promise of an outstanding future; though my situation looked pretty good on the outside, in truth, I was hurting a lot. The chaos of my interior world seemed to go hand in hand with my struggle to find clarity about young adult identity. During that first year after graduation, I taught an elementary school class of 29 kids whom I adored. All the while, I felt haunted by early childhood trauma and debilitating feelings of inferiority, and my personal confusion remained. The source of my inner conflict was mostly a mystery to me, buried somewhere in the recesses of the unconscious. With my emotions in turmoil, I ended up with an anxiety disorder and turned to alcohol for relief. At that point, I determined to head off around the world, and chose Australia as my first destination. The decision to escape Canada was perhaps based on the hope of discovering a geographic cure of some kind. Whatever the reasons, this marked the beginning of the adventure of my young adult life. I had just turned 22. I did not then understand that something beautiful was struggling to be born.

Indeed, a crisis of darkness often heralds the dawn of a new light. At the Orillia railway station I waved a sad farewell to my parents as I boarded *The Canadian*, a train that was to carry me on a long journey through northern Ontario across the prairie provinces to the west coast. Despite the dark force of my fears, I sensed a new wind blowing through my soul. From Vancouver I travelled to Hawaii, then on to Fiji. In the middle of the night, now almost two weeks after my moonlit walk on Lake Simcoe shores, I disembarked onto this small island in the southern hemisphere, and stared into the expansive nocturnal sky. I can attest to what I have since heard, that, while the stars in the northern hemisphere glow, those in the south blaze. I stood there awestruck, keenly sensing that my destiny was somehow tied into the grandeur of the stars. I was to live outside Canada for the next couple of years. During that time away, I had two pivotal experiences of awakening, two very defining moments.

The first breakthrough happened during my week-long stay in this mid-Pacific paradise. As I walked the sandy beaches, I felt a loneliness as deep as the ocean itself. As I confronted my own confused mental landscape, I was tossed back and forth between desolation and hope, and my thoughts wandered in many directions. Eventually, my mind came to focus on the question of happiness.

My sense was that life held an extraordinary potential for contentment, and that a wisdom of happiness could be found. A further insight suggested that my happiness would be more defined from the inside out than from the outside in. I observed that some people whose needs in life were well met were still very unhappy. Yet others, who suffered hardships of one kind or another, seemed to experience enduring fulfillment. Thus it became clear to me that happiness did not result from the absence of suffering, but rather depended on an ability to engage it creatively and negotiate its redemption. The good life, I then concluded, was not based on an accumulation of pleasures, power, and possessions; in fact, I knew that my obsession with certain gratifications at times drove me completely crazy.

I posed a further question to myself. Whom do I know who is genuinely happy? As certain individuals began to flash through my mind's eye, an unexpected insight intruded out of the blue: happiness belongs to those whose attention is turned towards the happiness of others, not their own. Right then I knew this to be the essential clue. A voice from somewhere inside me spoke: "Make your life an adventure of love." Like a fever that suddenly breaks, clouds of confusion lifted. The golden rule hit me at heart level. True peace is not about getting, but about giving. This new revelation of meaning allowed me to imagine my path into life in terms that transcended my personal ego drives. With this spiritual initiation, I felt ready to draw new maps of meaning.

I taught high school in Australia for a year and a half, in which I found much delight and new self-confidence. I drank a little too much beer, but slowly mustered the courage to meet my fears and ask for help. Many seeds of awareness were quietly planted, and I decided to head back to Canada. My homebound journey took four months: first traversing the Australian outback, then trekking through Southeast Asia, and finally catching an 11,000-mile bus ride from Kathmandu to London.

In Timor and Indonesia, I had my first taste of Third World poverty, and was shaken by the widespread squalor I witnessed. I travelled by railroad through the island of Java, and as my train slowly worked its way into the heart of Djakarta, I beheld the extreme destitution of those living alongside the rail tracks. Immersed into worlds so foreign to my own, I felt increasingly overwhelmed. This set the stage for a second defining moment, which occurred on my day of entry into India.

As I crossed a busy downtown intersection in Calcutta, a small girl grabbed onto one of my pant legs. She clutched my shin and stared up with wide eyes to catch my terrified gaze. Her eyes, which seemed to contain the suffering of the entire sub-continent of India, silently begged for love. I did not know how to answer her suffering. But I knew that my quest for meaning became fully alive in that sacred encounter.

Days later, in Nepal, as I stood watching the sun rise over Mount Everest, I was at a loss about how to reconcile the stark contrast of the mountain grandeur with the squalor of the urban ghettos. As the morning sunlight slid down the snowy Himalayan slopes and floodlit the lower valleys, I felt the presence of the young girl in Calcutta whose sorrowful eyes had invited me to discover what it means to be authentically human. What came to mind was Mahatma Gandhi's suggestion that we envision the face of the poorest and the weakest person we have ever seen, and reflect whether the next step we take in life will help that person restore control over her or his own destiny. That little girl represented such a person for me; ironically, it was she who helped me get a sense of my destiny. The encounter at the Calcutta intersection brought me the realization that compassion puts first those whom society puts last. With profound gratitude, I often remember that anonymous child, and thank her for teaching my heart to open.

where are you going?

I returned to India twice, at the ages of 26 and 48, and spent two six-month sojourns in the eastern Himalayas. My homes were in Darjeeling and Kalimpong, lying in a subtropical region whose rugged mountain beauty is matched perfectly by the rugged gentleness of its inhabitants. One of the striking characteristics of that northern region is the Tista (Tee-sta) River, whose features never failed to take my breath away. The Tista is often referred to as "the pure river," and in the dry season of the monsoon climate, its waters are an exquisite emerald descending rapidly from a source 17,000 feet above sea level. The Tista River is pure motion. Like all rivers, it keeps moving along, having somewhere it wants to go. The Tista's waters are alive and turbulent. They race their way downward between high banks to the plains, where they flatten and widen and then gently push along to meet the mighty Brahmaputra River in Bangladesh.

Like the ever-changing Tista River, human existence is in perpetual motion. Perhaps each of us can relate in some way to this image of a pulsing river whose fast-moving waters never let up. The French expression for whitewater is *eau vive*, which means "live water." The incessant force of evolution pushes ever onward, and despite our best efforts at maintaining the status quo we never stay the same. In truth, our unfulfilled longings leave us feeling somewhat restless most of the time. Physical reality undergoes continual change, and human consciousness exists in an unstable state of flux. Likewise, human relationships are built on somewhat shifting sands, appearing and then disappearing. As our shared meanings converge and diverge, we find our values undergoing steady revision. Certainly, life is anything but static.

A unique journey awaits each of us. As every river has its own singular mystery, so every human life holds a hidden destiny. Rivers, as they twist and turn, create a path of surprise: waterfalls, unexpected whirlpools, a variation of topographical features, the different light reflections of sun and moon, and always the unknown around every next bend. Human existence is much like a riverscape: steeped in mystery, always catching us somewhat by surprise. The Lepcha, a Himalayan tribe, refer to the Tista River as "Ti-Satha," which means "Where are you going?" This is a simple yet profound question that excites the curiosity of my spirit. I find the restless longings of my heart mirrored in the pulse of flowing waters – the vitality of a river seems to hold the energy of aspiration, ever inviting an adventure of self-discovery that requires only my willing consent.

the adventure of becoming

I recall a friend whose tear-filled eyes met mine, and, out of deep angst, uttered, "I'm aching to move on!" I, too, meet that ache of deep longing inside myself. Though the tale of our lives sometimes gets stuck, or deviates from its true course, nevertheless, each of us is given a mandate for maturation and evolution. There seems to be a never-ending sequence of transformations to undergo and thresholds to cross in life's steady thrust towards more life. While I have the capacity to go against that thrust, to refuse passage and resist the process, my true desire is to move ever onwards on a journey of awakening. In this spirit, the French Jesuit Teilhard de Chardin, writing in the *Hymn of the Universe*, prays for "... a blessed desire to go on advancing, discovering, fashioning and experiencing the world ... ."[1]

I am fond of the writings of Hermann Hesse, particularly his classic tale of Siddhartha. This story elucidates the journey motif, and has been instrumental in helping me come to appreciate both the rigorous challenge of responding to the call of authenticity, as well as the need to be patient with the awakening process. Most of all, Siddhartha teaches the importance of self-knowledge in cutting through spiritual pride, desire, hostility, and all the illusions of my ego-striving. This moving narrative tells the tale of a man in the various stages of life crossing over different thresholds of awareness. On the Samana path (a spiritual track of meditation, fasting, abandonment of the body), Siddhartha's initial quest for self-realization lacked authenticity and actually took him deeper into self-deception and pride. As he later acknowledged, it missed the mark of his true self. Going to the other extreme, Siddhartha plunged into a life of folly, where he was to learn more hard lessons. "Slowly, like moisture entering the dying tree trunk, slowly filling and rotting it, so did the world and inertia creep into Siddhartha's soul; it slowly filled his soul, made it heavy, made it tired, sent it to sleep."[2] After years of this folly, Siddhartha knew that the song of life had died in his heart. Through deep disillusionment and sorrow, Siddhartha came to realize that he was no longer able to love. This spoke the truth of his malaise.

Hesse describes Siddhartha's separation from the weariness of his illusions, from his attachment to teachers and doctrines, from his addiction to pleasures, and from idleness and acquisitiveness. We sense the intensity and momentum of the deep transformations taking place within him. Siddhartha learned with his eyes, heart, and stomach as well as his intellect. As he yielded to his destiny, new self-understanding emerged in the midst of desolation. Siddhartha's downward spiral into arrogance, misery, and despair slowly opened his soul to a deep stillness. With a new capacity to listen and be receptive, he discovered "… a secret art of thinking, feeling and breathing thoughts of unity at every moment of life."[3] In a final encounter with his dear friend, Siddhartha expounded on what he had learned: "It seems to me, Govinda, that love is the most important thing in the world. ... I think it is only important to love the world, not to despise it, not for us to hate each other, but to be able to regard the world and ourselves and all beings with love, admiration and respect."[4]

stable instability

I relate well to the journey motif seen in Siddhartha's life. I love whitewater canoeing, which has taught me how to dance with change. In this sport, one needs to perfect the art of eddying in order to negotiate swift-moving rivers. An eddy is a small whirlpool of water (or wind, fog, or dust) where the river bends back on itself. Where waters rush downstream, there's a corresponding upstream flow beside the stronger current. As downstream water impacts on and slips past a rock, some of the water spins around behind the rock and forms a back current. Canoeists use the jargon of "eddy in" and "eddy out" to describe a technique to stabilize oneself in fast waters. If you ever observe skilled kayakers manoeuvring in rapids, you will see how they throw themselves into the tumultuous flow of waters, and then tuck themselves back into an eddy. A split second later, they eddy out again into wild water, then eddy in behind another rock, following back currents caused by the configuration of the riverbed and banks. This is how they achieve a remarkable mastery, eddying in and out and in and out, continually stabilizing their canoes or kayaks in the flux of the river. As they negotiate each set of rapids, they succeed by pacing themselves carefully.

This image of eddying has demonstrated to me the prudence of pacing myself in the haste of task-driven life. A good stress-and-relaxation rhythm is essential both on fast-moving rivers and in fast-paced living. I never stop needing pockets of stillness in which to recollect my strength and wits. It is a question of striking the right balance between extroversion and introversion, and of holding the delicate tension between stability and change.

Without enough downtime, reckless speed inevitably brings me some measure of ruin, and unnecessary wear and tear. A parallel instruction came to me by way of a first-aid course, where I was taught the motto "Hurry slowly!"

What I have learned is the importance of holding a delicate tension between protection and vulnerability. The Jewish religious philosopher Avram Davis observes that stability and flux are opposite sides of the same coin. In *The Way of the Flame*, he refers to a central Jewish metaphor to capture the movement of life: "There is ebb and flow, but this flux, like a box within a box, resides within stability, and that stability in turn resides within flux, which resides within stability, and so on."[5] By its very nature, movement is destabilizing and involves varying degrees of vulnerability. The goal in life is not to avoid motion, but rather to move with a measure of steadiness or a minimum of commotion. Sound growth requires a stable instability. Inspired by this image, I often ponder how best to secure myself in the flux of change without compromising the forward momentum of my growth.

mud and sky

From time to time, I observe myself jockeying back and forth between feelings of omnipotence and powerlessness, somewhere along a continuum between hope and defeat. I once read these words on a wall calendar: "Determination is said to be finding your limits, and then exceeding them." To me, this two-sided coin suggests the paradox of my authentic limitations meeting my unlimited potential. Though my feet are made of clay, at the same time, my spirit wants to soar. I call this the tension between mud and sky.

Many argue that we can achieve whatever we want, that the sky is the limit, and that nothing is out of our reach. On occasion, all of us do experience a surge of power, a confidence in the realization of our wildest dreams. We taste our possibilities, and at times achieve the unimaginable. I know this to be true, for every once in a while, my "perfection" catches me somewhat by surprise.

On the other hand, any exploration of the unlimited ought to be grounded in the awareness of counterpoints of confinement. Beyond false bravado lies the need to respect our true limits. On a crumbling brick wall in inner-city Montreal, the phrase "nous sommes tous prisonniers" (we are all prisoners) was splashed with red paint in large lettering. It would not be too difficult for most of us to identify with those words, for we all experience those times of defeat when life brings us to our knees. Though hungering for freedom, we nevertheless find ourselves trapped in fear and fatigue, guilt and the grim drudgery of everydayness, and sometimes very real desperation. Such bondage to the earth inhibits the release of our spiritual potential, and sets up a face-off inside us between gravity and grace.

This is not to say that we should argue for our limitations, nor avoid taking on the challenge of excellence. I sense that I am frequently encumbered more by faulty beliefs than by actual limitations. One of the largest limiting factors is the belief that we cannot change. At the root of not being able to heal lies a core conviction about the impossibility of creating new possibility. And because the world seems more fixed than fluid, we do not co-operate with change. Or perhaps, not knowing how to change, we believe we cannot.

The serenity prayer highlights the interplay between will and surrender. "God grant me the serenity to accept the things I cannot change, the courage to change the things I can, and the wisdom to know the difference." This well-known prayer prays for the grace to let what is be, and the boldness to create what can be. It further invokes the power to differentiate clearly between what can and cannot be changed. This invocation, I find, brings a measure of peace, inviting me to respect particular givens, yet also dare my dreams.

It is said, "You can't push the river." The image of a river's indifference has struck me often: rivers go where they go, and flow in their own way. They show absolutely no mercy, though canoeists refer to some sets of rapids as more forgiving than others. Essentially, the art of "rivering" consists in knowing how to respond to rivers just as they are, with their distinct water dynamics and specific rock configurations. At some point during my whitewater initiation, it dawned on me that the river was simply being itself, and that all the rocks were exactly where they were supposed to be.

Proactivity points to personal power. I am subject to certain conditions and conditioning, but am not solely at the mercy of fate. In each moment I give shape to my life through my responses to the givens, and thus discover a measured power. Though frustrated by limiting circumstances, the plea of the serenity prayer is for a power of determination to take me out of the grip of powerlessness, so as to find the right equilibrium between effort and surrender. In the interplay between making-it-happen and letting-it-happen, somewhere a balance can be found. Paradoxically, as I learn to accept my limits, I can better embrace my unlimited potential.

A degree of freedom comes when we move from reaction to action. My dad must have told me a thousand times, "Act, don't react!" Every time he said it, I had a strong "reaction." He wanted me to understand that I was giving my personal power away. His basic claim was that action sources a response, while reaction fails to do so. Over some external conditions and inner psychic determinisms we have absolutely no control, yet the attainment of freedom rests on an ability to come into possession of our power of self-determination. Personal strength, I would learn in time, was a question of asserting myself from the inside out, rather than being defined from the outside in.

We have to remember that the change process begins with ourselves. A measure of frustration dissolves when we give up our manipulations and our need to control others. In relationships, knowing the boundary between what is me and what is not-me is of paramount importance. It is futile to try to change other people; our unacceptance of them only breeds resistance and opposition. In truth, others grow best in the soil of our love and consciousness, and the work that we do on ourselves makes that soil more fertile. In this way, we enable others to release their own potential. As power struggles and antagonisms are dismantled, new synergies begin to open up, and change comes about.

passionate rivering

Derived from the Greek *ek-stasis*, the word "ecstasy" has many connotations. It suggests feelings of bliss or beatitude, or the ending of a static situation. Stasis is stagnation, a dull state, a condition of boredom. It is found in the ditchwater of life-denial, where development is resisted and desolation results. Ecstasy is the experience of getting unstuck, moving from a standstill. It is the thrill of movement and change, the pulse of expanding one's horizons of possibility. It is the alive energy of being on a river adventure.

As we meet our inner emptiness and taste human vulnerability, we discover necessity, a passionate desire for higher integrity. Author and psychotherapist Robert Jingen Gunn, in *Journeys into Emptiness*, identifies four elements requisite for the journey to wholeness: a container, a teacher, a community, and a practice. The container is a place of safety and nurturance, a context that gives us a grounding, that protects and supports our story. Our psychological mentors and spiritual teachers guide the learning process, confront our evasions, and help us find a language of wisdom. They witness our journey. Community is where we learn to give and receive, where we learn to trust and become interdependent. We do not grow in isolation. A practice includes all the things we do to cultivate awareness, deepen our inner connection, and respond to the demands of authentic life. Gunn concludes, "... practicing the edge means constantly paying attention to our hopes, fears and dreams and pushing ourselves to whatever is 'next.' Practicing the edge requires constantly leaving behind the known, secure and familiar for the unknown that seems, somehow, to beckon."[6]

Human frustration pushes towards freedom and fulfillment. There arises a determination that becomes indispensable to the journey towards the integrity for which we hunger. To learn the art of passionate rivering requires a dance of awareness and serenity in moving waters. The journey motif beckons us to go beyond the present moment, with its inherent limitations, into new consciousness and creativity. Learning is true celebration, and in the adventure of becoming, the capacity to paddle the river is powered by passion.

voices of hope

During a second Himalayan sojourn, I visited Gangtok, the capital of Sikkim in the far north of India. Gangtok, a principal centre of commerce on the old trade route between China and India, lies 7,000 feet above sea level on a threshold to the high Tibetan plateau. My visit happened to coincide with National Children's Day, and I found my way to an open-air stadium where various children's groups were to stage a colourful set of artistic and musical performances. As the program neared its finale, a special introduction was given to the Gandhi Youth Ashram. Everyone was spellbound as the violins and voices of 30 destitute children from Kalimpong filled the Himalayan air with perfect rhapsody.

These young performers were gathered from the very poorest families, born of illiterate "coolie" parents condemned to poverty and toil. In a small Canadian-sponsored school, the children were being offered an education denied their elders, and the opportunity to develop their musical talents. As I watched their performance, the contrasting images of outer poverty and inner giftedness were most striking. The next day I picnicked with these youngsters on the banks of the Tista, and found myself enchanted in their spirited company. It was a joy to savour the exuberance of destitute children who had come alive in the affirmation of their talented potentials. Though born into hunger and human desperation, their small bodies were filled with music. Voices of hope emerging out of squalor, a radiance of beauty born out of poverty, flowers growing out of mud: these children became for me icons of promise, the image of that potential for development that invites wounded humanity to be lifted to noble life.

As a young adult, 22 years earlier, I had had an opportunity to live and work in northeastern India. That first encounter with Third World poverty awakened in me a new depth of meaning. I discovered that compassion is the way in which we are truly at home in the universe, and that there was an adventure awaiting my life. Now, years later, as I chewed my hard-boiled egg and chapatti, and watched the children splash and frolic in the icy waters of the emerald Tista under a deep blue Himalayan sky, I was again reminded of the summons of life: to awaken beauty, to develop talent and awareness, and to bring compassion to the sorrow of our world. This was a fresh invitation to me to play a part in alleviating human suffering.

2
Tension and Chaos …
Yourself to Discover

The temptation to live on the surface of life is clear enough. When we are pulled deeply into something, even love, it hurts and opens us up to great suffering. But the willingness to open to depth is the chief way in which dignity and purpose return to life … the chief symptom of our culture is banality. The chief antidote to banality is the willingness to accept the transformative suffering of depth.

James Hollis, *Creating a Life*

And when I had to stop my exploration because the path faded beneath my steps, I found a bottomless abyss at my feet, and out of it comes – arising I know not from where – the current which I dare to call my life.

Pierre Teilhard de Chardin, *The Divine Milieu*

There is a critical point in the increasing autonomy of the subject. It is reached when the subject finds out for him[her]self that it is up to him[her]self to decide what he[she] is to make of him[her]self.

Bernard Lonergan, *Existenz and Aggiornamento*

river of change

My heart beat rapidly as I walked into the principal's office, and I knew why. I was right at the edge, ready to jump. "Sir," I said with a slight quivering in my voice, "after a lot of agonized soul-searching I have come to the decision to leave professional teaching. I'm sorry to put you through this. I regret the disruption I am causing." I was 27, and this was the period following the return from my first six-month sojourn in India. My teaching position was at an inner-city Montreal school, and it was then just a little over two months into the academic year.

I was worried the students would feel very betrayed by my decision to leave. Knowing how difficult it would be to explain my departure, I argued to myself that what was best for me would also be best for them.

My ego was in for a beating. How could I make others understand? Everyone would have their own interpretations; I was particularly worried about parental disapproval. In letting go of my teaching position, I was discarding my security and standing once more at the brink of the fearful unknown. Once again it seemed that I was not able to get my life together – I was meeting grief, self-doubt, and fear inside myself. But, while on one level my sense of achievement was slipping, on another I knew that I was being asked to submit my ego to a larger truth, and to obey my life not as I had neatly planned it but rather as it wanted to express itself. A spirit of humility was needed to help me surrender to my calling – to a new refinement of meaning, and to a further elucidation of the creative tasks that awaited my future.

The principal was a man I was inclined to trust, someone easy to level with. Listening with remarkable compassion and understanding, he kindly affirmed the quality of care I had brought to my teaching, yet put forth absolutely no resistance to my decision. The principal, in fact, encouraged the change. I felt somewhat relieved, happy to receive his blessing. Yet he did have words of caution: "Such a breach of contract means that you will be barred from the teaching profession within the province of Québec for all time – you will have to pay a price." I made the leap, said my goodbyes, and shared some tears with my students.

My time in India had left its mark, some culture shock in reverse. I knew that my bliss was not in school curricula and examination grading. I was negotiating a whole gamut of feeling and a mood of deep disenchantment. It became necessary for me to redefine my understanding of what it meant to be a teacher. To me, the educational system lacked heart and put its focus more on a mind-made world. Learning, I believed, needed to be more attuned to emotions and the world inside ourselves: less logical, more soulful, less competitive, more relational. I deeply longed to help create educational opportunities that would reveal the essence of life to be an adventure in learning to love.

This discontent within myself pointed to the need to live my life in a different way. I began to see how the time I spent on the Asian subcontinent had marked a rite of passage into a new pattern of meaning. India had effected a more profound change in me than my conscious mind had acknowledged. Having been exposed to extreme human suffering, I felt myself drawn towards a new path of service, and indeed, new seeds of compassion seemed to be germinating.

I had no idea what was going to happen from then on. To stay in the same place would have been to compromise the truth of my calling. Beyond a narrow world of illusory security lay the unpredictable, the secret and sacred unknown towards which love was drawing me. This initiatory process invited me to let go of my ego's need for knowable patterns and control, and to allow my life to be ordered from within.

What followed was a series of extraordinary opportunities to bring my talents to bear in different areas of community organizing, awareness education, and spirituality. With each new social project came a fresh set of tests and trials.

going to the reef

Psychologist Eda LeShan, in *Divine Discontent*, suggests that we are required to go out to the reef from time to time, and that staying in a tight shell is a metaphor for stagnation. She tells this story:

> At a dinner party many years ago, I sat next to a man who was an oceanographer. At one point he asked me if I had ever wondered why lobsters could weigh one pound,

three pounds, even ten pounds when they had such a hard shell – how could they grow? I had to tell him this was a problem that was not very high on my list of priorities. He smiled and proceeded to tell me that when a lobster becomes crowded in its shell and can't grow anymore, by instinct it travels out to some place in the sea, hoping for relative safety, and begins to shed its shell. It is a terribly dangerous process – the lobster has to risk its life, because once it becomes naked, vulnerable, it can be dashed against a reef or eaten by another lobster or fish. But that is the only way it can grow.[7]

In response to the soul's longings, the undiscovered self seeks deeper meaning and demands change. The summons of life is ever to go on growing, to let go of attachments and leap over fear into new possibility. Change inevitably presents itself as an ordeal that engenders a degree of confusion and chaos. Even so, the status quo must be challenged over and over, allowing the human spirit to move ever forward. Each leap of faith involves a dying and a birth. The cost of any defence against development is boredom and banality, and the emptiness of meaning. Prolonged resistance to change creates an impasse in the psyche, a tension that sooner or later has to give. To dare the future requires a willingness to relinquish tired habits of thinking and feeling, and to allow values to outgrow their narrow confinements. Although having to endure the transitional chaos of change, we are rewarded with an increase of freedom.

Knowing when it is time to let go and leap forward comes from right discernment. Clinging and addictive behaviours are the result of a refusal to go to the reef. With excessive attachment to any matrix, we are reticent to break the bond with that which offers us comfort and sure security. Jungian analyst and writer James Hollis, in *Under Saturn's Shadow*, speaks of the extraordinary power of the mother complex, the enormous pull towards dependency in all of us. In times past, rites of initiation helped break these attachments to the comfort and nurturance of mother and hearth. Adolescents went through a physical separation, a staged kidnapping perhaps, and experienced a symbolic death of childhood dependency, which sometimes included a name change. During this ordeal, spiritual teachings were offered to make wisdom and energy available to them for the journey of adult life. In the modern age, this threshold is more difficult to negotiate without these rites of passage. When I think back on the transitions of my past, I recognize the large gaps in my awareness and see how much I lacked sound mentoring to support my maturation process.

The readiness for further growth springs from a tension between what is and what is yet to be. When the time comes to move forward, we are guided by our interests and attractions. A natural flow of charged psychic energy opens up the possibilities of life not yet entertained, revealing new spiritual directions. This growth tension, in a sense, pushes us beyond the status quo into change. Mythology scholar Joseph Campbell describes the pull that draws us as a counterpoint to the ego's posture:

> If you realize what the real problem is – losing yourself, giving yourself to some higher end, or to another – you realize that this itself is the ultimate trial. When we quit thinking primarily about ourselves and our own self-preservation, we undergo a truly heroic transformation of consciousness. And what all the myths have to deal with is transformations of one kind or another. You have been thinking one way, you now have to think a different way.[8]

Some of my community work has taken me into drug rehabilitation settings, where the addicts would talk about the need to get rid of the "stinking thinking." They would say, "It's the kind of thinking we do that's gotten us into so much trouble." In the Christian tradition, the scriptures speak of putting on a new mind.

to greater life

Life is ever on the move. In times of transition, I have certainly lacked a sufficient understanding of the dynamics of transformation, and the knowledge of how best to negotiate change. In *Magical Child*, Joseph Chilton Pearce, a prolific writer on child development, presents a map of the human journey through various life stages. His model of "matrix shifts," a conceptual framework that describes the process of human maturation, has helped me discern my own path and pace of change.

The word *matrix* derives from the Latin word for "womb." From *matrix* we get the derivative *mater* (mother), and "matter" (material, mother earth). The womb offers security, nurture, and a place from which one can begin to explore the unfamiliar world. The initial matrix shift is from womb to world. At birth, a baby cries as it meets an alien world outside the womb. Indeed, a newborn is more or less in trauma until it is able to bond anew with the mother, to re-establish its security. The previous symbiotic relationship comes to an end as one body turns into two. Outside the womb, a whole new language of interaction with the mother must be learned.

I recall an incident that elucidates the meaning of matrix. I had not seen Ray since his wedding a couple of years earlier. Kylie, his two-year-old daughter, was asleep when I arrived. When she awoke, Ray went to get her up. Kylie charged into the living room, but stopped dead in her tracks when she caught sight of an unfamiliar face. She ran back to her dad, who was following her, grabbed onto his pant legs, and peeked out from behind him. Kylie needed time to size me up. Ray said, "It's okay! It's just Steve. He's a good guy." Kylie slowly became more relaxed, though she remained close to her dad, needing to be further reassured. Before a half hour had passed, Kylie had climbed onto my lap, and we became fast friends.

I think also about my very first canoe trip on the Petawawa River. None of us had any real expertise in whitewater. All we had in our favour was a strong spirit of bravado, which unfortunately did not win the day. In fact, that bravado did us in, and two of our five canoes were destroyed in the first set of rapids. No one was seriously hurt, though there were small injuries, lost gear, and a degree of trauma within the group. Our instinctive response was to return to the island where we had camped the night before. In this wilderness, completely new to all of us, the only known landscape was the island that had been a twelve-hour home to us. Like Kylie grabbing onto her dad's pant legs, we returned to familiar ground where we were able to attain a measure of calm and psychic equilibrium before figuring out further strategies to recover.

Two conflicting drives, Pearce suggests, define patterns of human growth: the drive to interact with the unknown, and the anxiety drive. Kylie had been driven in two opposite directions. In her unexpected encounter with a stranger, apprehension propelled her back to dad in search of security. Once her anxiety was overcome, though, a natural desire to explore the unknown pushed her beyond the familiar. Because Ray was secured as a trusted matrix, Kylie was enabled to test new ground. However, without an absolutely safe place, insecurity grips the psyche and arrests new growth. In the experience of anxiety, our explorations shut down and we retreat to a known world.

As the rudiments of trust are learned and there is enough confidence to move to the next stage, we leave each stage of growth behind. Pearce suggests that the pattern of maturation is a lifelong series of matrix shifts, with each matrix loss followed by new matrix formation. Life has a forward thrust, its momentum constituted in an ongoing sequence of transitions. "Once a knowledge of the matrix becomes a firm structure of knowing, that matrix must be separated from … for a greater matrix, greater possibilities, and greater relations… . Life must be continually given up for a greater life."[9] True security lies in the confident ability to explore and be alive in expanding interactions with the unknown.

The concept of matrix shifts has helped me create a framework for understanding the dynamics of change in my own life. I see that there are times when I need to find my grounding and to build structure into my life: that is, times for matrix formation. And there is also a time to let go, to leave my security behind, and to leap into unknown territory. To strike the right balance between risk and retreat demands the exercise of prudent judgment at every stage along the way.

matrix loss

I worked for a couple of years at a hospitality house where the homeless were offered food, clothing, listening ears, and a warm befriending. On a day-to-day basis, I met many faces of anxiety: the whole question of finding a safe place was a continual drama for these street people. I recall a group of five men who had established their home on a hot-air vent outside Montreal's biggest arts centre, no doubt a welcome source of heat for these homeless men in the brutal Canadian winter. One day, it so happened, the police served notice that they could no longer sleep on those premises. Everything went haywire for the men from that point on. Due to their loss of the vent matrix, which had served as a secure home base, they fell into extreme anxiety.

Ultimately there are no nesting places, only resting places, for life is always on the move. All matrices last only for a time. Sooner or later, every position has to be surrendered. This applies to any matrix that constitutes security: a friendship, a set of ideas, an automobile, a particular social identity or self-image, the bed we lie down on each night, or a pair of blue jeans. Our emotional habits, too, are matrices of a sort, a routine of safety amid psychic flux. Intellectual paradigms help to create stability as new ideas bombard us from all directions, and moral frameworks serve to steady us in times of rapidly changing values. The house we live in constitutes a physical matrix, the community in which we participate a social matrix, the work we do a career matrix. But none of these has a permanency, and each is snatched away in the tireless procession of time. Continuous endings give way to new beginnings, and we stand ever at a threshold of one kind or another. Time is the great destroyer: over and over we die. The adventure of self-discovery is thus continuously renewed.

In the passages of time there are many separations continually propelling us into different sets of unknowns. As we shed old ideas, we construct new paradigms of thought that reflect developing insight. Our moral choices also undergo revision as we modify ethical judgments and draw up new maps of value. We die many times over, yielding again and again to new directions of meaning. The places and people we love, and the ideas and identities we cherish, have often to be placed behind us once and for all, to allow life to move forward. Each shift involves the death of an old matrix, the stress of change, and the disorder of a new creation. When a matrix is lost, there is a transition, a time of instability and disorganization until another matrix is formed. In every experience of painful loss, there is always grief work to do.

befriending chaos

My friend Trevor knows what it's like to be out on the reef. I happened to be reading about chaos theory when I found a letter from him in my mailbox. In it, he described the tension of an explosive inner struggle which he coined "the fight of the century." Shortly afterwards, we talked by telephone, and I asked Trevor how things were going. He talked about coming to the end of a cycle and having to make some big decisions about the track of his life, involving his career and personal relationships. Was he to go ahead, hold the pose, or turn back?

As Trevor worked his way through ambiguity and confusion, he experienced a range of chaotic emotions. Strong emotions go along with the experience of chaos, carrying loud messages from the unconscious. The rage he felt actually served to point him in the direction of a larger destiny.

Chaos has to do with complex dynamics, the disorder of multiple mixed-up interactions. Its dynamics are unpredictable – what Trevor described as so many different issues tied together in a seething mass with uncertain outcomes. Out of the chaos new patterns appear. The process, even while falling back into confusion, follows a path to a larger destiny. This is creative chaos. It oscillates between disorder and order, yet ultimately pushes towards a higher integration.

We only get through the chaos by participating in it. Despite resistance, a period of constant oscillation takes place, prolonged at times, between new courses of action and staying where one is. Trevor kept going back and forth, and back and forth, more or less stuck in the same conflict, unable to find resolution. Jungian author John Van Eenwyk has a good one-word definition to describe when one remains suspended between the new and the old for quite some time before a new pattern emerges. "The word generally used to describe this state of affairs is suffering."[10]

Trevor eventually was able to be set free from the demands of his old self, undo the impasse in his psyche, let his life evolve. Right in the eye of the storm, he became clear about needing to bear down on the development of his creative potential. This breakthrough of insight empowered him to make a brave decision. Trevor's psyche gave him affirmation to determine for himself a new path into the future. Like the sun rising after a nocturnal journey, this was an experience of newness, a rebirth. Van Eenwyk notes, "In his clinical work, Jung observed that some of his patients could experience a death-like descent into depression that was followed by a rejuvenation of healthy relationships with themselves, others, and life in general."[11]

Trevor's last remark in our conversation was most noteworthy. "You see some slight bit of order. You get one piece, and keep going." I agree with Trevor: there is no total clarity, only partial understanding, rough and approximate glimpses of a pattern. The imperative we all receive is to bravely continue the adventure of our self-discovery.

the undiscovered self

In all our lives, as with both Trevor and my young friend Kylie, we observe what are commonly called growing pains. The dynamics of development involve a great deal of tension, and indeed, a certain amount of suffering seems integral to any transformative process. Trevor's stress resulted from hearing an inner call that challenged him to follow his talent, to sacrifice security for creativity. Similarly, Kylie was pushing in the direction of her undiscovered self, learning to pace her exploration into the wide unknown. Often enough, on the river of maturation, Kylie and Trevor will again head into the fury of whitewater. Carl Jung describes the overwhelming stress that seems to underlie almost all growth as a "tension of opposites" within the human psyche. We are pushed and pulled in the direction of richer dimensions of being.

What are the opposing tensions? The word "ego" has a wide range of meanings, usually with negative connotations. "Being on a ego trip" is an expression that alludes to self-centred motivations. Egocentricity refers to holding a focus on self-protection and one's own ambitions. Ego thinks of itself as separate and special. On the other hand, healthy ego functioning suggests the development of personality in such a way that one becomes well-adapted, confident in one's own powers. An ego construct affords necessary stability, but there is more to us than form and function, and the ego must somehow transcend its restricted concern for self. We are asked to go beyond a narrow version of life.

Jungian psychology identifies ego and Self as the two main components of human personality. Essentially, Jung describes the ego as a very small subset of the total person. In the ego-bound condition, one lives in a marginal world of one's own, largely unaware of the deeper aspects of the human personality. The ego is the narcissistic and narrow self, building up defences to ensure its own survival. Its concerns are superficial, and it focuses on goals that are trivial in the long run. Because of the ego's incapacity to experience both a depth within self and an attention to others, isolation ensues. Restricted to the finite realm, this separate ego self lives in a world of fear, fatigue, and futility.

On the other hand, the Self, for Jung, indicates the whole person, embracing both the narrow ego and a wider undiscovered self. Usually, the ego is depicted as a very small circle, positioned off-centre, within a much larger circle representing the Self. The Self includes the innermost and outermost aspects of personhood. The journey into Self takes us into a world of confusion and creativity. It brings in experiences of meaning and mystery and miracle, of paradox and parables and poetry. Jung suggests that out of these spiritual depths spring universal compassion and the ego-shattering awareness of the unity of all creation.

The Self points to the essential, towards full authentic being. The ego is not the focal point. In fact, it is marginal to the much bigger reality of human destiny. The ego, then, is like the small tip of a huge iceberg. When we speak of dismantling the ego or becoming less self-centred, we refer to a movement from self to Self, from a small ego perspective to a much expanded sense of personhood. The Self, in fact, is a boundless world – the numinous realm where we touch on non-finite dimensions. Often the Self is talked about as the Imago Dei, the image of God within.

While we attain a measure of stability and order through ego functioning, we must escape an entrapment in its narrowness and plunge into the expansive unknown. Otherwise, we forfeit human potential. The ego, though not all bad, is incomplete. Indeed, confinement in ego-bound consciousness impoverishes human experience and leads to much suffering. The separate self, which is really just an illusion, cannot be enhanced at the expense of the whole. The evolving human story urges a movement from egocentricity into the experience of boundless love, enabling us to tap into the unlimited possibilities of human freedom. Our daunting challenge is to embark on a spiritual adventure that will build love on the planet and alleviate widespread human suffering. The task is to awaken a new consciousness that dis-illusions the strivings of the ambitious ego and leads us to the awareness of the interconnectedness of all life.

an unsuspected greatness

Benedictine monk Sebastian Moore proposes that our failure in attaining full potential reflects the unconscious refusal to find our own true selves; instead, we are powered by self-doubt and fear. We reject "some fullness of life to which God is impelling us and which our whole being dreads ... some unbearable personhood, identity, freedom... ."[12] The monk suggests that alienation is a condition revealing the radical distrust of our own goodness. We build walls around our lives and repress the sense of our true greatness: a greatness not to be equated with power and strength, but pointing to a boundless self beyond ego.

Moore believes that our habitual narrow self-images and limiting beliefs must undergo revision and expansion, and he invites us to confront the spiritual inertia that resists this creative process of grace. Sin is seen to be the repression of the true self, a closure on spiritual growth, the avoidance of our full freedom. St. Paul offers a somewhat similar perspective on potential: he invokes God's power to make the hidden self grow strong, a power that can do infinitely more than we can ask or imagine (see Ephesians 3.16, 20).

Marie Foley, a friend in Boston, suggests that a commitment to the process of uncovering the hidden self is required if transformations are to take place. She writes that in order to undo psychological habits and patterns, narcissistic and neurotic defences, traumas and illusions, we must put ourselves "in a position of openness and struggle."[13] The transformative process involves accessing the unconscious, repatterning the psyche, and harnessing new energies of spirit. The common goal of psychospiritual therapies and the human potential movement is to bring this undiscovered self into conscious awareness. Mystics point to self-knowledge as the key to spiritual realization – evolving awareness gives life its energetic momentum. The image of water as a symbol of the unconscious implies to me a lifelong journey along a river of awakening. My challenge lies in learning to ply the waters of my unmet self.

Returning to my river metaphor, a good understanding of river dynamics has helped me negotiate the pulsing flow of the unconscious. Symbols and stories, myths and metaphors have drawn me into and through the chaos of change. My emotions have served as chief sources of self-knowledge, and dreams and fantasies as windows into my hidden self. Spiritual disciplines, prayer and meditation, yoga, breathing exercises, art, experiences of solitude, travel, psychotherapy, music, nature outings – all have served to awaken in me a new depth of feeling and insight.

During the writing of this book, I spent two winters at Cedar Point, on Lake Simcoe, situated in southern Ontario. Car license plates in that province bear the words "Yours To Discover." I adapted this three-word motto to read "yourself to discover," and I have many rivers yet to run to encounter my hidden self. As I journey, from becoming to becoming, my adventure will entail much tension and chaos. I have only to trust that these rivers of change will lead towards an unimaginable fullness of life.

3
Right at the Edge ...
Resistance and Readiness

Life only demands of you the strength you possess.
Only one feat is possible – not to have run away.
Dag Hammarsjöld, *Markings*

You can't cross a chasm with two leaps.
Anonymous

In one success, a thousand failures lie forgotten;
In one refusal to try, a thousand successes may permanently die.
Anonymous

anxiety labyrinth

I am not sure what qualifies as anxiety disorder, but at the age of nineteen, I knew that I had gone over the edge. I started experiencing extreme nervousness, and my self-confidence was shattered. I was a somewhat timid kid, haunted by early childhood trauma and debilitating feelings of inferiority. My peers, for the most part, seemed to move out into life with an ease that I envied. I compensated for all that was lacking in confidence by pushing for perfection.

I drank to feel better. Addiction is one way to manage anxiety, and alcohol became my first line of defence. I drank to conquer insecurity. But all the while my fears grew, and I knew I was digging myself into a deeper and darker hole. Even as I attempted to achieve a false equanimity, to look good, to cover up my fears, I continued to be in the paralyzing grip of insecurity. Over time I was to come to terms with the notion that you can run but you cannot hide, and to realize that my problem was anxiety, not alcohol. Though I knew I had to deal with my drinking behaviour, I also became keenly aware of the need to confront my core inner conflicts. Ultimately, I realized there was no way to dupe myself. I had to get beyond denial and find a healthy way to manage my anxieties. The antidote to fear, it became clear, was to face my problems rather than to turn aside. The way out amounted to a way in, and the choice confronting me was to get real. Admitting that alcohol was a false answer to my problems, I felt ready to seek my freedom. At this point I decided to go dry, and I honoured that choice for the next four years.

I never like to readily admit feeling frightened. At this juncture in my life, however, I felt too great a measure of discomfort to be able to hide. I needed to give myself permission to be scared, and to learn to accept my fears and work with them creatively. Beyond the drama of the fearful ego, there was a bigger story that was my life. The choice to embrace my desire for true happiness brought with it the liberating revelation that peace comes from learning to love deeply. I committed myself to finding a connection with the energy of love.

Beyond subjective experience, I became attuned to the universal nature of fear as every person's response to the contingencies of the human condition. Our primal fears seem to reflect four key stresses: the satisfaction of physical earthbound appetites, a desire to belong, a yearning for meaning, and the dread of death. The litany of human anxiety seems somewhat endless: hunger, being cold, scarcity, physical pain, sickness, aging, lack, and helplessness. Deep-felt distress arises in respect to our relatedness with others: the fright of disconnection, abandonment, non-belonging. Issues around sexuality, intimacy, and loneliness stir a depth of apprehension: we dread separations and the decay of vital friendships. Interestingly, we fear success as well as failure. Most poignantly, we dread the void of meaning, both temporal and transcendent. Human beings long for enduring significance and that which points to the redemption of the whole cosmic process. Ultimately, it is death that frustrates our deepest dreams, and haunts us until we draw our very last breath. We puzzle anxiously over its secret meaning.

How, then, it might be asked, do we negotiate the darkness of our manifold fears? A somewhat similar question was once put to me: "Where did you find an opening of light to meet your personal darkness?" Both questions lead me to recall the words of American novelist and rights activist James Baldwin: "It is necessary while in darkness to know that there is light; to know that somewhere, inside oneself, waiting to be found, there is light."[14]

In my life, light has appeared in experiences of "connection": with family and friends, nature, my body, ideas, wisdom, and silence. From a young age, I received a spiritual instruction that emphasized the consideration of others; indeed, a pure light has shone in every exchange of compassion and gratitude, empathy and encouragement. Bonding with nature has also been truly redemptive. I recall, in particular, barefoot walks on long, empty beaches on the east coast of Australia, and the healing contact of my body with the sand and the sea. Over the years, the primal beauty of the Canadian wilderness has filled my senses, and I have counted tent, canoe, and backpack among my favourite possessions. Athletic endeavour has created boundless delight, and a powerful outlet for pent-up emotions. In the wintertimes of youth, living on the oxygen of shinny ice hockey, I would skate until my legs gave out. Reading also has been an integral part of my leisure, bringing the rapture of ideas and the consolations of wisdom. Travel experiences, too, have greatly expanded my horizons of understanding; an exposure to wide cultural diversity has provided an antidote to entrapment in a narrower private world view. Then there are those numinous experiences of inner connection, where the larger shafts of light have broken through – in the "grand silence" of prayer and meditation, my personal healing seems to have met its deepest source.

desperation and determination

With regard to this question of light coming into darkness, I think, too, about readiness and reluctance, choice and grace. On a little island in the mid-Pacific – a story I recounted in chapter 1 – I went into a black hole and battled my demons in an attempt to wrest meaning out of my inner turmoil. I had severed myself from the world I knew to risk an adventure into the unknown, and in that time of introversion I was gifted with some liberating insight. It has often been said that we have to hit rock bottom before a process of self-discovery can get underway. A devastating depression, a sudden accident or long illness, an intense emotional struggle, experiences of loss or trauma, enforced isolation, or the death of a loved one may provoke an inner journey. In the midst of these disguised curses are paradoxical blessings that emerge in reaction to chaos and crisis. "Few people come to counselling who are not driven to do so by some injury," writes Jungian author John A. Sanford. He continues,

> Others, who can maintain the illusion of self-sufficiency, will avoid contact with the inner world. They are too content and absorbed with outer things to pay attention to inner things. But those who first come to the inner world because they are forced to do so often remain to enjoy the feast. Though they are first motivated by some injury or failure in life, they may, through their contact with the inner world, not only be healed but also find the springs of creative living.[15]

Though many indeed go all the way down, not everyone does. Some seem to follow a more proactive than reactive path. Responding to an innate urge for personal development, they strike out on a journey of awakening without a trigger of tragedy. Deep positive emotions or new ideas, artistic endeavour, music or meditation, times of silence and solitude all have the power to disrupt ordinary consciousness and provoke movement. Where there is a strong and steady determination to move forward, a journey will quickly gather steam.

It is said, "There's a hard way, and a harder way." The general tendency might well be to pay attention to personal growth only when we are up against a wall. Often, it becomes a matter of "doing damage control" – on this harder way, we pay a big price for refusing inner attention. Difficulties in life, even disaster, inevitably follow. No doubt there are missed opportunities to grow that, in hindsight, we might all admit to: those neglected chances that cost us dearly or delayed our maturation. How do we find the less hard ways, and avert unnecessary pain? A commitment to a spiritual practice and a discipline of introversion enable us to encounter ourselves on a deeper level. It is imperative to find an inner guide within oneself. Some hear an interior voice in dreams and active imagination. We have only to find our own spiritual law and obey it.

Whether out of despair or by design, a motivation to find true happiness has impelled my healing journey. I observe, as I bend back on personal experience, that, whether born of both desperation and determination, whether goaded by negative experience or guided by inner callings, a force of creativity seems to keep pushing me in the direction of my undiscovered self. That which is unfinished within me both longs and looks for completion.

maximum tension

Malcolm, a friend from Saskatchewan, is an artist and a saxophone player. I asked him about the word "resonance" and what it meant to him. His spontaneous response went something like this: "It's a quality of sound that grows ... it amplifies itself rather than diffuses as it moves out into space ... sounds mixing and setting each other off ... sound which is alive, and takes on a life of its own ... sound which has a spinning quality ... it works magically, it's effortless, there's no friction, it seems like it can go on forever." And then Malcolm said something I would never forget: "I keep going through dissonance to get to resonance. Music that sounds syrupy resides only in resonance. Some music lives mainly in tension. Tension and resolution, that's what makes music live." He concluded by saying, "Once in a while I like to snap, when I'm in a state of maximum tension. That's where my creativity is, right at the edge. When I'm playing or painting, then all of a sudden I'm there! I'm connected. Then clarity and beauty break forth."[16]

Dissonance is defined as sound harmonically unresolved. I connected my conversation with Malcolm about tension and resolution with Ilya Prigogine's Nobel prize–winning work on the laws of entropy and syntropy. Entropy refers to a closed system experiencing progressive disorder and disintegration – a dead end. The law of syntropy refers to an open system that ingests new and eliminates unusable energies in order to further develop. Reflecting on Prigogine's theory, French-Canadian author Placide Gaboury comments:

> When the whole grows, it multiplies its interrelationships, upsetting the status quo, absorbing new cells; and the elements break up the previous cohesion. And this goes on continually: every "position" is continually shifting. Like a close-knit group, when a new member is introduced, the group must die to its previous harmony and include a disrupting agent ... a move which precisely, if it is well integrated, will produce a greater comprehension, a broader view, a more encompassing consciousness, a more universal growth.

> Thus, concludes Prigogine, a minimum of instability alone guarantees growth; and the more there is instability (without upsetting the total balance or metabolism), the more there is a chance for growth. This law is applicable to the spiritual path: one can only grow by outgrowing. One stagnates and suffers by clinging. One must continually let go.[17]

The insecure way marks the path to growth, an idea that goes somewhat against the grain of common thinking. Stress is healthy, and extremely necessary to growth, unless it turns into unmanageable distress. Distress reflects an imbalance, a pileup of too much tension without resolution, an unredeemed chaos. Life is maintained in a healthy balance between stress and relaxation. Commenting upon the law of syntropy, Gaboury advocates maximum instability, and urges us not to trade off the adventure of learning and living to satisfy the need for security. His recommendation to grow by outgrowing is qualified. He warns us not to go over the edge, but to live right at it. That's where Malcolm, the saxophone player, says his creativity lies.

one bold leap

In different ways, philosopher and author Jerome Miller suggests, we attempt to eliminate the future because of the anxiety we experience with regard to its unpredictability. We dread the future breaking in on us and overturning the present: "We approach the future with a plan for it precisely in the hope of escaping the radical throes of it; we hope to have a future that will not be disruptive, disturbing, or deconstructive."[18] Miller suggests that our need for control is to prevent the future from being any different from the present. So we try to get ahead, possessed by practical goals aimed at achieving a stasis. What we call progress really conceals our desire for more of that which is known, and is framed out of the fear of opening up to the unknown. It would be better, suggests Miller, to let amazement and self-abandonment guide us into a future, even though we may dread their unpredictability.

One bold leap can get us across the chasm, while two timid jumps will land us in the abyss. Sometimes there are no half measures. Authentic courage indeed walks tall in the face of despair and fear – it confronts obstacles and meets the challenge of change. Courage, from the same root as the French word *coeur*, means to take heart and enlarge our capacity to dare freedom. While fear wards off creativity, courage risks self-expression. Courage enables us to act against the regressive power of fear, and never betray truth. Though ready to venture a fuller life, courage is not about taking foolish chances. It does not risk for risk's sake. Courage does not dare danger with a false bravado, but rather pursues intelligent strategies. Authentic courage negotiates risk without diminishing challenge.

Andrew, a camping mate, speaks of his call to growth as a "chill of foreboding," as when he moves away from a campfire into the shadows of the forest and the blackness of night. He attests that when he leaves the security and light of the fire, the darkness, representing unknown possibilities, is both feared and alluring. Andrew also comments that the catalyst for change for him often comes in the middle of desperation,

> ... the awareness that I'm in a really tough situation, but I've got to deal with it.... It is just being aware that you're really, really stuck.... There may be a kind of blindness for a long time, as well as a lot of doubt, and the fear of not really wanting to face the struggle at all.... Then comes a readiness to face the struggle with a sense that this is exactly what life is all about, being ready to struggle and make something of it.[19]

In the school of anxiety, we discover that the ultimate antidote to being afraid is loving-kindness. As we listen to our fears and taste personal vulnerability, we become newly sensitive to the sorrow of others and are willing to get involved with their suffering. We learn that in bearing the burden of another's fear, we heal our own.

refusing the adventure

Along my river of transformation, I find myself frequently caught in cross-currents: something pushing me forward and something holding me back. I experience the urge to grow, a summons to life, a love into which I am being drawn. Conversely, there is also a deep-seated reluctance to go forward and to pay attention to what really matters. More than just being scared to change, I am at times just plain lazy.

Universally, for lack of determination and courage, we frequently give in to fear, and choose to live in denial or the dizziness of distraction. Cynical attitudes, chronic fatigue, depression, isolation, and destructive behaviours define different patterns of alienation. Evading the emptiness gnawing on the inside, we escape into work or worry, booze or busyness. The tendency to resist change and prefer inertia sets up patterns of avoidance that add up to a basic denial of the self. All too often we banish unpleasant experiences, bury feelings, narcotize pain, and bail out when the going gets tough. The allure of pleasure and our attachment to comfort sabotage our readiness for change. Denial becomes an easy habit, a way of life that covers up inner and outer conflicts.

Distraction plays a large part in the strategy of avoidance: fast-paced living, big projects, endless noise, lots of talking. Flooding oneself with stimuli is often a way to compensate for the lack of passionate living. Work becomes an obsession, part of a flight syndrome. We get horribly busy with a thousand and one things to do in the outer world, while inner reality is chronically avoided. The result of a life of denial and distraction is boredom and fatigue. Awareness becomes narrower, as we filter out our emotional worlds and refuse spiritual challenge. Thomas Merton, the well-known Trappist monk, says that people like to get around their spiritual responsibility "by entering into a routine of trivialities in which everything seems clear and noble and defined: but when you look at it honestly it falls apart, for it is riddled with absurdity from top to bottom … ."[20]

Sometimes psychological difficulties reflect that we have become caught up exclusively with the outer world and have failed to attend to our inner lives. When we ignore that we are not "feeling right" with ourselves, buried guilt manifests itself in uneasiness, physical symptoms, and depression. Deep-rooted resentments also confine our vital energies. We become stuck in the past and in powerlessness, and hold our stories back by lingering in a victim position. Jungian James Hollis understands that depression arises when psychic content gets trapped in the unconscious and is unable to find the light of consciousness. The refusal of awareness shuts down the energetic momentum of our lives. In response, the psyche proposes a healing journey to discover what the true self wants. Hollis writes:

> The depression is evidence of the dynamic character of the psyche which wishes life, and whose healing will come only when a person has been obliged to stop and ask why such a black mass has appeared ... [there is a need to] honour the depression for its insistence that one's life be changed ... the real story is what is occurring in the unconscious where time is timeless, where the internalized experiences of childhood reign, the more so as they remain unconscious. One can thus thank the depression as a gift from the psyche which wishes that the old wounding be healed. New life is already in the birth canal.[21]

We often speak of blessings in disguise. Sometimes, our bodies or our psyches will tell us when they are not pleased with our choices. Symptoms appear that will call us to change our life direction and styles. The process may be painful, but in the end it brings results very much to our liking.

the reluctant prophet

I love the Old Testament story about Jonah and the whale. Jonah is a prime example of someone who resisted his true calling. He was instructed to open the eyes of the people of Nineveh to their wickedness and urge them to repent, but he was not very happy about being asked by God to do this. Jonah, often named the reluctant prophet, refused this role and fled by ship in the opposite direction from Nineveh. Then, the Lord "unleashed a violent wind on the sea." (Jonah 1.4, Revised Standard Version) Jonah, knowing he was to blame for the storm, instructed the mariners to throw him overboard so that the sea would quiet down. The Lord "had arranged that a great fish should be there to swallow Jonah; and Jonah remained in the belly of the fish for three days and three nights" (Jonah 2.1, Revised Standard Version). The belly of the whale symbolizes the dark unconscious where truth that has been avoided is rediscovered. Jonah prayed to the Lord for deliverance, and the whale vomited him out on dry land. Not only did he want out; more important, Jonah realized that he was going against God's will. He then proceeded to Nineveh and fulfilled his mandate to deliver prophecy. If we, like Jonah, fail to heed our true calling, we can be sure that the going will get tough. Raging winds will blow to tell us that we, too, have to come to terms with the life we are resisting.

I am someone who identifies with Jonah quite easily. But when I avoid what I am supposed to do, instead deciding to do my own thing, I know there's always hell to pay. In the belly of the whale, we come to terms with our avoidances as our resistance breaks down. Joseph Campbell states, "My definition of a devil is a god who has not been recognized. That is to say, it is a power in you to which you have not given expression, and you push it back. And then like all repressed energy, it builds up and becomes completely dangerous to the position that you're trying to hold."[22] The unconscious will protest our refusal to obey what life asks of us, and disrupt our settled routine of avoidance. A black mass might appear in our psyche, and we, too, will have to undergo a time of purgation.

to shape intention

The desire to live authentically excites our imagination about possibility, helping to reveal that true path that awaits our recognition. How do our lives become more the outcome of consciousness and choice, and less the result of conditions and conditioning? The essence of proactivity is to shape intention, whereby we derive our life scripts from a vision of the future rather than from the limitations of the past.

The power of intention is crucial. Intention involves both dream and discipline. Avram Davis, in the *The Way of the Flame*, portrays the mystical tradition of Judaism describing "four qualities of consciousness."[23] One of these qualities refers to passionate intentionality (kavannah), which asks us to apply ourselves with our whole heart to every situation, and to do so with conscious intention. Avram suggests that a great deal of passion is required to imagine our lives. A declaration of noble intent allows us to move towards our chosen destinations. Steady determination and strong discipline enable us to hold tenaciously to the intentions that our guiding visions reveal. If we are ready to articulate our goals in words or symbols, and to make a commitment to follow the direction they inspire, we become powerful. Intention acts as pilot. Should we get derailed, we are provided with what we need to get back on track: a guiding spirit, necessary wisdom, circumstances instrumental in helping our journey along.

Through experience, I have discovered that once I make a fundamental commitment to pursue wholeness, continuous transformation ensues. Despite trials and obstacles, the right friends come along, the right situations present themselves, and the books that need to be read appear. If my intention is pure, it seems that the universe conspires on my behalf and offers abundant guidance to illuminate my path. In religious terms, this is called providence. A dictum from New Testament scripture suggests that we ought to seek the kingdom first, and the rest shall be given. (See Luke 12.31.) Yet I often go after "the rest" first.

Our resistance or readiness is very much a mystery. Whether the catalysts for growth are negative experiences or inner promptings, the timing and pace of each individual journey are different from every other. We are ready when we are ready. There is a saying that it is difficult to dislodge an unripe nut from its shell, but when the nut is ripe, the slightest tap will do. We are ripe for change when our resistances begin to break down. Journeys of transformation take time, and much long-suffering is needed to undergo the rigours of the process. The time we end up taking is precisely the time needed. We can only begin at the beginning, inspired by a dream of what we can do. A Chinese proverb wisely reminds us that "a journey of a thousand miles begins with a single step." This book began with a single word; we move along a river of awareness one insight at a time.

My island introversion in the mid-Pacific runs parallel to the experiences of Malcolm's maximum tension, Andrew's chill of foreboding, and Jonah's reluctance. In different ways, we have discovered that it is not always comfortable at the edges of growth. Yet each of us can learn to acknowledge our fear, and not run away.

4
Awakening Original Experience ...
The Hero Path

A single dramatic theme can stand in the background of one's life for a whole lifetime... . Individuals may have whole sets of values in the background, waiting for expression.
     Wilson VanDusen, *The Natural Depth in Man*

It's easier to ride a horse in the direction it's going.
     Anonymous

They've [King Arthur's knights] moved out of the society that would have protected them, and into the dark forest, into the world of fire, of original experience.
     Joseph Campbell, *The Power of Myth*

river of kindness

I recall my first Darjeeling assignment. The jeep had gone as far as it could go on the narrow, muddy road that was saturated from heavy monsoon rains. A 25-kilogram bag of grain was loaded onto my back, and I was dispatched to complete the delivery on foot to a small *bustee* (village) 500 metres farther down in the valley. I was grateful the trekking was down, not up. It was an arduous trek, but there was a hungry village awaiting much-needed food supplies.

This experience had the taste of something very real – I sensed that I was participating in something bigger than myself. It roused inside me a call to find my own true hero path. Of course, the ego is always around, and it was trying to steal some attention: if only everyone back home could see me now. But there was nobody watching me make my muddy trek, no one to applaud my achievement. The genuine heroes, in fact, were the village folk themselves, truly heroic in the way they carried their poverty and their suffering. I could only humbly accept their expressions of gratitude. I felt my heart stir thinking of the song lyrics of "Guantanamera": with the poor of the earth, I want to share my fate.

At that particular time in my life, aged 26, I was awakening to the vital realization that my life could make a difference to others. This insight was, in part, the result of finding myself in circumstances that called forth a response to human suffering. It grew also from encountering certain individuals who possessed exemplary hero qualities. India gave me exposure to both. Over time I have come to believe that the heroic abides inside each of us, within our very nature. However, we often resist our heroism. Its actualization sets forth a demanding task of recognition and response.

Not long after my initiatory experience, I met Sister Ivana at Jesu Ashram, a home for the destitute and dying at the base of the Himalayan foothills. Day after day, Ivana addressed the suffering of lepers, the sick, and the squatters who lived alongside India's railway tracks. I had a sort of mad love for this servant of the poor, what I would call a spiritual infatuation. A few months later I had the opportunity to become her apprentice. I was assigned a bicycle and a bandage box, given instructions on worm treatment, and sent into the suffering throng. "I can't do this. I am totally inept," I argued. Sister Ivana responded with the words "Stephen, they simply need the medicine of kindness."

I could only marvel as I watched Sister Ivana dole out her sweet compassion. Gratuitously, she came into my life to guide me onto the river of kindness. In every encounter, she bestowed dignity on the poor. Ivana did not discount the need for medical competence, but knew how integral care is to cure. The lepers received as much love from her as food rations, and the widows as much healing as help in building small thatched huts. Twenty-two years later I returned to Jesu Ashram to find Sister Ivana still devoted to doing her rounds (in her old age, with a motorized rickshaw), a tireless broker of gentle mercy to suffering humanity.

At a press conference in Washington, Mother Teresa was questioned by a reporter, "Some people say that you are a saint. What do you say?" She was quick to reply, "Well, I try to be, don't you?" Now, when I hear myself claiming to be just ordinary, I question if it is a strategy to avoid personal challenge. In placing expectations of the extra-ordinary onto others, do I disclaim my own responsibility to live heroically, and thereby discount my true potential? The hero's task seems less intimidating to me when I hear Mother Teresa's definition of heroism: doing small things with great love.

the hero archetype

As Sister Ivana slowly grew weary with age, the Canadian Broadcasting Corporation (CBC) sent a television crew to India to produce a documentary film portraying her life of devotion to the poor. I myself asked her about how she had embarked on this path of service. Ivana tells of the decision she made in her early 60s to give the rest of her life over to working with the destitute dying:

I had left the mountains for a three-month trial period, after which I couldn't make up my mind. In the end, I decided to return to Kurseong in the mountains. The work was too difficult and the heat of the plains too unbearable. As I was catching the bus, Brother Bob drove up on a scooter and said: "Sister, don't leave me. I need you to help me." Right then and there, I decided to stay and do the work, even if I should die! After that, I never had any problem doing the work.[24]

During that three-month retreat, Sister Ivana had sought new direction for her life. At first she encountered confusion and the fear of change, then hesitation, and finally a breakthrough of vision and courage. We find a similar pattern of the heroic throughout the Christian scriptures: Paul, John the Baptist, and Jesus each spent a lengthy time in the wilderness coming to terms with their callings. In the desert they underwent a rigorous formation in order to be strengthened and prepared for the tasks that lay ahead. Only then did they return to the community, inspired and confident, ready to offer their lives for the sake of love.

Through awakening a quality of compassion, Sister Ivana's story follows the pattern of the hero's journey, a life committed to the courageous discovery of the true self. Joseph Campbell defines the essential hero quality as a fearlessness to let go of familiar patterns in the never-ending quest of spiritual potential. "That's the basic motif of the universal hero's journey – leaving one condition and finding the source of life to bring you forth into a richer or mature condition."[25] The visionary hero has a threefold task: to retreat from ordinary everyday living, to awaken a power of vision, and then to return with an inspired message. The pattern is always the same: departure, discovery, delivery. Leaving traditional consciousness and habitual ways behind, one sets out into the dark unknown to seek a new power of insight. The quest calls forth an enlargement of consciousness, and the visionary hero eventually returns to share whatever truth has been revealed.

King Arthur's knights each went alone into a dark forest and entered it at a place where no one had ever done so before. "Then they rode out from the castle and separated as they had decided amongst themselves, striking out into the forest one here, one there, where they saw it thickest and wherever path or track was absent."[26] The castle symbolizes what must be left behind: the status quo, security, physical or emotional stagnation, inertia in one's living. A call is sounded, which most often summons radical innovation. The thick forest symbolizes the difficult challenge that the knight is about to face. Revelation is to be granted, but it will be found in a dark place, perhaps after a long ordeal. The pattern of the heroic indicates that often one finds one's treasure only at the bottom of the abyss. That darkness is frequently encountered in one's outer life when facing the challenges of new living situations or relationships, or changing personal identity. A hero adventure might also take place in an encounter with one's unconscious, solely within the deep recesses of the psyche.

The task of "awakening original experience" is an essential feature of the hero journey. It was considered a disgrace for the knights to go into the forest with anyone else, or where others had previously made entry. What was required of them was to risk that path that was uniquely their own. Each of us is called to go out with similar determination, to shape a life that reflects singular purpose rather than following blindly in someone else's tracks. We are to dare to go where no one has ever gone before. About this, Campbell writes,

> Original experience has not been interpreted for you, and so you've got to work out your life for yourself. Either you can take it or you can't. You don't have to go far off the interpreted path to find yourself in difficult situations. The courage to face the trials and to bring a whole new field of possibilities into the field of interpreted experience for other people to experience – that is the hero's deed.[27]

In some way, all heroes inspire fresh spiritual imagination and activate radical creativity. Obeying the call to growth, heroes go inward to discover themselves anew, daring to ask difficult questions that need to be asked. As vision emerges and self-understanding matures, old ways of seeing are left behind. A transformation of consciousness marks out the hero path, whereby serving others replaces self-interest. Ultimately, a call to the heroic is an invitation to love.

getting a life

Because of my unconventional path, friends sometimes tease me with the question "When are you going to get a life?" I reply, "I am working on it as fast as I can, but the river is slow to reveal its secrets." In truth, we might say that "getting" a life is more a matter of obedience than acquisition. To obey my life is to listen to the story it wants to tell, and to accept responsibility for shaping that story as my very own. It is to let the real me emerge from my inner depths. It is a question of allowing myself to be drawn onto a path that is congruent with my deepest intentions and meanings.

According to Danish philosopher Soren Kierkegaard, we cannot breathe if we forfeit a larger life. In submitting exclusively to survival needs, we shrink from bliss into the trivial, and so fail to find our true calling. Cultural anthropologist Ernest Becker, in *The Denial of Death*, offers an exposition of Kierkegaard, highlighting the compromise we make of our lives when, out of fear, we fail to shoulder the burden of our uniqueness. By playing things on the safe side, we default. Becker outlines the task of bliss:

> This, after all is said and done, is the only real problem of life, the only worthwhile preoccupation of man: What is one's true talent, his secret gift, his authentic vocation? In what way is one truly unique, and how can he express this uniqueness, give it form, dedicate it to something beyond himself? How can the person take his private inner being, the great mystery that he feels at the heart of himself, his emotions, his yearnings and use them to live more distinctively, to enrich both himself and mankind with the peculiar quality of his talent? In adolescence, most of us throb with this dilemma, expressing it either with words and thoughts or with simple numb pain and longing. But usually life sucks us up into standardized activities. The social hero-system into which we are born marks out paths for our heroism, paths to which we conform, to which we shape ourselves so that we can please others, become what they expect us to be. And instead of working our inner secret we gradually cover it over and forget it.... [28]

In place of letting life propose personal meaning, we try to impose a program on our lives. I have watched myself trying to "make up" a plot for my life, a false story that inevitably interrupts authenticity. Here my ego contrives and does the deciding, placing emphasis more on control and survival. Conditioning, too, tends to prevail over that which is native to us. Social coercion, the demands of culture, and family influences frequently have the effect of bending us out of shape. If we fail to work our inner secret, we miss the call to live a genuine life, and thereby neglect to find inner depth. As a counterpoint, Parker Palmer, a leading philosopher in education, suggests that vocation is not the outcome of will and grim determination. Rather, it is a voice calling: "Before I can tell my life what I want to do with it, I must listen to my life telling me who I am."[29] Our lives, then, are gifts to be recognized and developed. A hidden script abides within each of us.

what do you really want?

I once read that there are two invaluable guidelines to discern true vocation: aptitude and attraction. In becoming responsive to that which holds my fascination, the way of authenticity follows those true enchantments that open up a song within my heart. In discerning a valid path into the future, invariably the question arises: "What do you really want?" I have frequently posed this question to others, and almost without fail, the asking evokes poignant feeling, often a flow of tears to reveal deep-felt frustration and the lack of fulfillment. Indeed, our desire for happiness can be satisfied only by the attainment of a genuine life.

Some years back I found myself mired in a dead-end work situation. My creativity felt completely stifled, but I had not acknowledged how dispirited I truly felt. One day I overheard someone say, "I think I am in the wrong story!" The words hit me like the force of a powerful wind, and I recognized that it was time to let go. It was necessary to strike out in a bold direction, for the work I was doing no longer held any fascination. It became apparent that I would be punished with more disenchantment if I refused to take a new step.

Cosmologist Brian Swimme, in *The Universe is a Green Dragon*, highlights the theme of allurement:

> You do not know what you can do, or who you are in your fullest significance, or what powers are hiding within you. All exists in the emptiness of your potentiality, a realm that cannot be seen or tasted or touched. How will you bring these powers forth? How will you awaken your creativity? By responding to the allurements that beckon to you, by following your passions and interests. Alluring activity draws you into being, just as it drew the stars into being. Our life and powers come forth through our response to allurement.[30]

The universe is developing through the mysterious longings that permeate our lives and that cannot be explained. Somehow, that is the way the world binds together. Particular attractions spark events, set relationships in motion, and thus reveal our places under the sun. However, there are false lights, fatal attractions. Only genuine allurement gives momentum to our journey into love. The good tugs at us, but the counterpulls of egotistic striving can often be seductively masked. True authenticity points to the fascinations of the spirit, not the fascinations of the ego. Swimme suggests that the basis of one's vision must be transformed from self-interest to service – that ignorance, fear, greed, prejudice, rivalry, inordinate affections, and addiction to profit ought to be replaced by spiritually energetic values, by loving-kindness and altruism. In addition, we can be blinded by the fear of the suffering that any transformative process entails. Thus, we need both discernment and daring.

Ironically, we frequently find our right way in life after landing in the wrong story, or following a fatal attraction. In times like these, we discover who or what we are not. An old teaching story from India tells of a conversation between a king and a sculptor. The king was much impressed by the work of the sculptor and wanted to know the secret of his artistry. The sculptor replied,

> For a long time I do nothing but observe this block of stone and study it from every angle. ... Then, slowly, very slowly, I begin to notice something in the substance of the rock. ... an outline shows itself to me. ... The outline grows stronger. ... Oh, yes, I can see it! An elephant is stirring in there! Only then do I start to work with chisel and mallet, always clinging to my sense of that outline. ... with utter singleness of purpose, I chip away every last bit of stone that is not elephant. What remains will be, must be, elephant.[31]

This point is echoed by the monk Sebastian Moore. He puts his slant on the not-elephant image by suggesting two ways of understanding asceticism: "The conventional view is that it means denying ourselves things we want. A more discerning and disconcerting view is that it means dropping things that we no longer want, admitting to ourselves we no longer want them, and thus giving our journey, our story, a chance to move on... ."[32]

suffering and meaning

Following the three years he spent as a prisoner in a concentration camp at Auschwitz, Victor Frankl pioneered a psychological movement called "logotherapy," which focuses on the will to meaning. The goal of logotherapy is to identify a purpose in life surpassing the narrow aspirations of mere functional living, instinctual satisfaction, and social adaptation. Frankl observed that some prisoners detained in the concentration camps, through caring for their fellow prisoners, were able to transcend their own grim suffering. Logotherapy is based on the premise that the pursuit of contentment is secondary to the task of meaning. An existential vacuum could well be described as the experience of meaninglessness. Different forms of neurosis, Frankl believes, result from the failure to actualize meaning, especially finding the meaning of suffering in our lives. In fact, we often try to avoid our suffering. The will to pleasure, power, or money often compensates for a lack of spiritual focus.

In logotherapy, three different avenues of meaning are proposed: the achievement of a deed, the realization of value, and the embrace of suffering itself. I remember well the story Frankl told to a Montreal audience of a garbage man in Paris who salvaged broken toys from the trash bins he emptied on his daily rounds, repaired them after hours in his little workshop, and then distributed them to children living in the poor ghettos. The life of that garbage man was imbued with meaning. Individuals often identify the peak moments of their lives as experiences of beauty, truth, love. For Frankl, the most poignant depth of meaning is found when we come to terms with unavoidable suffering. Of this, he writes, "For what matters above all is the attitude we take towards suffering, the attitude in which we take the suffering upon ourselves."[33] Expressions of sacrificial love enable us to interpret and bear suffering purposefully, and redeem ourselves as victims of its pain.

Psychic life has an ebb and flow, asserts James Hollis in *Swamplands of the Soul*, and no one is exempt from being pulled down into dismal places of grief and guilt, fear and betrayal, anger and anxiety, despair and depression, and the like. Though it is tough going, we must go through these swamps to find a purpose that dignifies our lives. If we refuse to go down into grief, and if we want only to avoid pain and flee our suffering, we create a basis for addictions, neuroses, and the failure to mature. No matter what swamp we find ourselves in, there is a need to identify a task that will increase our understanding. Hollis writes, "Wisdom arises through the assimilation of suffering. Suffering assimilated enlarges the personality, brings amplitude to the soul."[34] Suffering enables us to gather insights and healing images that bring us across those dark abysses where we discover new depth. Thus, we move from the past to the present, from reflex to creativity, from the regressive to the progressive. The specific tasks and meanings suggested by each swampland state all point to the goal of reimagining our lives.

However unmerited our suffering, we are challenged to embrace the losses we undergo when life is interrupted, refused, or destroyed. The answer to meaninglessness is, paradoxically, right in the middle of our suffering. On that island in the mid-Pacific where I faced my inner turmoil, I began in earnest to search out my personal truth. It was in that swampland of deep discouragement that I found a path oriented to meaning. Meaninglessness is equivalent to illness; thus, the challenge of reclaiming authenticity lies in awakening personal meaning.

sacrifice and rapture

The message on my telephone answering machine was vibrant. It was Malcolm calling from Saskatchewan: "I've just quit my job. Now I can live the life of a transient, migrant freelance musician-artist, and all those sorts of things – and it's exciting again!" A pivotal theme of Joseph Campbell's scholarship in comparative mythology is "follow your bliss"; Malcolm was feeling the exuberance of choosing to move into the adventure of his life. By obeying his inner call, he was awakening his deepest spiritual energies. Campbell advocates, "... get rid of the life that you have planned in order to have the life that's waiting to be yours."[35] Like Malcolm, I recall taking a momentous leap when I decided to leave professional teaching. I was scared, but I knew I was ready to risk a new adventure.

Travelling a river of bliss entails both the relinquishment of security and the requirement of sacrifice, but also holds the promise of rapture. If we focus on digging for gold, we more or less die. More than once, I had to forgo a salaried position and jump over the edge to spark my creativity. This does not cancel the obligation to attend to the practical side of life. Campbell makes the point this way:

... it's very important for a young person to have the courage to do what seems to him[her] significant in life, and
not just take a job in order to make money. But this takes
a bit of prudence and very careful planning, and may delay
financial achievement and comfortable living. But the ultimate result will be very much to his[her] pleasure.[36]

The realization of bliss goes hand in hand with sacrifice. It
comes at a cost, and requires of us a measure of suffering. In
fact, it is often necessary to endure some big setbacks and a lot
of disappointment. I recall a conversation circle when one of the
guys became quite irritated as we discussed this notion. "I don't
get this bliss business," Nick protested. "I work long hours at the
restaurant and I don't have any time for fun in life." Nick was
the father of two daughters, and tireless in his loving devotion to
them. "Your girls are your bliss," I responded. Right away Nick
understood the link between bliss and sacrifice.

If we cultivate our bliss no matter what others say, Joseph
Campbell postulates, we will experience the rapture of being
truly alive. Again he is urging us to hang on to that which makes
us genuinely happy. When our outer lives find congruence with
our deepest levels of inspiration, we bring joy not only to ourselves but to everyone we encounter. Few people would disagree
with this principle, but many would say its practice is next to
impossible. We will have to see if Malcolm gets a payoff for stick-
ing his neck out. From my own past, I know that whenever I have
obeyed the longings of my heart, I have been richly rewarded.

the riverman

My hero path builds on a riverman image. I like to make the
contrast between canals and rivers: canals go in straight lines, and
are artificial and humdrum; on the other hand, rivers are always
full of new promise. They wind unpredictably and take longer to
run, and you never know what lies around the next bend. While
a canal is somewhat boring, a river makes for a lot more fun. I

am slowly giving up travelling in canal-like straight lines, and trying to stop being too neat and efficient, always in control. I realize that it is not necessary to get to where I am going as fast as I can. As a riverman, I am becoming more comfortable living in mystery – after all, the hero task is to ply the waters of the great unknown.

No one person is able to save the world, yet each of us is called to respond to particular challenges and bring forth unique creativity, a special gift. Heroes are ordinary persons who develop their talent for the sake of a love that is always bigger than themselves. The hero is everyone, and is found everywhere: in office or marketplace, at home, in school or factory. Their varied callings are to intellectual endeavours or concerns of social justice, to entrepreneurial or athletic achievement, to manual trades or scientific research. The passionate pursuit of goodness and truth, and the practice of charity, mark out a hero's path.

My life has been graced to travel in the company of an enthusiastic band of rivermates, including those with hero contributions described in this chapter: Ivana, brokering the wisdom of kindness; Malcolm, affirming the truth of his artistic creativity; and Nick, embracing sacrifice. Many unnamed others have inspired me with their courage, most especially those broken people of the earth who bravely carry such huge burdens of suffering. The vast majority of heroes are unsung, as they quietly dedicate themselves to labours of love. Each of us, although having many differentiated life tasks and talents, is invited to continue the journey of awakening our true potential. What we have in common is the hero call: to do what we do best, with great love. There are many miles of river to go before reaching the ocean.

5
River of Images ...
Symbol and Spirit

A man's work is nothing but this slow trek to rediscover through the detours of art those two or three great and simple images in whose presence his heart first opened.
    Albert Camus

I didn't know that there is a place deep inside where one's real life goes on, much like an underground river in parched, dry country, which flows whether one knows about it or not.
    Sharon Butala, *The Perfection of the Morning*

... there was always deep in the background, the feeling that something other than myself was involved. It was as though a breath of the great world of stars and endless space had touched me, or as if a spirit had invisibly entered the room ...
    Carl Jung, *Memories, Dreams, Reflections*

mental landscapes

"My mind races like a train that doesn't stop at stations," a friend of mine commented. I thought how very aptly that image would describe my own mental landscape, connoting the fast momentum of its non-stop "train" of thought. "How do you ever get off the train if it never stops at stations?" I asked. "By getting derailed, and that happens often enough," my friend replied.

This leads me to wonder if I am actually able to choose the train I ride on, and if it is possible to change my mental landscape. Bob Marley, in one of his well-known songs, refers to mental slavery and suggests that only we ourselves can free our minds. This idea makes me wonder about the role the imagination plays in generating pictures that define the direction or misdirection of my life. In order to find a freedom path, I need to come to know the train I am on, and to learn to distinguish between the different states of mind that either foster or negate human happiness.

Ideas and mental images shape the passion, the movement, the direction of our lives. From moment to moment, the choices we make are driven by the pictures that capture the heart and imagination. They release vision and vitality, and significantly shape our attitudes and actions. Certain symbols are charged with energy towards which we experience intense emotional attractions. It is not always easy to recognize the imagery concealed in our emotions. Our inner mental representations reveal hidden values. Seed images fashion our tastes and habits, and frame the way we picture ourselves and our possibilities. The power of a mental image to define our behaviours cannot be underestimated.

My mind likes to dance from one place to another, always enchanted by an assortment of tunes. In fact, my pictures of myself keep changing all the time. In the flux of self-images, I have borne many identities: good guy, achiever, rebel, hero helper, scapegoat, helpless victim, loser, teacher, trickster, wounded healer, learner, and wanderer. Each character builds itself from a bundle of images to create an amalgam called personal identity. If some of the pictures reflect the true self and others a false me, how do I discern which is the right train, the one with a destination to peace of mind?

The challenge of authenticity is to find those mysterious images that release the spiritual energies of life, and that harmonize our relationship to self, to one another, and to nature. But identity can often be based on the deceptions of the ego that compete with finding a genuine life. Whether chasing after an illusory high, confined by negative emotional habits, or trapped inside our own self-defeating defences, we readily encounter many obstacles to freedom. For some reason, we resist making ourselves completely available to contentment. Nonetheless, the inborn desire for true identity lies in wait and calls forth the task of personal transformation. The litmus test of freedom is measured along the spectrum of our experience of happiness.

Relating these thoughts to my personal story, the experience of shame in childhood years left a deep imprint on my boyhood identity. Robbed of self-esteem, I locked into a pattern of negative self-perception that engendered a sense of helplessness. I felt at odds with life, and found it very hard to trust my own worth. Such a distorted self-image ran a lot of interference in the process of self-actualization.

Yet, in this mud of self-alienation grew the longing to find a way out of negativity. As I sought healing wisdom, I encountered a spiritual warrior inside myself that dared me to open my heart. Teaching stories from various healing traditions guided me into the exercise of positive imagination. Many parables within the Christian spiritual tradition graced me with a heritage of values that were instrumental in helping me transcend self-deprecating attitudes. As I tapped into deeper levels of energy, more integral pictures of myself emerged, and fear gradually gave way to trust. I slowly came to perceive the future as open, not closed. As a new mental pattern emerged, I learned to relinquish the victim position and assume the responsible authorship of my life. Most important, through re-picturing the past and the healing of memories, I became empowered to forgive. Various symbols of wholeness came as gratuitous blessing, and, in this way, I was able to grasp the knowledge that genuine identity builds itself on the image of love.

symbolic fire and rain

The fire of hope is often symbolized by the flame of a candle. A regular practice in my work with the terminally ill has been to introduce symbols of hope, to help light a way of passage through the ordeal of illness and death. In diverse spiritual rituals around the planet, candles are lit to invoke blessings of compassion.

They flicker as wordless prayers and express the deep human longing for light to dispel our dark suffering. Our candles seem to blaze strongest in places of black despair. In some ways, we are all watchers of the dawn, waiting for the break of day.

I first met Don just after he had been jolted with the news of an inoperable brain tumour. Suddenly, he found himself on "death row." In the days that followed, Don was in shock, wrestling with his grief and fears. We talked a little, not a lot, and he processed his feelings mostly in silence. Don asked me about my work with the dying, and seemed intrigued when I described to him the ritual in India of blessing one another with the "fire of life." Lighting candles was an integral part of my ritual expression; how appreciative Don was when I told him that I had a candle burning for him. As his disease progressed, and body and mind disintegrated, he would simply open his eyes and ask if the candle was still burning. He would smile when I replied, "Burning strong," for the candle had become the symbol of his hope. Identifying with the light of the candle, Don seemed to be negotiating his victory over death's darkness. His son David recounts that, days before Don died, in a barely conscious state, he opened his eyes and simply uttered, "I am a candle burning in the night."

A positive symbol enabled Don to leap from the known into the unknown, to move beyond the obvious to things hidden. Symbols introduce new thresholds of perception and mediate meaning from our unconscious depths. One of their functions is to deconstruct the conventional perspectives of ordinary consciousness and bring us into contact with the essential aspects of our lives. In the ebbing of his life, a symbol appeared to Don, and he latched onto it. As his identification with the body faded, the candle became a powerful focal point in an awakening of spiritual identity, a sign of Don's emerging consciousness.

Metaphors leap over ordinary consciousness and lead us into new worlds of meaning. The river is my core metaphor depicting the movement of life and the many challenges we meet in negotiating its winding courses towards open water. Water must keep moving to remain pure, and my life, like a river, is an adventure that is on the move, a journey of ongoing self-discovery. Letting the metaphor expand, I visualize a river travelling not simply over the earth's surface, but through the atmosphere. Every river, in point of fact, is a small aspect of a much larger set of dynamics – the hydrological cycle reveals that water moves in an awesome circle. Precipitation, in many different forms, falls from the atmosphere to the earth. It seeps into the ground or creates the run-off in a watershed area feeding springs, streams, and rivers that flow oceanward. The rain causes the earth to flower, giving seed to the earth and bread to humankind. All this water eventually evaporates, returning to the atmosphere to condense and form cloud, and once again to fall from the sky. The prophet Isaiah employed the hydrological cycle as a metaphor to describe the sacred purposes of the word of love, which I like to call "spiritual rain." Love falls like the rain. I ride on it, swim in it, and ascend on its wings.

the power of image

Images jump at us from the outside world and also arise from inside ourselves. In an emerging global village, the images are mixed and many, and aggressively compete for our attention. As our lives move faster and faster, indeed we are being spun around by the rapidly changing pulse of world views and values. Modern communications technology dramatically accelerates the flow of this great tide of imagery and ideas that assails us from without. In the contemporary scene, we frequently feel unsure of individual identity shaped by such a steady flux of visual stimuli and cultural icons. A further tide of energy arises from our inner depths, and the psyche spontaneously produces a flow of symbolic imagery. How we negotiate these representations of memory and longing, born of past experience and our anticipations of the future, determines to a large extent the pictures we have of ourselves. They play themselves out in positive and negative ways, either to inspire fulfillment or to beget alienation.

A woman once came to me and stated that her life was "not going anywhere." As she described her situation and her feeling of entrapment, the image of a pool of stagnant water appeared inside her imagination. She visualized the water in this pool building up to a critical mass and looking for a channel. This mental image formed into a dam that was about to break. At that moment, the woman exclaimed, "It's me that wants to burst; it's me that's about to give!" Here is a case where tension builds up in the psyche, and the trapped unconscious energy is seeking to find a way out. New self-understanding was struggling to be born, and the tension between the unsatisfactory status quo and the not-yet-imagined future was about to snap. As the woman groped for clarity, this image spoke to her. Metaphorically, as the trapped energy heated up, the journey motif became activated and invited the woman to dare her unknown future.

Wilderness trips always seem to create the magic of igniting the metaphor of life's call to adventure. Awakening primal fire, the immersion into lake and forest invites us back to live in a more instinctual and natural way. Nature outings inevitably seem to stir a strong longing for wholesome living, and spark a desire to reimagine our lifestyles. Trip participants frequently talk about tapping into unmet inner resourcefulness to brave the elements and varieties of challenging weather conditions. Such memories seem to engender new self-trust and courage in meeting the trials of life. Margo typifies the benefit: "I'm not going to avoid difficult challenges anymore. On the other side of every storm, there was sunshine waiting. So I am going to take life's bad weather as an opportunity to learn to become more resourceful. I feel more daring now, not so easily defeated by things." Larry put it this way: "I got rid of a lot of bad attitudes and limiting ideas about myself. The trip was amazing. It gave me a lot of vitality. I feel really excited about the adventure of my life that lies ahead."

the energies of life

I have always been somewhat intimidated by the word "archetype," and struggle to get a clear grasp of its meaning. The word makes better sense when I think of archetypes as the songs of the spirit that I hear deep inside myself. Archetypes describe the energies of life pouring through us: the wisdom, creativity, bliss, talent, and beauty that bubble up from within. These energies are activated if we listen to their inner melodies calling us to authentic life. Archetypes point to wonder, to where the mystery of life wants to take us. They are the patterns of life and of meaning found within the human heart and its symbolic representations. They indicate life's profound spiritual orientations.

We ride the world of matter and spirit on a river of images. The archetypes, representing patterns of symbolic imagery, spark spiritual imagination to guide our development. The symbols springing up from the unconscious disrupt the orderly world of rational definition. They are dynamic and have a rather unpredictable quality. Beyond conceptual thinking, symbolic understanding leads us into the expansive unmapped territory of the non-rational, a world of chaos, ambiguity, and paradox. Introducing both disorder and transformation, symbols take us to the edge of certainty. Our lives are hidden in obscure mystery.

Archetypes are universal and timeless, depicting the overarching patterns of human experience. The hero adventure, for example, describes a life lived in self-discovery, awakened in the power of one's self-determination. Heroic tales are told of those who have risked their necks to bring forth new powers of creativity. Mythic heroes lead the way for us, and exemplify what it means to live authentically. The hero myths inspire in us the courage to live bold, innovative lives. This pattern is the same through different ages and cultures. Other examples of spiritual archetypes described throughout this book include the journey to wholeness, the resurrection motif, sacrificial love, forgiveness, the creative warrior, and the wounded healer.

We also refer to psychological and biological archetypes, patterns of experience within the psyche and body. Puberty would be an example, indicating a stage of human growth having the same pattern the world round, whether one is born in Lima, Melbourne, or Cairo. Similarly, the underlying spiritual themes of human life are everywhere the same. The same truths are revealed through various symbolic images, truths bigger than any particular geography, cultural tradition, or historical moment. Archetypes have motifs that are common and constant. They are not created by the individual or any particular cultural tradition, but are, as it were, spiritually organic. They enter by way of mythic symbols, dream personifications, storytelling, or by way of direct experience.

Beyond the mundane, spiritual archetypes guide us towards the vision of our own creative fulfillment. These songs from within open our hearts to compassion, and invite us into a deep communion with all of life. Introduced to a world beyond immediate appearance, we leap from the banal world into transcendent realms. Powerful positive images capture our imagination, sweep us up in a luminosity of insight, and enliven us with inspiration. Archetypes guide us to larger meanings so that everyday life becomes an epic adventure of love.

discernment of symbols

Symbols have their pulls and counterpulls. They give us both direction and misdirection, compelling our attention and activity towards both true and illusory values. It is most important, cautions Robert Doran, a Jesuit scholar, not to give free reign to the psyche. He points out the danger of being swallowed up by the unconscious and swept away by emerging feelings and fantasies. Some images mislead us completely and incline us to false values. We imagine our happiness in the wrong place. Opposites reside within the human psyche: villains and heroes, greed and generosity, bad and good. Vulgar images can seduce us, deluding our imagination and passions, and giving us wrong guidance. At other times, we are caught in the power of psychological complexes, driven by anger, fear, resentment, or hatred. Or, we become hooked into an addictive grab for money, food, alcohol, sex, or drugs to offset the desolations of life.

On the positive side, we receive images that guide us to find ways out of our emotional confinements and release us from possession by mere instinct. Spiritual practices such as meditation help us to purify our intentions and to discover a noble path. They inspire us to build genuine and generous relationships that reform our world in the image of love. As we mark out a direction of love, luminosity dispels inner darkness.

Nocturnal dreams give us a window into a world bigger than that of ordinary consciousness. In sleep, dreams spontaneously produce symbols within the psyche that can portray new depths of being. Symbolic images evoke feelings, and are evoked by them. Dreams are ultimately about the dreamer, whose hidden aspects are symbolized in her or his dreams. In dream interpretation, we tend to let rational consciousness dictate its messages. But the language of symbols can be deciphered only up to a point, and should not be dishonoured with black-and-white explanations. Plain language and literal interpretation cannot adequately clarify their meanings. It is better to observe dreams and avoid quick and often naive interpretations, instead letting dream impressions slowly filter into images. Their discontinuous messages are progressively revealed, and thus require patient attention. As mentioned above, the gift of discernment helps sort out positive and negative directions of meaning. It is not a question of figuring out, but letting the symbolic images take us beyond words into mysterious places where new dimensions of awareness open up.

educating imagination

The word "myth" commonly has been distorted to represent that which is not true. Ironically, the essence of genuine myth points to that which is most true about life. A myth may be a story of fact or fiction, but essentially it is employed as a metaphor of meaning. The accuracy of historical detail is irrelevant. What is significant is the spiritual value suggested, the wisdom a myth contains. Myths speak to our experience of life, and assist us in the art of living. They are time-honoured maps geared to open us to authentic existence. Mythic stories teach us how to read the movement of life, how to steady ourselves in the day-to-day flux, and how to realize the full depth of ourselves. They help us to traverse thresholds of transformation and undergo ordeals of change.

Through myth, we activate symbolic images. Myths, says Joseph Campbell, are "masks of God" opening up eternity as divinity pours into temporal time. Myths awaken us to wonder, to beauty, and to the transcendent. "This is the final secret of myth – to teach you how to penetrate the labyrinth of life in such a way that its spiritual values come through."[37] Myths about the sublime are often taken as literal fact or historical truth, and their intended meanings become grossly distorted. The wisdom of myth is principally symbolic, meant to put us in accord with the inner mystery of ourselves, with the natural world, with the social good, and with the movement of life. Myths help us resolve deep inner conflicts within self and within society. They develop a language and ethic of harmonious relationship.

We live in a demythologized age, and symbols that once excited our imaginations and vision no longer command the same attention. Sometimes our construct of reality comes more from media and advertising images than from our own spiritual depths. We tend to trust external images more than those that arise from inner imagination. Refined scientific insight has rightly rendered obsolete many past formulations of meaning. But, as a result, we have lost our appreciation of symbols and blunted our myth-making skills. By putting too much faith in science and what it "knows," we are in danger of being cut off from regions of the human psyche and spirit. Logic and language will get us only so far. A one-sided emphasis on hard knowledge has diluted mystery and meaning.

As we meet the difficult challenges of our contemporary times, we frequently find ourselves unprepared, confused about direction and lacking the right clues to find our spiritual paths. In losing access to the imaginative world, we forfeit wisdom. In losing sight of the significance of symbol-making and ritual, we fail to tap into the level of essential meanings, and thereby fail to harness our spiritual potential. Development is necessarily impaired when we do not penetrate beneath the surface of things. When inner communication shuts down, a healthy interplay no longer exists between the worlds of instinct and spirit. They split off from each other, inducing a crisis of anxiety and disillusionment. Without a song of the imagination, we quickly lose touch with our inner depth.

The genius of the spirit helps us reclaim our health and vitality. Otherwise, we remain stuck in our muddy emotions. Stephen and Robin Larsen, in their biography of Joseph Campbell entitled *A Fire in the Mind*, highlight the importance of mythic imagination: "When we are confronted with a profound or even a naive manifestation of the myth, we enjoy a deep sense of recovered composure, health, power, and enthusiasm for life…."[38] The authors emphasize the contrast between "mythos" and "complex." A psychological complex reflects the woundings and traumas of personal biography. In my life, when I was not able to find my authentic story and follow its fundamental truth, I became confused, experienced a crisis of anxiety, and felt bereft. Only by working through my anger and resentment consciously could I recover my composure. Myths and stories provided images of healing that enabled me to negotiate these disturbed feelings, and move beyond their grip and irritation. Otherwise, I would have remained disturbed and possessed by negative emotions. Myths educate the imagination. With healing symbols, we activate the wisdom of the heart enabling us to learn to love.

informed maps

A map is a set of images, a limited representation of a particular geography. Maps are used to guide our movement over unknown physical or spiritual terrain. They provide pictures that simplify a multi-dimensional world, and thereby enable us to better see where we are going. The maps that others chart can benefit us up to a point, and help us avoid dangers and dead ends. We are able to learn from the experience of those who have gone before us. But every journey, in a sense, is new and like no other. Each of us will also need a map of our own making to penetrate the personal labyrinth of our own unprecedented life.

From the poet, the priestess, and the philosopher, we receive inspiration and rich instruction. Shamans, scientists, and saints all communicate a bounty of insight and truth. Inspired teachers, artists, and storytellers create fertile soil for our own individual discovery, and the understanding actualized in their consciousness moves out to us. Joseph Campbell points to literature for guidance. "I'll tell you a way, a very nice way. Sit in a room and read – and read and read. And read the right books by the right people. Your mind is brought onto that level, and you have a nice, mild, slow-burning rapture all the time."[39] We also receive clues of direction from those special friends and companions who share with us the energies and symbols that fire their own imaginations. In short, through the guidance of tradition and common hard-won wisdoms, we learn much more than what we can find out for ourselves. We derive extraordinary benefit from the lived experience and dynamic consciousness of others.

However, to discern the deep personal truth of our individual lives, we need to critically evaluate our received maps. Outside wisdom must be confirmed in our own developed understanding. While map-making relies on communal pools of insight, our lives are ultimately in our own hands – we must draft our own blueprints, and continually revise them as we acquire new insight. During our river expeditions, we carefully scout every set of challenging rapids. Each canoeist first studies the water dynamics on her or his own, then compares the individual reading of the waters with the interpretations of other canoemates, and lastly checks the map of a river guidebook. As each of us acquires river expertise, our growing knowledge allows us to trust our own judgment as it matures in a dialogue with the experience and insight of others.

Mythic stories speak to eternal principles, but lose their purity when their messages are distorted through the authoritarian imposition of ideas and values. Cultural systems sometimes tend to be more closed than open, and thus impede the integrity of an individual's quest for value. When we are told what the symbols should mean, myth is employed to force interpretation, to control norms of conduct, and to dictate morality. A living dialogue with immediate experience is replaced by standard evaluations. Mythic stories frequently become contaminated with institutional propaganda in the service of preserving unexamined tradition. Then, the reference becomes more to the past than to the present, more to historical than to spiritual significance, and more to static interpretation than dynamic symbolic creativity. Since the journey of life ever travels over new topography, our maps of meaning are always under revision. We are constantly demythologizing and remythologizing to find a way over ambiguous terrain. Some mythic maps have an enduring quality; others are useful only for brief excursions. Each of us must enter into careful discernment to clarify which maps of meaning are valid.

It is our map-making expertise that makes all the difference in finding sound direction in the movement of life.

The question we have been asking centres on the manner in which we awaken authentic identity and find genuine happiness. My search has gone down many rivers of lost meaning before finding what I think to be my true river. I have bought into illusory images, followed many false lights, and used wrong maps. No doubt, for all of us, right wisdom is hard won. As we shatter our illusions, one by one, and tear up our faulty maps, we begin to taste the law of inner harmony. Saving grace lies in our ability to educate the imagination, to awaken the creativity of love within ourselves, and to go where the mysteries of life want to take us. We have only to beg the spiritual gifts of wisdom and discernment to guide the great adventure of becoming real.

Part 2

Inspired Quest: Integrity

6
To Live the Question ...
Awareness Power

... we are body-spirits and the energies of desire permeate our being. The desires and longings which we have for what is beautiful, for what makes sense, for what is true, for what has value, and for what has ultimate value are at the heart of what it means to be human.

Vernon Gregson, *The Desires of the Human Heart*

What is it I need to know ...
what is it I don't know I need to know?

Mary Oliver, *The Leaf and the Cloud*

Beings endowed with self-awareness become, precisely in virtue of that bending back upon themselves, immediately capable of rising into a new sphere of existence: in truth another world is born.

Teilhard de Chardin, *Hymn of the Universe*

awareness power

"What is your success rate?" was the frequent question of visitors coming to our drug rehabilitation centre. I found myself resisting this question and would offer a slightly provocative response: "About a hundred percent these days." My answer was usually met with a quizzical look. "Well," I quickly added, "it all depends on how you define success." To elucidate my thought, I would continue, "There are some individuals who have been drug-free or sober, say for two years, but who are not doing very well. There are others just rebounding from a slip who are making good progress." The point I wanted to make was that the criteria for success ought not to be reduced to one indicator – the time period of abstinence. A better measure would reflect an individual's readiness for true self-encounter, I suggested. Beyond the tendency to look for fast self-understanding and happy-ever-after outcomes, success lies more in the activation of a deep healing journey. Beyond symptom management, it is necessary to address the root conflicts underpinning drug behaviour. More than a superficial resolve of bad conduct, genuine rehabilitation embraces the quest to find one's true freedom. It is a process that takes time. Everyone grows at a different pace, and results are achieved as they are achieved. I like what Gandhi said about full effort being full victory.

A huge emphasis was placed on will power when I was growing up. The basic teaching suggested that control and change were simply a matter of will. "Where there's a will, there's a way," was a frequently used adage. Through time, as I observed my own noble efforts to change, I began to question whether willingness and determination were enough to win self-mastery. I also noted that many individuals, caught up in addictions of one kind or another, were unable to change despite very determined resolution and effort. From personal experience, I knew that after many exhausting inner power struggles, I had yet to tame the beast. There was more to self-control than clenching my fist, gritting my teeth, and simply powering through. How, I asked, are our impulsive drives brought under control? How do we get out of the victim position? What are we to do with anger and jealousy and fear, and all manner of unruly emotion?

I did not get any fast answers, but just asking new questions felt good. My desire for a grasp of richer understanding set a process of dialogue and discovery in motion. It became clear to me that awareness gives energetic momentum to the unfolding of our lives. Indeed, by awareness we evolve, and our willingness to change seems to grow in proportion to our self-knowledge. Awareness power, combined with the will to change, creates the master key. We have then to awaken that fascination for self-discovery that energizes transformation, for it is the longing for wholeness that drives us to plumb our inner depth. In observing the flow of outer happenings and inner experience, and probing the yet unknown, our lives become defined by an aspiration for enlarged consciousness. It is in this expansion of consciousness, it seems to me, that our true creativity is released.

looking for a conversation

One September morning in 1982, in a moment of keen aspiration, I contacted 22 friends, suggesting we form a conversation circle. The journey of personal transformation was to be the subject of the proposed dialogue. I felt somewhat timid in taking this initiative, but I was eagerly looking for a conversation.

Inside a therapeutic setting, I had enjoyed a privileged intimacy with young drug abusers through the previous five years. The abundant healing nurture I had received left me feeling alive as never before. That is how I came to appreciate the value of sharing with others the different maps we each use in search of happiness, harmony, and force of character. A new friendship circle, I hoped, would create a similar opportunity for intimate sharing. My plan was not to set up a therapeutic encounter, but rather to create a relaxed dialogue on themes of personal development. I proposed putting an idea or question into the centre of our circle each week, around which we would pivot our conversation. Our inquiry was to focus on the transformative process, exploring the kinds of effort that would help us to heal, unlock inner creativity, and realize personal happiness.

The response to my invitation was extremely enthusiastic – nineteen individuals jumped into the process. Two circles were formed and met weekly for the next nine months. Thus, a dialogue – which we called IASIS, derived from the Greek, meaning "a place where one is restored to wholeness" – was born. The dialogues were lively and energizing, no doubt because we were talking about what really mattered most to us, and sharing with each other the world inside ourselves. In the excitement of self-discovery, our questions and ideas were carried outside the circle to kitchen tables around Montreal, and the conversation kept gathering steam. A third circle was formed, and a fourth. The momentum continued, and over the next few years, 50 circles had been created throughout Québec and Ontario.

As the dialogues evolved, participants, each in their own manner, sought to understand ways to open themselves up to self-knowledge, healing power, and the energies of life. Our guiding questions reflected on the challenge of realizing personal authenticity. In an atmosphere of relaxed trust, the chance to exchange personal experience acted as a powerful catalyst for change – a pool of rich insight served to stimulate individual inquiry. Through self-encounter and our intimate interactions with one another, we tapped into a wealth of wisdom, allowing each of us to find new inner depth.

In the autumn of 1995, thirteen years after the initial IASIS circle, the conversation went to the East. As the rainy season lifted from northeastern India, I returned to the eastern Himalayas, and immersed myself in a cross-cultural dialogue with mountain folk throughout the Darjeeling region: students, social development workers, teachers, spiritual communities. Our learning circles comprised an extraordinary mix of people drawn from a wide diversity of experience and culture, both spiritual and secular. Through encounter, as we exchanged maps of meaning with one another, we tasted the oneness of human aspiration. Through appreciating our cultural differences, it became clear that we have a common story and a collective purpose. For myself, I came to sense that the pressing challenge of the modern age lies in developing a global sense of family. Out of that Himalayan conversation, extended through the waxing and waning of six cycles of the moon, what became truly apparent to me was the critical importance – as cultures intersect more and more on our shrinking planet – of articulating a new global spirituality.

counterpoints of view

Imagine yourself sitting in one of these circles. In the centre of the circle, on a small table, is a cup. You are asked how many flowers you see on the design of the cup, and you respond, saying, "One." Catherine, the person directly across from you, is asked the same question. She responds, "Two." Paul, the person a quarter way around the circle to the right, acknowledges seeing a part of two flowers, while Debbie, the person quarter left, attests to seeing only a part of one flower. A second question is asked to the members of the group: how many handles do you see on the cup? You and two others say, "One"; the fourth person states that there is no handle. Clearly, the group is divided in the way it sees the features of the cup.

Each individual has an original point of view, a lone angle of perception. Hence, the data feedback is mixed. The cup reveals a variety of faces, and the ensuing conversation is quick to produce disagreement. The range of perceived images highlights the uniqueness of every angle from which the object on the small table is viewed. Each person sees from a single vantage point, and captures only small aspects of a much larger reality. Over and over again, participants in this exercise have expressed the shock of realizing the tiny size of their subjective perspectives, quite literally a *point* of view.

A further question is asked: "In light of the conflicting perceptions, who is right and who is wrong?" At first there is a quick and common consensus that everyone is right and no one wrong. But Catherine hesitates and qualifies her answer: "Each one sees what each one sees, so no one's really wrong. But no one is really right, inasmuch as everyone is very limited in what they see." Debbie raises a further question about the accuracy of perception: "Is there such a thing as misperception? Can one's subjective vision be faulty? How are we going to find out the real number of flowers and handles?" Paul pipes in, "We could all be wrong!"

Admittedly, there is tension when people come together to live, work, learn, or play. Differences often rub the wrong way and leave us at odds with one another. The wide diversity of viewpoints in all human affairs creates stresses that frequently play themselves out in bitter arguments or violent power struggles, if not all-out war. A disintegrative factor in relationships and group living reveals itself unless tensions of dissemblance are in some way resolved. On the other hand, integrity is achieved where there is a keen respect for divergent perceptions, ideas, judgments, beliefs, and values. As we ponder and probe and put our eyes together with others, we come to see through a wider lens.

An argument can point to healthy debate, but, more often than not, the word "argument" carries a negative connotation – it suggests an adversarial exchange that lacks genuine communication. At the bottom of any argument embedded in narrow-mindedness is a fundamental deficit of affirmation and respect for the perspectives of others. Arguments of this kind are everyday events, whereas positive debate is perhaps a rarer occurrence. Whenever irrefutable claims are made to one's own understanding, attempts are made to impose ideas and beliefs on others. With rigidly held opinions, the interplay between individuals becomes an arena of war, involving to one degree or another dynamics of win-lose, attack-counterattack, and offence-defence. Making oneself right tends to be matched by an equal effort to make others wrong. An unhealthy argument, in short, implies an interpersonal power struggle that degenerates into two stubborn monologues.

Conflict, however, need not be divisive, and when properly understood and managed, actually helps to build relational integrity. Paradoxically, differences inspire the drive for truth, and questions needing to be asked are brought to light. The catalytic tension of varied views representing a range of human experience invites interactive inquiry, enabling wider wisdom to emerge from narrower perspective. Chaos theorist John R. Van Eenwyk states, "When we begin to see the perspectives of others, chaos becomes a discussion."[40] Authentic dialogue is born as different points of view find expression in positive confrontation. Where humility and respect are present, power struggles are transformed into creative human encounters leading to extraordinary breakthroughs of insight.

Every perspective is an entrance into wider understanding; however, misperceptions, deceptions, and biases need to be identified and weeded out. While affirming the validity of subjective experience, we still face the challenge of arriving at some notion of what is real and of moving beyond private understanding. In *To Know As We Are Known*, Parker Palmer argues that "Too many of us subscribe to a weak doctrine of pluralism, to the simple notion that truth looks different when viewed from different angles. Because this notion concedes diversity without calling us into dialogue, it leaves us in isolation and destroys community... ."[41] Palmer suggests that we too easily concede our differences, and settle for a truth that consists of little more than our own private perceptions and needs.

Truth is then both private and communal. Palmer dares us to recognize that differences invite a dynamic play of inter-subjectivity. The effort to clarify our diverse notions of truth involves a co-operative process of mutual transformation. It is vital to go beyond ideas that were once thought valid. Truth lies inside and outside ourselves, somewhere juxtaposed between opposing views. Any quest for truth involves long and exacting observation: noticing from one angle, and then another, and another. Patient inquiry and careful discourse are indispensable to success. As points and counterpoints listen to each other, new understanding emerges to enhance the accuracy of judgments of fact and value. There can be no doubt that openness to the questions and critiques of others empowers correction and development. Through creative dialogue, ignorance and illusion become exposed, engendering wiser insight and more prudent courses of action.

the narrow mind

"Are there any narrow-minded people in Sikkim?" I asked a class of graduating high school students living high up in the Himalayan hills. "Sure, I live with some!" shot back one student. There was a roar of nervous laughter, but after some initial shyness, there ensued an outpouring of self-expression and, as it turned out, it was impossible to cap the conversation once it got underway. I invited the students to define the nature of narrow-mindedness. The gist of what they had to say was that narrow-minded people live in closed systems, and show an extraordinary intolerance of insights not congruent with their own. They are rigid, and lock into a way of seeing and doing things. They block relationship and stifle dialogue. Threatened by and unable to assume other viewpoints, narrow-minded persons want to exercise control: they attempt to overpower others and to manipulate situations. As they become entrenched in fixed positions, they build identities that need to be heavily defended. Their best defence is an offence, and they often go on the attack. One student neatly summed up the matter: "All violence in relationships seems rooted in attitudes of intolerance and domination."

I was amazed at the penetrating insight these young people possessed. When further asked to define the opposite of narrow-mindedness, they suggested that supple-minded individuals are open to growth and new understanding. They welcome encounters with others and always seem ready to dialogue their truth. In order to experience the other side, they are able to suspend their points of view and listen with care. It is not a question of lacking a position or giving up their convictions, but rather a matter of not being inordinately attached to one position. An open mind takes us beyond narrow and fixed interpretations, beyond reductive explanations and rigid definitions. When we are able to let other viewpoints be, and to enter into a lively exchange of ideas and experience, we demonstrate a readiness to learn. Continuous learning is always in search of a new way of looking at things.

What of our convictions? Can we have a firm belief, solid values, and still be open to other viewpoints? To have a conviction does not mean being inordinately attached to our present views. Nor does it mean being definitively correct, and making what anyone else believes categorically wrong. When we are in touch with and able to affirm an inner sense of truth, we do not feel the need to defend ourselves. A basic postulate is that truth speaks for itself. Indeed, we can be loyal to our own personal truth and be passionate about our ideas, and, at the same time, converse confidently with other positions. The juxtaposition of opposite points of view is fertile ground for expanding insight. In dialogue, we can both challenge and let ourselves be challenged by others. The virtue of humility enables creative confrontation that invites openness and results in a mutual modification of outlooks. It is the insecure fundamentalist who avoids dialogue and shores up fear with non-negotiable beliefs.

One of the Sikkimese students drew our attention to Gandhi, who exemplified a firmness of conviction and a readiness for confrontation. Gandhi argued that truth born in inner dialogue must find outer expression. In his view, it was vital to take a stand and clearly articulate one's ideas, beliefs, and values, even though it requires great courage to hold one's truth in the face of evil and error. However, this task of self-expression, Gandhi emphasized, must be rendered with humility and without resorting to violence. To be humble does not mean negating our inner truth, but rather relinquishing any arrogant claims to absolute rightness. Most of all, it requires us to respect the right of others to be different. The exercise of true humility allows us to listen with sensitivity to all oppositions to our truth, and even to suffer lies and the aggression of enemy attack. In the end, Gandhi's life and death invite us to trust the integrity of the truth process.

collaborative learning

I used to be quite attached to a self-image of being ruggedly autonomous. I prided myself on the ability to stand on my own, and, retreating into a private world, would attempt to figure most things out by myself. The dialogue circles helped me break out of my self-enclosed world. I began to recognize that in isolation, learning lags. Left to ourselves, we live in a smaller world, unable to receive and benefit from the wisdom of others. The creative exchange of positions and counterpoints moves us into the experience of mutual transformation. The circles also gave me the opportunity to learn the art of careful listening and skillful self-expression.

Exposure and encounter facilitate the enlargement of awareness, and create a feedback loop that enables us to be present to ourselves in a new way. I need other persons, especially to get to know myself. Without interaction and mirroring, self-knowledge narrows. In the interplay of my awareness meeting the awareness of others, I am no longer a stranger to them or to myself.

Beyond my direct interactions with others, living an open life means letting myself be exposed to a broader community of consciousness, to the rich insights of poets, intellectuals and artists. Jesuit thinker Bernard Lonergan highlights this notion of wide learning: "Again words express not merely what we have found out for ourselves but also all we care to learn from the memories of others, from the common sense of the community, from the pages of literature, from the labours of scholars, from the investigations of scientists, from the experience of saints, from the meditations of philosophers and theologians."[42] Through a communion experience, I learn to value the deliberations and discoveries of others along with my own.

primal wonder

I am fond of the expression the "art of noticing." It suggests the practice of bringing wakeful attention to whatever is happening. I notice my hunger, or anxiety, or the longings of my heart. I observe my thoughts and mental processes, and listen to the flow of my feelings. I note my breath, feel heat and cold, and watch inspiration come and go. As well, I notice the people I meet, the conversations I have, and what is going on around me in the external world. Just noticing seems to create a large leap of awareness.

Primal wonder ignites the human mind in its dynamic longing to understand. Wonder sparks the quest for order and meaning. We reach into the dark unknown to explore, question by question, the hidden mysteries of the universe and our own enigmatic self-perplexity. Relentlessly, we search out answers in an attempt to undo the suffering, confusion, and disorder in which we find ourselves mired. Taking us beyond routines of perception, wonder sets off a flow of questions about anything and everything. I am graced when I have others with whom to share my questions.

Questions create disquiet, tension, inner conflict, instability. Questions leave room for movement, expansion, the enlargement of perception. The mysteries that our questions probe are infinitely complex, and our answers are never big enough. The knowledge we come upon stands up only so long, and our tidy explanations all wear out. What we think is clear returns to confusion, becomes stale, is no longer adequate. Our answers are not sufficient to grasp the whole truth of anything. They fall apart time after time, exploding ever again into mystery beyond the nets of human understanding. The monk Thomas Merton proposed that we fear asking questions because they might not have answers.

The tension of wonder keeps us on the edge of insight. To be truly alive is to be in a process of continuous learning. With age, I learn to feel somewhat more at home in the mystery of the unknown. It is natural to grieve the loss of secure answers, but are we not also compelled to search beyond our knowing for what is missing in our understanding? Wonder is the lively spiritual libido that excites us and pushes us towards the horizon of the infinite unknown. We are invigorated by questions, forever tantalized by the secrets of the universe. Since meaning and value are never fully grasped, the task of inquiry is never complete.

Wonder seeks insight – it begins the quest for truth. It evokes questions that enable us to appropriate what is obscure and to bring the dark unknown to light. Curiosity emerges from an inborn unrestricted desire to know that guides our awareness towards genuine value. This desire is oriented to the task of recognizing the good, discovering freedom, and building sound integrity. For Plato, that freedom consists in finding a way out of our dark caves into light. For Bernard Lonergan, freedom is achieving human authenticity.

The longer we are able to hold the tension of a stubborn question, the greater the depth of our emerging insight. When confusion refuses to yield to clarity, it is all the more important to sustain inquiry and stay with the process. Things eventually begin to make sense in a new way. Wisdom breaks in to bring a gift of understanding and new orientations of meaning. We are always delighted when insight arrives, and in the middle of that delight we find an even deeper thirst for what remains unrevealed. There is no answer sufficient to put an end to the questions sparked by wonder. Inquiry, unless stifled, moves ever onwards.

Questions do not survive where self-righteous attitudes prevail. Locked beliefs often form on the heels of "right" answers, and further questions are refused. Dogmatic thinking clings to answers, and proposes rigid methods for achieving desired results. I love the story of the rat in a maze, running down this tunnel and that tunnel in pursuit of cheese. Finally, the rat finds the cheese, and comes to associate cheese with the tunnel where it was discovered. But one day, the cheese gets moved. The rat heads down that familiar tunnel several times before realizing there is no more cheese to be had there, and that it ought to start looking elsewhere. If we build faulty beliefs about where the cheese is to be found, we keep going down the same tunnels forever, even long after the cheese disappears. Human beings easily get attached to their own right ideas and right answers. We lock into fixed notions of the good, even after our beliefs fail to deliver their promises, and then proceed to tell everyone else that they are looking in the wrong tunnels. Worse still, our righteousness makes it categorically wrong for others even to entertain the notion of exploring another tunnel. But, in the end, what counts is finding the cheese. Our first loyalty ought to be to truth, not to being right.

a bride to amazement

The following of wonder is a lifelong expedition, a pilgrimage to the heart of the universe. In "When Death Comes," the poet Mary Oliver writes of her hope to live all her life as a bride to amazement. It is awe that sends us forth on the quest. Beyond closed-mindedness, we become moving viewpoints. This theme of openness also resonates in the writings of Marilyn Ferguson, author in new age themes:

> Molecules and stars, brainwaves and concepts, individuals and societies – all have the potential for transformation. Transformation, like a vehicle on a downward incline, gathers momentum as it goes. All wholes transcend their parts by virtue of internal coherence, cooperation, openness to input. The higher on the evolutionary scale, the more freedom to reorganize. An ant lives out a destiny; a human

being shapes one. Evolution is a continuous breaking and forming to make new, richer wholes. Even our genetic material is in flux. If we try to live as closed systems, we are doomed to regress. If we enlarge our awareness, admit new information, and take advantage of the brain's brilliant capacity to integrate and reconcile, we can leap forward.[43]

For me to become genuine demands vigilant inner attention in obedience to the desire to discover who I am and what I am to make of myself. Not content with incomplete observation and partial truths, my task is to root out illusion in order to come to know what is ultimately worthwhile in my life. The eros of wonder, when I am faithful to it, allows me to discover new layers of value that usher in progressive wholeness. The hard part, we might all agree, is the requirement of perseverance and patience, for an adventure of awareness involves a protracted discipline. I have come to appreciate that my apprenticeship will last a lifetime. My new mantra is "keep rivering," by which I encourage myself to be tireless in effort, to stay awake, and to keep rigorously honest. Self-discovery is unrestricted, and the mystery of life's meaning ever expands. The challenge is to listen long, to live the question, to let go, and to leap into the wonder of love.

7
Insight and Action ...
Alienation to Authenticity

The notion of self-awareness ... is not a looking at myself but a being with myself.

Sebastian Moore, *The Inner Loneliness*

Our knowing is oriented toward action: we desire to know because we desire to act, and act intelligently. Our experiencing, understanding, and judging are directed not to just what is, but to what is to be done, not just to knowing reality, but to creating reality, and creating ourselves in the process.

Vernon Gregson, *The Desires of the Human Heart*

Love is clarity of perception and accuracy of response.

J. Krishnamurti

dynamic knowing

Shortly before turning 50, I wrote to friends about feeling restless, and mentioned that my mood was to "go for broke" as I entered the next decade of my life. Be careful what you pray for, the saying goes. Three months later, my life was on a new trajectory, both because of an unexpected birthday gift and the initiation of my "River of Awareness" writing project.

The gift was a sponsored trip to Boston to attend The Lonergan Workshop. At this conference, I found myself in the company of philosophers and theologians from around the world who gather once a year to reflect on the writings of Bernard Lonergan, a deceased Canadian Jesuit. I had neither read nor heard of Lonergan, but my benefactor recommended this week-long workshop to spark my interest. In his life devoted to a study of human understanding, Lonergan had probed the disillusionment of the modern age, which showed much evidence of personal and social decline. Observing the growing vacuum of values and meaning, he strove to understand the dynamics of this deterioration. Arriving at the conference with a store of limited street knowledge, I felt somewhat intimidated to be in the company of these scholars. But as I met and conversed with workshop participants, I discovered that we shared many common questions regarding alienation and authenticity. Contemporary modern life indeed seemed marked by widespread disenchantment. I would often wonder what we needed to learn in order to find more personal peace and social harmony. How might I live life in a more soulful way?

I have always been interested in questions related to understanding how we learn. So I was delighted to discover Lonergan's focus on the learning process, outlining a method of discernment and decision that guides sound insight and purposeful action. In his pivotal work, *Insight*, Lonergan explores the natural human desire to know as it searches for genuine value. How are we empowered to comprehend and choose what is truly worthwhile? I was excited to find the IASIS dialogues congruent with Lonergan's model of dynamic knowing. There is a pattern, he suggests, in how we come to understand, that is built right into life, a pattern we can easily verify in our own experience. The process is driven by the power of intention. It focuses on the notion of an engaged dialogue with our questions in search of meaning. Lonergan's model of dynamic knowing suggests an open path of self-discovery leading us ultimately into the experience of love.

To follow this path is to first be attentive to one's own concrete experience – to question and come into an understanding of that experience. My school education always seemed abstracted from the questions I really needed to ask about life. So I was pleased at the Lonergan conference to explore the notion of self-inquiry. Beyond observing and questioning our experience, we are invited to verify the soundness of the insights we glean. This step of discernment is of paramount importance, and I know from personal experience that its lack accounts for some large gaps in my self-development. I have had to suffer some hard lessons. The final step in Lonergan's intentional consciousness is to dare to do the right thing, that is, to live out of the notion of good that we discover, to walk the talk. This decision of action is sometimes the hardest step of all, only because of the human tendency to prefer the easy way out, or perhaps because we get caught in the rut of chasing after habitual satisfactions.

The more questions I ask, the more insights I acquire. Learning grows out of an inborn desire to know, and my knowledge constantly advances as I co-operate with that natural desire. On the other hand, if I refuse questions and avoid investigating what I do not yet know, my spontaneous inclination to learn wanes. In restricting curiosity, possibility is narrowed down. I then settle for easy, once-and-for-all answers. Conceptual thinking tends to focus on knowing as content more than as desire and process. Conversely, Lonergan places full emphasis on nourishing the desire to know, and guiding the development of that desire.

The second reason I so appreciated the Boston conference was that it converged with my question about what it means to live genuinely. From my own life experience, I know that the advancement of meaning and value has accrued as a result of being attentive to my concrete lived experience. In Lonergan's view, authentic living demands such attentiveness to enable us to find a path of love. The more we head into the direction of love, the more we come into true possession of ourselves. Inauthenticity occurs when I brush aside questions, make rash judgments, and avoid self-inquiry. Authenticity falters if I choose satisfactions over value, and go against the grain of personal meaning. Through further appreciating the powers of attention and intention, the conference served to strengthen my commitment to wide-eyed living.

The final benefit I derived from the week-long workshop was a heightened realization of how my religious experience had introduced me to another realm of knowing found through prayer and meditation, through ritual and liturgy, and foremost in the experience of love. The Christian tradition, which has been my heritage, speaks of the Love of God being poured into our hearts by the Holy Spirit. Among the gratuitous gifts of the Spirit are wisdom, understanding, sound judgment, wonder, and awe. These amazing graces arrive as gifts rather than a fruit of human striving. I was able to appreciate in a new way the spiritual legacy that has blessed my life. I felt a new sense of gratitude for the rich inner and outer instruction that has guided me gently along my river adventure.

primary awareness

Primary awareness is mere experiencing, and precedes reflective consciousness. Before we think about what's happening, we are involved in self-presence. We simply witness what is going on in our bodies, our minds, our emotions, and our external worlds. We observe experience before we attempt to make sense of what is happening. In the last chapter, mention was made of the art of noticing, where we witness ourselves being hungry, feeling angry, or worrying about something, for example. Experience is simply any situation or state of being in which one finds oneself: sensing, dreaming, thinking, feeling, acting. Primary awareness observes the data of our physical senses, our mental processes, and the flow of consciousness within interior psychic and spiritual realms.

Self-awareness creates what Sebastian Moore calls "the vibrancy of myself."[44] It is not a matter of figuring myself out, but rather a "being with" myself. In the first stage, we simply witness the flow of inner and outer experience. The observation of experience is the starting point before we analyze and try to figure things out. Lonergan describes the first level of awareness:

"It is a world of immediate experience, of the given as given, of image and affect without any perceptible intrusion from insight or concept, reflection or judgment, deliberation or choice. It is the world of pleasure and pain, hunger and thirst, food and drink, rage and satisfaction and sleep."[45] It is direct experience, a spontaneous presence to the raw moment-to-moment goings-on within and outside ourselves. It is observation in front of interpretation.

We cannot easily sustain non-judgmental attention to the now moment. The goal of practices of mindfulness is to stay highly awake and alert, and not offer any resistance to what is happening in the present. That means letting go of both future and past, of worry and regret. I often remind myself to meet "the river as it presents itself," a sort of mantra by which I try to allow everything to be as it is. Though my taste of the now is rare, it is liberating simply to practise witnessing my moods, desires, and reactions without judgment or aversion. As I acquire a measured power of self-observation, I learn to let things be and to be with myself. A participant in one of our dialogue circles suggested that IASIS can be sounded another way: "I-as-is."

the delight of insight

Beyond observation, we begin to question our experience. We are propelled by curiosity, an intent pushing us out of ignorance to seek what we do not understand. Attracted to deeper awareness, we reflect on our personal experience – biological, emotional, intellectual, aesthetic, spiritual – and ask questions for understanding. These questions set the process of inquiry in motion, and are crucial to insight. This second level of reflective awareness represents an intensification of knowing, and the natural drive to see how things fit together often requires prolonged investigation and painful effort. But asking questions, sooner or later, always leads to the delight of insight. Teilhard de Chardin speaks of this second level of awareness as a "bending back," and attests that acts of reflection enable us to effect a transformation in depth.

There is something mysterious about the arrival of insights – they often emerge out of nowhere. Though we puzzle over matters and work hard to try to make sense of what's happening, when insight arrives, it seems to come quite gratuitously. Out of the blue, something clicks, a connection is made, an idea dawns upon us, a pattern of meaning is comprehended. Our behaviours are influenced as such insights emerge and expand. In the unexpected leap of understanding, we experience a release from tension and feel a joy we want to share with others. Yet, even as a piece of the puzzle gets solved, we are impelled to ask new questions. Over time, the insights we gather combine and build on one another, cumulatively enabling us to better clarify what is going on as well as to get a better grasp of situations. Going a step further, we begin to identify patterns of experience and build conceptual frameworks of understanding.

The artist, too, responds to the desire to know, and intends to interpret and place value on human experience. Artistic formulations do not attempt to define truth, but to reveal it. Artists employ the language of images and symbols rather than methods of theory to explore the truth of life. Artistic insight, scientific discoveries, and spiritual illumination are all peak experiences, moments of delight as we glimpse the unknown universe.

crucial discernment

The validity of any insight needs to be questioned, to undergo reality testing. Any grasp of understanding is only partial, and sometimes suffers gross distortion. Some of the insights we have are sharp and on the mark, and some shabby. How do we tell the difference? Lonergan's well-known remark that "insights are a dime a dozen"[46] highlights his emphasis on the crucial importance of developing an acuity of insight. We can always deceive ourselves. There are oversights as well as insights, mistaken beliefs and false solutions. Sound understanding is often lacking. Thus, in search of true clarity of perception, we need to be tentative about the conclusions we make, always verifying the data we gather and the judgment we exercise.

Where there is miscomprehension, ineffective paths of action result. Distorted insight sheds false light on the realities of our lives, and we pay dearly for poor judgment. Only a fine quality of discernment can uncover truth. The choice to live authentically entails a commitment to critical and honest self-inquiry. When facts are evaded or not respected, or when we are closed to new information, development is arrested. If we make false assumptions or, avoid questioning what we already know, learning shuts down. We also fail to grow when we rashly jump to quick conclusions, or, through indecisiveness, postpone evaluation altogether. Lastly, misunderstanding arises in the refusal to raise vital questions. All manner of running away from insight precludes intelligent choices, and so leads to folly. Disintegration ensues and is marked by disenchantment.

To address the web of error in our knowing and doing, a proper method of discernment is crucial. Our dime-a-dozen insights must be critically verified with hard evidence. Intellectual morality begs a thorough and rigorous testing of the truth of our insights, requiring us to "never make a judgment that outruns the evidence."[47] We must ask, "Have I got this right, and does my insight mirror what is really going on?" Lonergan's analysis of operations of experiencing, understanding, and critical reflection correspond with the process used by investigative scientists as they gather data, make hypotheses, and verify their findings by careful experiment. Each interpretation will either find affirmation or be rejected as false. Eventually, we arrive at a probability of correct understanding, guided by the clearest thinking of which we are capable. A scientist today speaks of probabilities, not of absolutes. At some point we must say that such and such conclusions represent the best available understanding, and then take a stand. Such evaluation brings to an end a particular line of inquiry.

Things are often not as they seem, and indeed, all that glitters is not gold. What we see cannot always be believed, for knowing goes further than mere looking. Hence, continuous reality checks are necessary. The exercise of sound judgment in human affairs requires deliberation, discernment, a set of criteria for coming to what is truly so. As we work from level to level through this dynamic structure of knowing, awareness expands in new directions, grows in richness. In a succession of discoveries, insights gather cumulatively, progress results. In a self-correcting process of learning, the crucial activity of discernment exposes mistaken ideas and the limitations of any one insight. The process spontaneously evokes the further questions that lead towards a more comprehensive understanding. Exposing one error tends to reveal related errors, enabling us to undo a web of false views.

psychic conversion

A friend was recently diagnosed with congestive heart failure. On the evening before a quadruple bypass operation, I visited her in hospital. The medical technology was most impressive – modern biofeedback supplied comprehensive data enabling precise diagnosis. The surgical team, with a remarkable base of knowledge and skills, provided treatment marked by excellence. It made me wonder if it would be possible to acquire the same precision of insight in the realm of the human psyche. I suspected that the process would look much the same: good data, sound interpretation, and skillful means.

The psyche is the source of a spontaneous flow of images and intentions, feelings and fantasies, thoughts known and hidden. The psyche writes its own biography, and sometimes throws us for unexpected loops. Robert Doran, a Lonergan colleague, refers to the psyche as "the pulsing flow of life,"[48] a complex world of motion and commotion: memories and anticipations, wishes and longings, dreams and symbols, imaginings and sensations. With attentiveness to what the psyche is revealing, psychological self-knowledge provides the basis upon which new direction of meaning can be found. The psyche makes a lot of noise. It is our task to listen to the inner din, and, through acts of self-understanding, we begin to see patterns to the noise. How we understand the dynamics of this inner flow will determine our capacity either to find or to lose a direction of meaning in our lives. The material of the psyche provides the data to be noted and interpreted. As quality medical treatment depends on complete data and sound diagnosis, similarly, in the realm of the psyche, we must pay keen attention to the world inside ourselves and carefully interpret what is going on. This is Doran's notion of "psychic conversion." The greater the knowledge we have of our psyches, the better our ability to make good choices.

Insight is needed, though it is not always wanted. Repression, like congestive heart failure, acts to block the flow of images and energy produced within the psyche. Old habits of thinking and feeling hem in parts of the psyche needed for developing consciousness. Certain contents of the psyche are unwelcome and thus censored. If I fail to see what is going on inside myself, or misinterpret what I see, I lose myself in misdirection and meaninglessness. The essence of authentic existence, for Doran, is finding direction in the very movement of life, and for this, self-knowledge is vital. In this way, I am not simply swept along by the pulsing psychic flow, but orient myself to wellness through acts of understanding and love. I will either find a path of meaning or lose my way.

connection to feeling

All of us are, in part, a bundle of feelings. A wide range of emotion accompanies our attitudes and ambitions, our inclinations and intention. A flow of feelings runs through every experience. Feelings themselves beget feelings, building momentum in both positive and negative directions.

Feelings can lead or mislead us. They push and pull us to what is worthwhile or worthless. They point to those things that either add value to or devalue our lives. Connection to inner feeling opens the way to health; we are able to get in touch with ourselves, and with our true values. Consolations and desolations reveal patterns of feeling that, when discerned with care, can give us clues to find a right direction. But when we are at a distance from our feelings, our choices become disconnected from the substance of our lives. Cut off from feeling, we are prone to follow illusory satisfactions and seductions. As we open up to the world of the psyche, feelings reveal how we are being moved and what directions we need to move in.

Unconscious feelings paralyze growth, and drag us down. Denied fear, resentment, anger, guilt, and sadness hold us in their grip. Such feelings go underground as we resist insight, critical judgment, and decisions of courage. A disordered psyche refuses or is incapable of the journey of self-presence: it stifles questions, ignores higher values, and thus the noise within the psyche gets turned up. Inattention to the inner psychic processes is similar to neglecting the symptoms of a physical ailment and to evading diagnosis. Whatever impedes wakefulness and blocks intelligent self-inquiry feeds a momentum of negative disintegration. Doran evaluates this situation in the following way:

> Psychic disorder can now be understood in terms of complexes of psychic energy that interfere with, block, or prevent the sustained performance of the operations through which direction is found in the movement of life: the operations of intelligent inquiry and insight, of critical reflection and judgment, of responsible deliberation and decision, of love.[49]

This brings us back to ask what it means to be truly authentic. Along the path Lonergan describes, authenticity begins with paying attention and asking questions. That which is genuine

> ... does not brush questions aside, smother doubts, push problems down, escape to activity, to chatter, to passive entertainment, to sleep, to narcotics. It confronts issues, inspects them, studies their many aspects, works out their various implications, contemplates their concrete consequences in one's own life and in the lives of others.[50]

Knowing is never static, and we are willing to throw away old answers. Protecting what we know only hinders our ability to grow. Indeed, our knowledge is ever incomplete, our learning never-ending. Our openness thus must be unrestricted, for no answer is complete enough to silence further questions.

The river of authenticity follows the way of inquiry and insight, deliberation and decision. It is the path to love. What is discerned as worthwhile needs to find affirmation in action, and there must be a leap from "knowing" to "doing." As consciousness evolves, conscience forms and asks to be followed. This point introduces us to the field of morality, which is nothing more than a language of value. Moral deliberation allows us to discover the best possible choices. Our theories of the good have then to be translated into decision and deed, and to find expression in acts of moral courage and love. It is a matter of understanding the right thing to do and daring to do it.

the art of deciding

Any venture of consciousness recognizes that there are limitations on present awareness. Because these gaps exist, our decision-making should be handled with extreme care. Sound decisions require a comprehensive understanding of the complex matters that come into play in any particular evaluation. In my own decision-making, I have come up with what I call the 5D process: data, delay, deliberation, discernment, and decision.

The first step involves the gathering of good data – getting the facts and information right, observing circumstances carefully, and paying attention to detail. From experience I know that if the data is wrong, any decision I take is doomed from the start. This leads into the second step, which is to delay. I try to be particularly mindful here. The key is deciding not to decide in order to allow an adequate time frame to listen long to the question at hand. I heard a radio report delivering the same message: don't make decisions, sleep on the question; the subconscious is a think tank. The French say, "La nuit porte conseil" (the night brings guidance). I first get clear about when the decision needs to be taken. I then designate a suitable time interval to allow for an open-ended exploration of all options, a period in which to probe and wait for insight. The Great Law of the Iroquois contained a dictum that the more important the decision, the more slowly it should be made. They stressed the importance of wide consultation and collaboration to ensure the quality of their evaluations and choices.

The deliberation phase entails holding the tension of alternatives, listening to a wide range of images and ideas and feelings, and letting my viewpoint expand. Critical questioning reverses closed-mindedness and avoidance of truth. I stick to my questions to avoid wavering back and forth between hastily drawn, premature conclusions. The fourth step is the task of discernment: an effort to weed out any bias and blind spots, and check my judgment. Sound discernment exposes the ways in which we narrow down consciousness and resist its call for continuous enlargement. The final step translates into being decisive. At the designated time for deciding, I follow what my best understanding indicates and embrace a choice. From here on, we should not doubt the decision taken, but act with strong resolve.

daring to be free

Getting real involves renouncing inauthenticity. When I am out of touch with where my life story comes from and where it wants to go, I forfeit my personhood. As I refuse to heal the past and to build a future, development is replaced by drifting. We are all drifters, to one extent or another, inasmuch as we deny our possibilities. Drifters fail to find themselves, their own decisions and deeds. They are defined from the outside in, and conform to what everyone else is thinking and doing. Inauthenticity reveals the want of self-determination. Authenticity, however, demands open-eyed living, and invites a strong core commitment to learning. In place of stumbling along, we embrace the challenge of unimagined possibility. As the quest for integrity intensifies, we move into the possession of our autonomy, and become the centre of our own self-determination. Our discoveries, decisions, and deeds make us who we are to be.

A critical point in my appropriation of personal autonomy is reached, Lonergan emphasizes, as I come to realize that it is up to me to decide what to make of myself. A path of self-determination combines the ways of attentiveness and wisdom and love, those higher integrations of my being that are realized through dynamic learning. Faithfulness to my journey of self-discovery enables sustained attentiveness, inspired discernment, and a steady intention of the good. My choices need to reflect the courage to opt for true value over that which is simply pleasing. Beyond mindless action and aimless drifting, as I choose conscious living, my capacity for genuine love keeps on growing. In place of endless futility, the good is intended, opted for, acted toward. Through finding a direction of meaning, I discover my true freedom.

Inspiration is as much a part of us as breathing in and breathing out, but we are not always conscious of the process. The emergence of personal authenticity is probable if it is sustained by an expansion of interiority. Interiority persuades the search for integrated psychological and spiritual wisdom, and invigorates outward action to make our external lives vibrantly free. An inner vision defines our task of meaning, and calls forth discipline. As I search for and move towards love, I allow myself to reimagine my possibilities. Ultimately, I am not defined by biological and psychological conditions – I do not exist simply as effects of causes and conditioning. Rather, spirit in each of us triumphs over mind and matter; our intellectual and artistic formulations enable us to break out of limiting self-images and beliefs. Each of us becomes a maker of history and meaning. We each create a life.

The Dhammapada, a Buddhist text compiled in the third century BC, instructs, "By faith, by virtue and energy, by deep contemplation and vision, by wisdom and by right action, you shall overcome the sorrows of life."[51] I love the promise of these words. They persuade me to live an open life, letting myself be guided from challenge to challenge. They encourage me to dive into inner mystery, energetic action, and moral meaning – to make my life into a work of art.

8
Feelings Are Stories ... Buried Fire

... Self-awareness is insight. Such persons with little of it are repressed and not insightful. They are difficult to deal with as persons. Persons with greater insight are easier to deal with in depth. They have rich moment-to-moment impressions. There is no defensive hiding. They are available to themselves and to others.

... Feeling can soon be recognized as the background accompaniment of all perception, all thought, all action. The relaxed perception of this background allows our feeling to clarify its own meaning and directions.

Wilson Van Dusen, *The Natural Depth in Man*

You don't repress feelings, you negotiate them.
You find out why you feel the way you do.

Robert M. Doran, *Dialogues in Celebration*

Alas for you lawyers and Pharisees, hypocrites!
You clean the outside of the cup and dish,
which you have filled inside by robbery and self-indulgence!
Blind Pharisee! ... you are like tombs covered with whitewash;
they look well from outside, but inside are full of dead man's bones
and all kinds of filth.

Matthew 23:25, 27

rain and rage

Chinese medicine says to be aware of two dangers: climate and the emotions. Wilderness trips sometimes bring extremes of both. Warm sunshine burning away a morning mist, soothing breezes, the intoxicating smell of the forest after a gentle rain each create a special delight. But I recall a particular canoe trip where the weather was foul and a lot of nasty emotion was kicking up in my psyche. A storm of anger at a friend threw me into turmoil. It rained hard all that day, and neither the rage nor the rain let up.

Out in the back country, there is no running away from a storm. You are stuck with the world of nature, and with yourself and your canoemates, for better or for worse. On that trip, I was able to escape neither the cold wet weather nor my hot anger. Much as one wants a way out of discomfort, negative emotions have a way of not allowing us to ignore them. I was upset with a close friend – feeling hurt, misunderstood, wrongly accused, isolated. I didn't know what to do with all these messy emotions. My anger went unabated. I walked through the soggy forest, skipped supper, and crawled into my sleeping bag before sunset. I tossed and turned through the night, and my anger seemed to have an even harder edge the next morning. I was holding on to it, justifying it, wanting to lash out. I felt ashamed of not being in control.

Indeed, I was in ego territory, wanting to hide the un-ideal me. On pure adrenalin, I walked a muddy 3,000-metre portage non-stop with a canoe on my head! Gradually it started to dawn on me that the enemy was within, not without. I experienced partial relief when my "holding on" became a "letting go" as I released some of my violent thoughts towards my friend. But the rage seemed to then turn inwards. Still afraid of giving up its false pride, my ego did not want to admit the muddy me. More was needed: to learn to care for my anger as one would have compassion on a wounded companion. I would have to release my resistance to my emotional discomfort, to hold and explore it, to transform it.

Sometimes it is so hard to stop the momentum of negative emotion, and choose to let go. Once again, I was being taught that I do not need to hide from feelings or run from myself – my task is rather to befriend my emotional experience, and read and interpret the data of the psyche within a framework of memory and understanding. I had to let go of my ego's need to conquer negative feelings; the challenge was to accept them and negotiate their meanings.

emotional literacy

Emotion is like the movement of a river running inside ourselves. Frequently that motion turns into commotion, perhaps chronic emotional discomfort, as we become choked up with anger, stuck in grief or regret, embedded in fear or melancholy, or paralyzed by resentment. If feelings are shunned or misread, the forward momentum of living slows down. We remain emotionally illiterate, disconnected, weary, and disturbed when we are unable to read the stories our feelings tell. However, in dialogue with our emotions, we become aware of their patterns. Self-observation lets us attend to the data of our psychic flow as we begin to decipher our feelings within an interpretive framework. In this way, we can free up emotional blockages and discern new directions of meaning.

On the phone answering machine, I could feel an agony of the struggle in Mike's voice. He indicated that he was three days drug-free, and "it's mental now!" Feelings of rage were surfacing, and Mike felt very raw and vulnerable. "Maybe I'm just destined to self-destruct," he uttered.

Mike's drug addiction hooks into a deep resentment that has had him in its grip for a long time. An experience of deep shaming in early childhood put him on the sidelines of life, and he felt denied the enjoyment of common pleasures. Mike has always spoken of his need to turn to drugs as a way to contain his violent emotions. "If I didn't use drugs, I'd go crazy. I'd lose it completely, and all hell would break loose."

Resentment is indeed a very costly emotion, for it chokes our very freedom. It is a "raw deal" feeling based on getting the short end of the stick. It arises in situations of injustice, both real and perceived. Examples of such injustices include being disadvantaged or exploited, taken for granted, short-changed in terms of recognition or opportunity, inappropriately punished, underpaid or unacknowledged, grossly misunderstood, or deprived of privileges and the good fortune that others enjoy. In loud protest of life's mistreatment, resentment knows a dark chemistry of anger and envy. At its worst, it lashes out at those who have the long end of the stick, feeding on hatred and a desire for vengeance. In the grip of resentment, like a broken record, we rehash the past, going over and over the injustices experienced. If we keep replaying our stories of victimization, the plot of our lives turns into a melodrama of helplessness and tired protest.

"I don't know how to not think this way," Mike lamented. He felt trapped both in his resentment and in his addictive behaviours. Mike did not know how to go about the huge task of learning to accept the loss that held him in dark grief. That healing process entails seeking to understand why he feels the way he does. It involves an effort towards self-knowledge in search of the liberating insight that will enable him to let go of his sense of being prevented from living happily. In some way, Mike's feeling of strong entitlement to what would be "more fair" will have to melt down. Carlo Carretto, a Little Brother of Jesus, in *Letters from the Desert*, proposes, as an answer to injustice, the compelling image of shifting from a *victim* to *victor* position, through letting go of what one thinks one deserves. The way out of emotional discomfort requires finding a love that is larger than the fairness that resentment demands. In order to claim a sense of personal control over his life, Mike will have to choose not to stay in victim identity. That freedom was yet for him to recover.

The range of human feeling is awesome. We feel apathetic, proud, jealous, shy, optimistic, regretful, guilty, confident, embarrassed, frustrated, angry, grateful, envious, lonely, helpless, exuberant, mischievous, peaceful, enthusiastic, bored, paranoid, infatuated, hungry, confused, determined, resentful, nervous, glad, or sad – often many of these at the same time. The list could stretch on ad infinitum to depict the colourful drama of inner experience with its subtle moods, its varied rhythms, its lively tempo. Laughter and tears are both born out of our feelings. Feelings introduce us to our full humanity, revealing lamentation and longing, suffering and joy, disenchantment and ecstasy. Any stream of feeling knows both welcome and unwanted emotion.

Feelings are neither good nor bad. We feel what we feel what we feel. In themselves, feelings are not dangerous. However, actions that are prompted by unrecognized feelings can be very dangerous. If we get down on our feelings, or deny them, or dramatize them, we cut ourselves off from vital awareness. Habits of repressing or acting out feelings lead to personal and interpersonal dysfunction. We tend to split off parts of ourselves by banishing feeling: "It's silly to feel that way ... there's no reason to be feeling angry like this ... stop crying, you're okay ... have a cookie, and you'll feel better ... there's nothing to be afraid of ... you shouldn't be feeling guilty ... why don't you stop feeling sorry for yourself?" I was taught that feelings should be subordinated to reason. I have since learned that when we relegate feelings to an inferior importance, we deny our passions and split off a part of who we are. Indeed, large aspects of personhood are rejected and lost. In so doing, we meet only a part of ourselves, and thus, we have less intimate encounter with others. The effect is a flattening of the personality.

composting muddy feelings

"I just want to feel it through," a buddy of mine remarked when terminating a long-term relationship with a girlfriend he had been dating since high school. I asked my friend what he meant by feeling it through, and he responded, "I have a lot of sadness in me. I just have to let it in and let it go." I liked his way of saying this. As described earlier, I have never found it easy to climb inside my feelings and work them through. When growing up, I was taught that feelings are a poor test of reality. I was told to think rather than to feel. I was never taught to befriend my emotions and factor them into the equation-making of my life.

Connection to feeling, I now know, is vital to identifying the movement and momentum of my life. Every feeling is a story. The demanding task of self-intimacy is to listen to those stories. Like the five senses, our feelings are an indispensable means of self-knowledge. They are spontaneous signals from within that connect us to our natural inclinations. Feeling, states Van Dusen, forms the background accompaniment to the end-products of thinking and acting. A sensitive attunement to the world moving inside ourselves helps us paint an honest portrait of self. The feelings that spring from our unconscious depths guide us to what is congruent with our natural bent – they amplify the perspectives of our narrower conceptual outlooks.

As I take cognizance of inner feeling, I come into possession of myself. Beyond denial, I simply need to be alert to what is going on inside me. Once emotions are identified, Robert Doran suggests that we negotiate with the psyche to persuade our feelings. We should not just drift along with them, nor let ourselves be swept along in their undertow. Feelings can either guide us or drag us along. They, too, can be seductive, and lead us astray. Reason helps us to sort out and order our emotions, and to discern whether our feelings are attracting us towards true or illusory value. As we develop a framework for understanding the messages of our emotions, we become empowered to make choices. To summarize, to take our emotions seriously means to carefully monitor and identify them, and to interpret them as accurately as we can in order to find right direction in the movement of life.

I like to remind myself that it is out of mud that flowers grow. The image is compelling for me because it suggests that healing is not achieved through eliminating the negative aspects of my experience. Healing does not mean getting rid of unwanted emotions, or overriding the turmoil inside myself. On the contrary, it is to come face to face with those inner worlds of muddy feeling. The trauma and tension of emotional wounding call forth a new ordering of life. As manure is composted into fertile soil, in like manner, alienated feeling can be converted into positive energy. The challenge of cultivating negative feelings into a beautiful garden entails learning the art and science of composting. It is good to remember that rotten garbage makes good fertilizer.

the self unaware

Carl Jung coined the term "shadow" to denote aspects of ourselves, both dark and bright, that we do not care to see. He was referring to that part of the human personality, the realm of the unconscious, which goes into hiding. The psyche is divided between the conscious self, a mere tip of the iceberg, and the unconscious self, a vast inner world hidden below the surface. The term "bright shadow" denotes an individual's undiscovered positive potential and disregarded talent. On the other hand, the dark shadow is a composite of all that is undesirable within ourselves. The dark shadow conceals the unacceptable. We seem to prefer more angelic images of ourselves, and therefore disassociate from our messy human nature. When we deny that our feet are made of clay, and try to live up to impossible ideals, it becomes difficult for us to confess our faults – our mistakes cause us to squirm with shame and to hide from ourselves. Those muddy feelings, unkind thoughts, narcissistic attitudes, and uncivilized desires that intrude upon our innocent self-images are disowned.

I know that my self-image is tied to the ideal world. I need to put on masks of goodness, and to present myself always in the best possible light. In trying to live up to family expectations and cultural norms of appropriateness, I camouflage the bad and the ugly. Even though I keep pushing the non-ideal out of sight, it does not go away. My mom used to say I had a whited-sepulchre personality: his room looks nice and neat and tidy, but don't look inside the closet. Over and over, Jesus condemned the Pharisees for their game of trying to look good. Needing approval and attempting to avoid the risk of reproach, I, too, hide my undesirable *humus*, a looking-good strategy to win the regard of others. Every time I put my stronger foot forward, I pretend even to myself that I do not have a weaker foot.

In the end, disowning aspects of oneself comes at a cost. As we deny a part of our experience and rationalize aberrant behaviours, we risk shutting down awareness. In so doing, we engender self-alienation.

> The person who suppresses the animal side of one's nature may become civilized, but does so at the expense of decreasing the motive power for spontaneity, creativity, strong emotions, and deep insights. A person cuts oneself off from the wisdom of one's instinctual nature, a wisdom that can be more profound than any learning or culture can provide.[52]

As Malcolm, the saxophone player, spoke of his need to go through dissonance to get to resonance, the tension of imperfection, too, complements our search for the music of love.

the nun and the prostitute

Sister Mary Rose recounted to me the story of meeting her shadow in a most unexpected way. "I was getting more and more upset. I was experiencing a lot of disruptive emotions and feeling really uneasy in my own skin." The religious nun continued to describe how she had become progressively more unstable, moody, and dysfunctional in day-to-day living within her spiritual community. Eventually, she decided to leave her religious order and seek help from a therapist. The former nun told of meeting in group therapy another woman whose story resonated almost completely with her own. That woman, who for years had been a prostitute, was now digging up a past that indicated a history of sexual incest with her father. The prostitute's telling triggered deep emotion in Mary Rose as she relived the same painful experience buried deep in her own memory. Later she remarked that "The prostitute and I the nun had simply put on different 'habits' to cope with our experiences of abuse. Here we were, outside our social masks, both faced with the task of coming to terms with the deeper issues which had defined our defensive survival posturing."

The nun and the prostitute were engaged with their father complex. A psychological complex refers to a pocket of emotional energy that builds up in the psyche. Memories of the past, charged with feeling, define patterns of experience. We think we know who we are and that we are in control. Yet, we are in fact owned by our complexes. Repressed memories live autonomously inside the psyche – they have a life of their own, and unconsciously shape our choices. When they remain unrecognized and untamed, they covertly control us. Thus we are bound by past memory, and our self-determination in the present is undermined. A negative complex will take over ordinary consciousness and temporarily possess us. What gets split off in the unconscious runs a lot of interference, says Hollis, "… for what is not integrated will be projected onto others or leak out in dangerous behaviour," or will be "… internalized in debilitating ways."[53] We see this, for example, in persons who have buried their anger, but whose repressed rage surfaces in a bad temper or violent outbursts, or turns into self-destructive behaviour. The poison of resentment, feelings of inferiority, reaction to authority, grief, guilt, fear, and frustration build on past experiences of victimization, humiliation, being dominated, loss, blame, intimidation, lack of recognition, and the like. They cripple present living, for the past gets replayed over and over again. The fact of the matter is that we do not heal memory by banishing our painful emotions and the unpleasant aspects of the past. Our feelings get buried alive, and remain active inside us.

restriction versus repression

A wisdom teaching says, "Keep your friends close. Keep your enemies closer." We repress our uncivilized urges in order to control these unwelcome impulses, yet the catch is that repression itself renders us less in control. If we act without being conscious of our motives, we become blind to our own behaviours, attitudes, and habits of thinking and feeling, and thus become largely unaware of what is driving us. In a sense, instead of being the driver, we are being driven. Only with consciousness can we attain a measure of self-mastery.

Any repression of the flow of insight will stifle inquiry, ultimately narrowing comprehension and consciousness. Repression, or what we might call shadow-making, blocks from awareness that part of the personality that fails to conform to our idealized self-images. This includes characteristics such as aggression, guilt, envy, narcissism, lust, deceit, hatred, anger, jealousy, resentment, fear, greed, and inferiority, to name a few. What is not ideal is sent into exile and stored in the unconscious. Shadow-making occurs when we fear losing control of our passions, or when we want to cover up what we think is bad in ourselves.

Acknowledgment counteracts repression. As the shadow becomes unmasked, the self is befriended. The conscious personality is required to stop lying and to get in touch with the contents of the unconscious. Not to do so is to court chaos. It's easier to slay the devil you know than the devil you don't. In connecting to our unconscious depths and relating with the shadow, we become less one-sided and more rounded. Our consciousness grows much wider. Ending our pretence of perfection, we begin to see ourselves as we truly are.

What you do not know about yourself will hurt you. Initially, the psyche will tolerate repression and the inner world will stand in the wings, while one's outer life will run along somewhat smoothly. If ignored persistently, a mutiny will eventually arise from within. The shadow personality is dangerous when not acknowledged, accepted, and assimilated by the conscious personality. Obsessive thoughts, addictions and compulsive behaviours, moodiness, violence, chronic depression, emotional disturbance, and mental illness ensue. Only by recognizing our impulses and our more primitive energies do we prevent repressed content from finding circuitous expression in negative behaviours, disease, or interpersonal dysfunction.

Sebastian Moore makes a clear distinction between restriction and repression: "Restriction means recognizing honestly that I desire something, and deciding then that the prosecution of this desire is not appropriate; whereas repression means pretending to myself that I don't have the desire."[54] When repression gives way to expression, that content emerging from the unconscious needs a discipline of restriction to find appropriate declaration and expression. We had a rule of thumb in our drug rehabilitation program: verbalize your feelings, but don't dump them, don't dramatize them, don't act them out.

circumstantial bottle-openers

Patterns of emotion form configurations within the psyche that become grooved in a certain way. Our feelings are often emotional replays from the past, simply new editions of old emotions. They are often repeating something that happened earlier, and do not solely apply to the person or situation onto whom they are being transferred in the present. How do we put these repetitions behind us? Are we able to repattern the mind and discard emotions of the past?

When we relive the emotional experience of a distant past, these replays give us a wonderful opportunity to climb inside our feeling worlds. As we go down "... long, long corridors extending into deep darkness,"[55] we can then begin to make some sense of our enigmatic emotions. Rosemary Haughton coins the term "circumstantial bottle-openers," referring to the particular situations that trigger stored-up emotion.[56] Powerful constellations of repressed feelings erupt from one's inner depths, activated by an event, big or small, that parallels the past. A circumstance of the present often affords a micro picture of surface reality, but alludes to the macro picture of a hidden world of complex feeling.

What is important to understand is that the immediate cause of feeling is not the only cause. When the charge of emotional energy is out of proportion to the triggering circumstances, we know a bigger story is being told. The sadness when a close friend moves away might activate some buried grief related to an earlier loss of a loved one. The action of an inconsiderate motorist can draw out some pent-up anger associated with earlier abuse. An unkind put-down might stir up old feelings of shame. Behaving in a way that contradicts one's code of ethics could well touch off a deep-rooted guilt complex. As old forgotten feelings surface in the present, and we relive the past, we have the opportunity to develop emotional insight that can help heal painful past memories.

A story comes to mind from a healing circle in which I had facilitated a conversation focused on circumstantial bottle-openers. After laying out a theoretical scheme, I suggested we come up with some examples to bring to life the idea of emotional self-knowledge. I have never forgotten the story that Brendan told:

> I was sitting in a restaurant on Sunday morning with my girlfriend, and we were hoping to have a nice quiet conversation. We ordered toast and coffee from the waitress, and I told her there was nothing else we wanted. Shortly after my friend and I had begun our conversation, the waitress returned. She dutifully asked, no doubt as she was trained to do, if everything was all right. I felt a little irritated, and impatiently asked her to leave us alone. We have everything we need! The waitress left and we resumed talking, though I was feeling a little agitated. Well, would you believe, after about fifteen minutes, she returned once again, cheerily

asking: sure I can't get you something else? I exploded!
And with some very colourful language, I expressed my
extreme annoyance. I was besides myself. I had told her in
plain and simple English to leave us alone. She then fetched
the manager, we were both thrown out of the restaurant,
and I have been boiling with anger ever since.

As Brendan was relating this story, now four days after the
event, his face became redder and his voice grew angrier. I asked
the group to try to differentiate between the "circumstances"
and the "bottle." The immediate situation included a restaurant,
a Sunday morning and an exchange with a waitress. It quickly became clear to the group that the waitress did not cause Brendan's
anger, though he himself thought it was she who had made
him angry. The group came up with two insights: his anger had
something to do with boundaries and not being listened to. He
had basically put out the message, in plain and simple English,
to stay away. The waitress had returned and invaded his space.
Brendan had not been heard. Brendan's girlfriend was in our circle, and she started to giggle. She was seeing something. Brendan
was open, and encouraged her to express whatever she wanted
to the group. She explained that they had three little kittens at
home, and that every time Brendan was on the telephone, they
jumped up on his lap, and drove him absolutely crazy. He remedied the situation by erecting a partition around the telephone
to keep the cats out. Another member of the group remembered
Brendan the week before, lamenting living in a "one-horse town"
where everybody knows everybody else's business.

Brendan was coming to some new personal insight, and
then something clicked inside him. He announced to the group,
"Do you know that all my life I have been trying to keep people
away!" The upshot was that Brendan recognized his anger as a
pattern of feeling, and that it was his own to heal. The waitress
had not made him angry. His catharsis was not caused by her.
It was only associated with that Sunday morning set of circum-

stances. Brendan's charged emotion suggested that there were bigger issues from the past which begged for healing. He was excited about expanding his awareness further, and he had some good clues to help him investigate his own wounded emotional patterns.

Emotional awareness opens up in many ways. In this instance, the steps included naming the feelings, narrating the circumstances, dis-identifying the triggering situation as the cause of the present feeling, yet using the narrative to find clues to discover overall emotional patterns. This method allowed Brendan to get beyond blame, and to become more conscious of what was driving his negative emotions. In this way, he was empowered to repattern unwanted habits of feeling, and enjoy new emotional freedom. Brendan had been owned by his anger, and now he had become its owner. He was mightily relieved to be set free from his long-standing confinement inside the prison of anger.

9
Intellectual Darkness ...
Bias and Decline

This ambivalence is a reflection of our attitude toward truth per se: we want to know it and at the same time we don't because it hurts, can frighten us, places excessive demands on us, and robs us of the security of our cherished illusions.

Alice Miller, *Thou Shalt Not Be Aware*

We don't know that we don't see.

Gerald Heard, *An Anthology of Devotional Literature*

It is not demanded of us that we always be in a state of the heart which grants us vision and self-mastery. It is only demanded of us that we know the state we are in.

Jacob Needleman, *Lost Christianity*

a new habitat

I did some heavy drinking as a young man, and then went dry for four years to begin a healing journey. I resisted labelling myself an alcoholic though I knew there was a problem I had to face. Labelling is locking, it has been said, and assuming fixed identity seemed to me to undermine the potential of transformation.

Subsequently, my work in the field of drug rehabilitation brought me into relationship with a large number of young persons whose lives had gone out of control for one reason or another. Alcohol and drug abuse were the common denominators that qualified one to join our program. But all too readily we seemed to slap a label on these young abusers, locking them into identities premised on a belief in personal powerlessness. The unexamined assumption was that, if your life was messed up, and you drank or used drugs excessively, you were an addict. It seemed expedient to put everyone into the same mould, and assign common identity. However, the causes underpinning abuse behaviours are complex and multiple, and the required healing strategies equally as varied. I have clearly seen how the imposition of "addict" identity, especially one which becomes fixed over time, amounts to a form of branding that can do great violence to the individual. Narrative self-understanding indeed often becomes self-fulfilling.

All too often we argue hard for our limitations and lock the future into narrow possibility. Through over-identifying with the negative aspects of experience, we block belief in positive potential. If we let ourselves be reduced to the name of a disease, we risk *becoming* our sickness. It's one thing to address misbehaviour, and another to define self as the problem. When we build negative images around notions of self-defeat, we do not just *have* problems, we *are* our problems.

I like to think about rehabilitation as a question, not an answer. Essentially a process of open self-inquiry, it begins with listening deeply to my inner affliction. It is important to carefully identify my personal conflicts in order to initiate a healing process in search of keen self-understanding. Sound therapeutic strategies, I believe, prefer description to definition, and acknowledgment to explanation. This boils down to more observation, less interpretation. If the therapeutic focus isolates symptomatic behaviour, it fails to investigate the underlying causes of dependency. Such reductionism overlooks an individual's core conflicts. If the singular goal of rehabilitation is to get sober or stay straight, the whole point of a comprehensive healing journey might well be missed.

What is crucial to the modification of abuse behaviour is developing a framework of understanding that addresses its complex multiple causes. In contemporary society, large numbers of young persons go through the painful experience of family breakdown, and many resort to alcohol and drugs as a way of coping. Others are victims of abuse or trauma, and carry deep emotional woundings. Most suffer low self-esteem. For many, drugs and alcohol become a way to manage anxieties, to soften hurt, to numb grief, to escape painful reality. The drug or the drink become all that matters for the afflicted person, but underlying patterns of alienation set up habits of compulsive behaviour. The far-reaching task of rehabilitation, then, is to discover the root imbalances that are throwing the life of an individual into confusion and chaos. In my case, I had the honesty to admit that alcohol was a problem, and the readiness to seek a path of healing. In time, I was able to get to the heart of my inner conflict, and to face the feelings of inadequacy that led to my excessive drinking. Mind you, there are individuals who need to assign themselves addict identity to properly acknowledge chronic compulsivity. But that was not so in my case.

What is important, it seems to me, as a rehabilitation process gets underway, is to start at a place of saying we do not really understand what is going on. Even the simplest human behaviour is hugely complex. Life is dynamic, matter and mind and spirit are always on the move, and each individual is involved in multiple reactions and interactions. Rehabilitation is finding a healing milieu that offers compassionate presence, critical questioning and insight, and steady encouragement. It is finding a new habitat, a safe space, a healing circle in which to explore the sources of disintegration within oneself, then to negotiate new health. The circle helps its members learn to attain new depths of self-understanding. The circle comforts and challenges. The circle shares in a wisdom quest to find sobriety, balance, meaning, integrity.

I don't want to hear about it

It is often said that ignorance is bliss, a rationalization that suggests the strong human tendency to avoid uncomfortable knowing. For the more we know, the more we feel compelled to change. A don't-want-to-hear-about-it attitude seems to reflect a deliberate cover-up of truth, the refusal to search out the knowledge that requires change. Rather than being a case of not knowing any better, it so often turns out to be a case of not wanting to know, a matter of willful denial. Short-term self-interest so often seems to prevail against the way of wakeful attention. Conversely, if in fact it is truth that ultimately sets us free, is it not our ignorance that sabotages our true bliss? Do we not trade our short-term satisfactions, which we defined as bliss, for genuine value? Do we not rob ourselves of lasting happiness?

From time to time, I catch myself thinking, "If only I knew then what I know now." Indeed, we suffer for what is missing in our awareness. Consciousness is a part of the makeup of human freedom, and presents us with the option of developing depth understanding or refusing to do so. Over time, it has become clear to me that I have the choice to be attentive or inattentive, critically reflective or lazy in my thinking, wise or rash in judgment, honest or self-deceived, decisive or indecisive. Shabby attention, deception in understanding, and poor discernment exact huge costs. Looking back on my past, I better understand how the distorted ideas and false values I embraced made my life dysfunctional to one degree or another. I have paid for my don't-want-to-hear-about-it attitudes, my refusals of awareness motivated by self-interest or the reluctance of effort. Careless thinking, self-deception, and mindless busyness have exacted their toll.

Human ingenuity builds on the confidence that problems have solutions. But if we refuse to examine our lives and to put our grasps of insight ever to the test, consciousness contracts and possibility becomes constricted. Frozen thought, rigid interpretation, and unquestioned beliefs lock us into narrow frameworks of understanding. Quick explanations put an end to questioning and short-circuit intellectual endeavour. If the activity of philosophical, artistic, and scientific expression is stifled or undervalued, truth becomes distorted. Intellectual darkness results when we conform to what others think, and refuse critical reading and reflection. Self-knowledge is vital to human development. Our lives are very much diminished when its importance is downplayed.

development and decline

Integrity is found when a spirit of inquiry is alive, and when questions about value are asked. The word "integrity" is usually associated with honesty, speaking truth, sincerity, and harmony. To integrate connotes movement towards unity, while disintegration denotes fragmentation. Mathematicians speak of whole numbers (1, 2, 3 or -1, -2, and so forth) as integers. Their undividedness differentiates them from fractions. Integrity is then a quality of wholeness, of being undivided. Integration is that creative process of getting it together. Entropy defines disintegration, a falling apart that is unredeemed, an uncreative process of breakdown. Conversely, syntropy entails that disintegration that growth itself demands, and that is part of the creative process. A transitional chaos must be navigated, and order and stability surrendered. This involves letting go of a hold on reality, and pushing beyond the edges of the known world. To open up to what lies beyond, an old integrity dies in order to yield a higher integrity. This we might call creative disintegration.

The creative task points to learning what is not yet known, and to finding solutions to problems. Either we are realizing our creative potential or we are failing to develop. According to Bernard Lonergan, we move in one of two directions: development or decline. Development is to find and implement the insights that solve problems. To develop is to attend to the sources of disintegration in ourselves and within our social milieus. Progress gathers insight, not one but many, and moves forward through a series of transformations. Decline, on the other hand, marks the disorder of incomplete development. As integrity is compromised and our questions brushed aside, oversights and blunders abound. Truth cannot be grasped by minds that are closed. The evasion of questions and subsequent insights sets decline in motion. Reliable judgment about what is worthwhile becomes absent, and satisfactions are sought in place of genuine value. Consequently, when sound knowledge is lacking, growth and moral capability are inhibited, and we become confined to a cramped life.

The reversal of darkness requires a gentle patience in sifting through our personal experience and insight; only with courage and a steadfast heart are we able to sustain our practice of awareness. A commitment to honesty is essential to dig down into the pile of self-deception and root out the lies we tell ourselves. This may sound like a rigorous process, but the habit of awareness acquires its own energetic momentum, and does indeed set us free. In the end, the task of consciousness turns out to be much easier than drifting along in a mindless way.

the four biases

To speak of the biases of consciousness is to suggest that we all, indeed, carry a poverty of awareness. We can only take in so much reality. We are more unconscious than conscious. Much truth is beyond perception, or is filtered out for different reasons. The data of our own experience is partial, our interpretations distorted, and our judgment far from sound. Insight is impoverished by bias, which breeds in the mud of egocentricity, as well as the soil of ignorance, self-evasion, and closed-mindedness. Lonergan describes a scheme of four biases that shut down growth and constitute decline. All four serve to compress awareness, and set in motion a wheel of decline that obstructs progress.

First is *dramatic bias*, which alludes to the fact that insight is not always wanted. In fact, it is often shunned. Through shutting out aspects of the self, we repress images emerging from our inner depths and dodge voices calling from the unconscious. Dramatic bias, similar to repression, refers to the evasions of insight that involve a censoring of the psyche to block out self-knowledge. Shadow-making is the selective awareness welcoming what we want to see and banishing undesired knowledge. We exclude questions, flee insight, block out painful memory. Past woundings and traumas in the body or psyche, which we are not ready to heal, set up this self-defensive blocking strategy.

A flow of consciousness loses its dynamic momentum when there is an exclusion of insight and a censorship of unwanted self-knowledge. We select what we are ready to admit into awareness, and at the same time block unconscious psychic content trying to push its way into conscious recognition. Lonergan refers to this spontaneous exclusion of knowledge as a scotoma, a blind spot. While the control and selection of unconscious content is necessary to establish a suitable pace for growth, distorted censorship involves the outright rejection of shadow content: insight is "… brushed aside in an emotional reaction of distaste, pride, dread, horror, revulsion."[57] Such defensive posturing entails a refusal to break out of settled routines, but if understanding is not sought, misunderstandings multiply rapidly. The cure for scotoma is the breakthrough of intellectual and emotional insight, which illuminates the darkness and reverses the previous flight from knowledge. Sometimes in-depth therapy is the only way to negotiate such impasses. An analyst is often needed to outwit the dramatic bias defended through resistance and transferences. Good and honest friends, too, can be helpful in making us aware of our blindness. As psychic trouble is linked to a refusal of understanding, recovery involves an openness to a comprehension formerly unwelcomed. Blindness, and the disorder it entails, are undone by relinquishing our defences and relaxing our efforts of censorship to allow needed insights to emerge. A new possibility of order opens up as misunderstanding gives way to new understanding, as oversight becomes insight.

Second, there is *general bias*, which denotes an antagonism of common sense towards rational inquiry and reflection. Common sense, when it is overvalued, focuses on the immediately practical, and ignores the lengthier search for broader understanding. We often fail to examine our lives and to take a good hard look at what is going on. Intellectual darkness occurs when learning is incomplete. Lonergan suggests that what goes for common sense is quite often "common nonsense." The general bias comes into play when common sense belittles ideas and theoretical investigations, and when it mocks the long tasks of philosophical and scientific inquiry. As we focus on the here-and-now, progress is sacrificed to the short view, and becomes sluggish and stagnant. General bias points to the fact that we are often more inclined to look for quick answers and to refuse the more difficult task of thorough understanding. In a war situation, for example, smart bombs replace the social analysis that is vital to help understand and resolve the complex dynamics of inter-group strife.

Individual bias has to do with egocentricity, and is the third bias that contributes to decline. Here, the individual fails to grasp the reality of interconnection, and private advantage is sought. Insights that threaten perceived self-interest are shunned. The individual is focused on his or her own self-fulfillment, ready to take but not give. The needs of others are excluded, and reality is filtered through the narrow prejudice of one's narcissistic satisfactions. Attention becomes confined to selfish and short-sighted motivations, and situations are exploited to personal advantage. Jean Belair, a Montreal nurse, depicts the difference between self-centred and compassionate care: "The orientation of the nurse may be towards self-regarding values or she may choose self-transcending ones. Either way her practice is a work of art. But the one is dull and lacklustre, devoid of feeling and meaning; the other is bright and energetic, charged with joy and meaning."[58]

The last is *group bias*, which promotes the good of one group or social class over and against the well-being of another segment of the populace. This is the case when a privileged nation exploits a less developed one to promote particular advantage. They put their own well-being first. Bound in a narrow consciousness of separateness, vested-interest groups turn in on themselves and shut out a concern for the wider human family. When one group is elevated and given more legitimacy, its interests are promoted and protected, all at the expense of another group that is undervalued and whose talents and resources are unrewarded. Power and recognition become skewed in their distribution, leading inevitably to social disharmony and moral corruption. There seems to be no end to social injustices.

To describe these four biases is to say that we can be enthusiastic about truth, but very blind to it. However, through understanding the dynamics of decline, we become empowered to unmask bias. We first must be willing to enlarge our understanding, ready to usher in a new way of looking at things. Revolutionary perception is based on innovative and imaginative thinking, and a discipline of effort. We have to work at it. Of course, we never arrive at the full truth of anything; nevertheless, we endeavour to head in that direction. Intellectual integrity thrives when our knowledge is subject to constant critique. True progress is the fruit of conscious living.

justification and ideology

Invariably, we rationalize doing what we do, excuse what we say, or explain how we got to be this or that way. The worst use of reason is to set up cause-and-effect explanations to serve as justifications for our wrong actions. Incessant "becauses" try to legitimize our addictions, our violence, our maladaptive behaviours, or systematic injustice. Our failed lives are defended by endless rationalizations that serve only to protect the status quo. A single cause can be argued to justify a whole life not working.

Explanations can set up and support limiting beliefs that assign causes that keep us trapped in narrow interpretation. It becomes clear that self-justifications rob us of awareness.

Likewise, the avoidance of insight is revealed when we offer blind allegiance to dogmatic belief, an ideal, or unquestioned notions of divine will or the common good. Ideologies prescribe truth and freeze personal interpretation. When critical reflection is lacking, we go along with the thinking of others without careful attention to our own experience and our own questions, and thereby fail to develop insight. When we buy into ready-made ideas and values, truth is proclaimed rather than pursued. When questions go unasked, we are prone to buy into common illusion and deceptions.

The function that ideologies play in justifying our dark deeds is seen in the way we develop beliefs to legitimize and perpetuate violence. Philosopher and professor Michael McCarthy points out the hideous way in which ideological falsehood reinforces our moral blindness:

> Moral evil includes both the wrong that we do alone and the wrong that we do together. And just as we can do greater good by cooperating with other people, so we can do greater evil. ... There is perhaps no graver moral evil than ideology, the false beliefs that we use to justify and even make systematic our destructive wrongdoing. For ideologies, both personal and collective, keep us from acknowledging the harm we do. They keep us from repenting our sins, asking forgiveness, making reparations, amending our lives. They tell us the terrible and seductive lie that we are right, even noble, to inflict suffering, injury, irreversible death on our fellow humans. For after all, they deserve it.[59]

an open path

We hear people talking more and more about the two hemispheres of the brain. The left brain is involved with linear thinking, cause-and-effect, logic, and analysis. The right brain is associated with intuition, gestalts of understanding, and synthesis. Author Robert Ornstein, in *The Psychology of Consciousness*, suggests that these two modes of consciousness, the analytic and the holistic, are complementary to each other. Just as day and night are incomplete without each other, so, too, right- and left-brain processes belong together. During daylight hours, the brilliance of the sun obscures the stars from view. Hence, if our investigation of the stars happens during the daytime, we will fail to locate what is visible only in the dark of night. Both daytime and night-time perspectives are invaluable.

There is a variety of modes through which I come to know the many different ways in which awareness breaks in: biological sensation, gut feelings, common-sense knowing, artistic interpretation, symbolic imagery, intuitive understanding, emotional intelligence, spiritual wisdom, prayer, and, occasionally, mystical illumination. There are deep rhythms of life and vast unexplored regions of human experience that lie beyond rational appropriation. Profound experiences of beauty, love, or suffering open up huge new dimensions of being. Confronted with such experiences, humility teaches me to acknowledge the limits of rational consciousness and to relinquish thinking that I know. While language and theory are useful in helping me identify and interpret my experience, consciousness offers different paths of insight to help me penetrate more deeply into the mystery and meaning and miracle of my existence.

As we have seen, the task of consciousness always calls for critical discernment. Whatever knowledge we glean from our bodies, emotions, intuitions, dreams, and revelations begs us to take pause. What we think we "know" always only approximates the truth. The many paths by which we come to know reveal partial truth, and we never acquire a complete grasp of insight. Whether through left- or right-brain functioning, through the net of logic and language or intuitive grasps of meaning, through reasoned propositions or artistic imagination, or through sudden gestalts of understanding, our knowing is subject to self-deception and bias. Similarly, on the spiritual plane, we must discern holy spirits from evil ones, and root out false claims on God's will. But as we unmask the illusion and deceptions that slant our interpretations, we let a truer light break through.

As we move around the circumference of our experience, we grasp only fragmentary aspects of the whole. There is always a danger of becoming stuck in any one take of reality, captured by a particular image or concept that dominates perception. Optimum awareness travels along a spectrum of perspective, inviting us to open as many windows of insight as possible. An expanding consciousness implies a long journey of discovery to avoid any rush to interpretation, any jumping to conclusions. Easy answers are more comfortable than stubborn questions, and it is not uncommon for us to narrow down the truth of our experience. We are prone to refuse the more difficult questions and challenges. Authenticity involves focused intention and a steady commitment to being with ourselves in honest inner dialogue, as well as to being outwardly attentive. We notice with clarity what is going on in our bodies, our thoughts and feelings, our relationships, and the world around us. The practice of awareness puts us in touch with the pulse of unfolding meaning in our lives.

To practise mindfulness is to practise love, says the Buddhist monk Thich Nhat Hanh, whose spirituality pivots around a practice of insight meditation. This practice seeks "how to understand, how to love, how to make understanding and love into real things."[60] It involves looking deeply into any situation in order to question its true nature. Hanh suggests that we become very rich, and very, very happy, if we develop such habits of mindfulness. Our faulty perceptions bend reality out of shape, whereas accurate perception gives us a grasp of reality. We receive a certain amount of data from sense perception that helps us adapt and respond to our environment. If the data is not registered or is received in a distorted way, we quickly lose touch with reality. In relationships, bad feelings are commonly engendered that are very often the result of misunderstandings. Faulty perception sets up gross misinterpretation, and much interpersonal suffering ensues. So reality checks are needed. Looking deeply means carefully working towards insight that gets it right. With enlarged and sensitive understanding, compassion arises.

To live an open life demands that we live our questions. Responsive to life's intoxicating wonder, the genuine philosopher embarks on a quest for authenticity that entails a commitment to sustained inquiry that holds the tension between the known and the unknown. Any answer is the temporary resolution of a question's tension, a place of rest until new data comes along. With new input, a new unrest develops until a new insight again brings rest, at least for a while. This is the rhythm of tension and rest in learning.

Our world does not need more philosophies, but rather more philosophers. And the philosopher is every person. In welcoming critical intellectual and artistic reflection, I show that I am ready to challenge my established ideas, my habits of thinking and rationalized prejudices, my biases of consciousness. I must be willing to critique my own personal interpretations in order to expose any blind spots that may thwart insight. It is this unrestricted openness to truth that leads to a more intelligent ordering of my life, and that empowers the development of my talent potential for making a better world.

The journey of awareness follows an open path. It relaxes into a stream of consciousness that ever pushes towards new horizons of understanding in a reach for greater illumination. A comprehensive consciousness unlocks our habits of intellectual darkness, and seeks to reverse our flight from insight. It marries analytic and holistic understanding, science and art, reason and faith. Paradoxically, consciousness grows in the midst of ambiguity, and what we know continually explodes into mystery. We can shine light on mystery, but not explain the inexplicable. Wisdom is less what I figure out by myself, and more the gift and voice of the gods. On my "river of awareness," I always stand in need of more illumination to dispel the limitations of my seeing.

10
Fragile Bodies ...
The Healing Force

The material body is a river of atoms, the mind is a river of thought, and what holds them together is a river of intelligence.
Deepak Chopra, *Quantum Healing*

In therapy, the problem is always the whole person, never the symptom alone ... a personality, a life history, a pattern of hopes and desires lie behind the psychosis.
Carl Jung

Exceptional patients do indeed want to be educated and made "doctors" of their own cases.
Bernie S. Siegel, *Love, Medicine & Miracles*

the sturdy chair

"Make your body one of your best friends," exhorted the assistant headmaster addressing a student assembly in Sydney, Australia. All 700 high school students were gripped by these words that came from his heart of grief. Tom was undergoing a serious health crisis at the time, and as he spoke, those present felt his acute sense of loss. Wellness, Tom proposed, was one of the two most important values in life, and he urged the students to find a healthy lifestyle. I was a young teacher at the time, and was grateful for the assistant headmaster's message. It was one I would remember through the years. Yet I was left wondering what the second important value was.

Now, nearly four decades later, I like to pass the message to others, and scatter seeds of health consciousness. Throughout mortal existence, each of us lives in one and the same house. The odyssey of my life takes unique form in the physical being that I inhabit, a body that grounds the entire adventure between birth and death, and as such is worthy of diligent care. The physical organism longs to heal, to feel strong and spirited, and to know love. To harness my health potential, I can activate and guide the process through co-operation with the body's inner intelligence. Tapping the inherent wisdom of nature, I awaken deep vitality. The best medicines I have found include both gentle and vigorous exercise, wholesome food, and sound rest. As biospiritual creatures, we require a host of other sources of nurture: silent meditation, friendship, the healing of memories, forgiveness, the beauty of nature, storytelling, spiritual reading, emotional support, self-expression, and loving touch.

I once attended a talk where the metaphor of a chair with four legs was employed to describe a strategy for health. The speaker pictured the seat of the chair as the body, and the four supporting legs as representing nutrition, exercise, rest, and psychospiritual input. He went on to point out that when one of the legs was shorter than another, it made the chair very wobbly.

During my time in India, I did a three-month stint as a paramedic. My medical rounds brought me into an intimate encounter with large numbers of lepers and with the squatters who lived along the railway tracks. There were also long queues of kids with scabies. Mine was a very hands-on assignment, and I was soon able to identify many of the diseases with which I was coming face to face. In this world of endless suffering, I longed to understand how some of this misery could be prevented. The lack of biological knowledge, adequate food supplies, medicines, uncontaminated drinking water, and proper hygiene all contributed to the widespread physical affliction. As well as witnessing the ravages of malnutrition, I had a hard time maintaining my own intestinal health. I needed to learn about nutrition, the first leg of the chair. I keenly wanted more insight into what foods make the body well.

The body shuns idleness. It is made for movement. To move with the natural grace of the body is to discover an elegance of motion and form. The second leg of the chair is exercise. Through inertia and immobility, our muscles knot up and we experience physical lethargy. "If you don't use it, you lose it," goes the old saying. If energy is blocked, illness ensues. Conversely, we experience well-being when energy flows. I know that when I am in shape, I thoroughly enjoy my embodiment. Our bodies are naturally dynamic, seeking their fulfillment in graceful movement and vigorous toil and exuberant play.

In mid-life, I began to practise yoga, and was pleased to find how much it helped me both relax the body and focus the mind. In yoga, I discovered a balance that combined stretching and strengthening exercise, together with the observation of breath to help bring the mind to stillness. Yoga also enabled me to let go of a lot of pent-up feelings stored in the cells and musculature of my body. In releasing accumulated tension, I had more space within my body and felt lighter.

The third leg of the chair metaphor represents the body's need for rest. In this time- and task-driven age, we disregard the body's need for a healthy stress-relaxation rhythm. When I began lifeguard training, lesson one caught me by surprise. It focused on how to defend oneself from a victim thrashing about in the water. The rationale, though, quickly became apparent: before a rescue can be undertaken, a victim must be calm. Otherwise, efforts at rescue are futile and risk two drownings. In a similar way, healing begins with a strategy to cultivate deep relaxation. Stress plays a big part in the anatomy of any disease, and prolonged distress compromises the immune system's capability. Towards this goal of calm, it is essential to find a matrix of healing and sources of restful repose.

The old adage "early to bed and early to rise makes a person healthy, wealthy, and wise" perhaps gives us the best wisdom about rest. The sleep debt in our non-stop modern times has reached unprecedented levels, and seriously compromises our health. Modern technology has made us into creatures of the night as we sit in front of television sets and computer monitors. As much as we shortchange our sleep, we jeopardize the body's immune function and hormonal balance. Disconnected from nature's light-and-dark rhythm, we are left chronically rest-less in this age of time-famine. The body falls victim – stillness and sleep are replaced by stimulus and stress. We have yet to learn that sleep is far from a waste of time.

The fourth leg of the chair indicates the holistic nature of health. Our bodies are linked to mind and spirit, joined together in a pattern of interconnected complex functioning. Spontaneously striving for balance and harmony, a healing force guides us towards wholeness. To be "out of" shape is to lose touch with the rhythms of the body and its vital connection to the spontaneous psyche and inborn spiritual intelligence. The task of healing probes the multiple sources of disintegration that exist on interrelating body-mind-spirit horizons. Disease is not restricted to the biochemical body. Sickness builds on negative thinking, the afflicted emotions, toxic attitudes, and spiritual imbalance. Unattended inner conflicts and unresolved interpersonal discord manifest as maladies on the physical plane. Any effort towards integral health becomes a venture of wide attention. To be "in" shape is to be in touch with the regenerative and degenerative rhythms of body-mind-spirit, and to listen imaginatively to our deepest healing possibilities.

The sturdiness of the chair depends on the strength of all four legs: nutrition, rest, exercise, and psychospiritual healing. As the journey of wholeness calls, we best respond by moving in the direction it encourages. Health is a process, a continuous effort towards optimum well-being. It is not just the absence of illness. Health care does not exist solely within the framework of the curative domain. In fact, prevention and education are its cornerstones. The chair stands strong when well-maintained, but, if not, is prone to wobble or collapse. I know that, as I continue to age, I need to keep a close eye on all four legs.

law of cure

The Chinese speak of the "law of cure," in which they refer to illness as a "healing crisis." Physical symptoms are the body's messengers, acting to signal a health imbalance. Symptoms give expression to unhappiness in the body, reveal malaise, and make an appeal for remedy. These messengers help us to access and activate the body's healing power. The law of cure introduces us to the notion that disease is the challenge, however difficult, of bringing the body back into harmony. Such an attitude empowers the hope and confidence of healing.

The intelligence of the body is activated by a conscious determination towards health, and it is up to us to enter dynamically into the healing process. Much of what we need to learn about our physicality is hidden. Self-insight is found through listening to the wisdom of the body as well as tapping into the deep pool of acquired medical knowledge. The biological and physiological sciences, the healing arts, and spiritual practice all help us actualize the wisdom of cure.

Our physicality is not as frozen as we think. Though certain injuries leave permanent disability in their wake, in truth our bodies have a rather fluid quality. How do we learn to appreciate the body's sheer resilience and trust its amazing regenerative capacity? In every moment our physical organisms are creating new cells and replacing old ones. Even when there is a permanent diminishment or loss of body function, there exists a steady force of healing that pushes towards a restoration of vitality. The body continuously reinvents itself from a wellspring of original health.

Good sense would suggest that the more time I invest in learning and healing, the greater the dividend of wellness. A core health strategy lies in taking time to learn about my physicality and what nurture my body needs to thrive. Sometimes, even when I have symptoms that scream for attention, it seems I cannot afford the time to heal. Though the wisdom of cure is sometimes slowly revealed, perhaps all of us tend to short-circuit the process with our impatience. If we fail to give ourselves time or permission to be sick, we are prone to abbreviate diagnostic inquiry and look for quick fixes. The modern pace of life indeed fails to sanction time for health recovery – we would do well to listen to our bodies when they claim a need for cure, a need for time out and regenerative nurture.

whole-health

Health is a complex process, directed towards achieving balance and wisdom. Each thought, feeling, and attitude talks to the body, alters brain chemistry, and somehow rearranges our physicality. We fluctuate between stasis and destabilization in an untamed flow of molecules and mental processes and meanings. Thus, healing is a continual balancing act, a learning process that requires steady intention and attention.

Mind and matter are intricately intertwined. In continual flux, the body is responsive at every moment to the pulsing flow of psychic energies. We can cite many examples: mental striving affects respiration, healing intent alters enzymes and hemoglobin values, a threat of danger creates the dramatic rush of adrenaline, sexual interest speeds the heart, and fear tenses body muscu-lature. Both pleasure and pain talk to the body. Experiences of delight create chemical substances known as endorphins that shield us against invading viruses and germs. Our wounds of the past are held within the cellular memory of our bodies – the habit of repressing negative emotions plays a significant role in the anatomy of sickness.

As we factor the spiritual dimension into health, we witness its astonishing impact. Against all odds, the sheer will to live at times creates a triumph of wellness. Noble challenges invigor-ate us with remarkable strength. Experiences of inner purpose and peace have been seen to override the reality of pain, and indeed modify brain-body chemistry. Many speak of miraculous transformations through their experience of prayer and meditation. For me, what is most truly compelling is the power of compassion, a force that breaks through physical and emotional constraints to heal us at a very deep level.

Conversely, spiritual malaise creates significant negative impacts – the loss of belonging, intimacy, dignity, and meaning set physical and psychological decline in motion. Experiences of isolation lead to deep despondency, and unrelieved loneliness to lower immune response. More and more, it is recognized that hopelessness and helplessness breed disease, and that unhappiness does indeed cause us to be ill.

Health difficulties develop when life itself becomes blocked in some manner. Though the body may be subject to germs and infection, though it suffers from poor nutrition and insufficient exercise, the psyche itself is subject to grave woundings and deficiencies of esteem, forgiveness, and trust. In his essay titled "Paranoia," Ernest Becker describes healing in mind-body terms, and talks about mental confusions as problems of a total lived experience:

> If you are at ease, comfortable, feel you belong, sense the plenitude of your powers – then your thoughts are generous, warm, broad, rich, tentative, and open. If you are cramped, trapped, weak, overwhelmed, underneath your experience – then your thoughts are mean, chilly, poor, humourless, dogmatic, and closed. Mental patients almost always say "my mind is confused, something is wrong in my head." That's where the symptoms are, but not the problem. The patient does not know that the kind of thinking you do depends on the seating of your whole body and being in the world.[61]

Whole health involves matter and mind and meaning. Healing, for Becker, is a biospiritual process that requires relaxing and steadying the whole organism, and learning to understand our pathologies in their many aspects. Healing includes a mellowing of mood, a restored sense of trust, and the recovery of physical and emotional ease. It is knowing that our contributions to life are wanted and needed. This entails finding a sense of purpose and place, and an abiding sense of belonging. Essentially, healing is learning to value ourselves.

earthen vessel

The plot of our lives is a tale of unceasing change. Through the different seasons of life, our bodies are being formed and re-formed, all the while experiencing a continuous cycle of physical development and decline. Suffering is certain as our bodies go through different varieties of physical dis-ease, contagion, and limitation. Many of our afflictions cannot be undone. Through new attitudes, awareness, and action, however, our physical woes can be diminished. Unfortunately, we are not always willing to bring a discipline of mindful attention to our suffering. The body, split off from awareness and subject to neglect and abuse, can remain a huge shadow area. Often, in fact, more energy is expended in complaining about suffering than in coming to terms with it.

One way to avoid dealing with the afflicted body is to pamper it, to console it with false satisfactions. Arising out of an aversion to suffering, we look for quick symptom relief and manufactured consolations. The use of prescription drugs, food, and alcohol to escape pain often turns into patterns of abuse that only augment our total suffering.

Aging, with its process of diminishment, is hard, but harder yet if growing older becomes synonymous with sickness. It has been said that our illnesses are not simply a matter of aging; rather, our aging is more a matter of the illnesses we experience. Though physical degeneration takes place through time, the discipline of loving the body and learning its wisdom makes a degree of health available at any stage of life. An attunement to our true physical needs allows us to realize a fuller potential of creativity. However, in disregarding the body and denying its requirements, we suffer not only a greater intensity of pain, but also the sullenness of unlived life. Unactualized health potential translates into diminished happiness.

Of course, we all face inevitable decline, and there comes a time when it is necessary to let go of the body. Though physical cure may not be possible, the self is able to heal in other ways and reach for new depth of meaning. Even as our bodies falter, our aspirations and values undergo profound reorientation. The birth of new purpose helps us reframe our understanding of an illness, and indicates the evolution of life towards a larger meaning of well-being. We do not know the ultimate significance of our lives. We have only to learn to trust the body as the earthen vessel in the journey of our becoming.

Central to a notion of spiritual health is the reference of the body to ultimate mystery. It is thus that we are able to experience death itself as a healing rite of passage. To befriend the mystery of life is to make friends with death. Our mortal bodies, as we know them, are not for keeps. They are temporary "houses" belonging to the imperfection of the finite world. The body carries us on a sacred journey progressing towards its own mysterious transfiguration. Physical life is perpetually being restructured, and undergoes both degenerative and regenerative phases. The denial of death, built on resistance to life's eternal rhythm, itself underlies many of our physical diseases and cultural pathologies. Learning when and how to let go of the body is integral to health. Healing thus honours diminishment and death, relinquishes form, and participates in the body's reinventing of itself as life leaps from a finite to an infinite horizon.

the inner doctor

The primary doctor resides within ourselves. An astonishing power of healing that originates from deep inside each of us waits to be identified, awakened, and realized. Self-healing refers to the concept that we, as individual owners of a body, are principally responsible for harnessing our own health potentials. It is up to the self to generate healing. We might well ask why the notion of self-healing has been commonly discarded. Generally, we seem more inclined to ascribe the achievements of healing to outside agency and intervention: to the doctor we consult, the treatment we undergo, or the medicine we ingest.

Put another way, we have become objects of treatment rather than the responsible subjects of our health. To a large extent, we seem ready to turn our bodies over to others, relying on their insights and judgments more than our own. However, only when we understand the personal nature of healing are we ready to take charge of our bodies and activate true healing power. What is necessary is to accept responsibility for knowing ourselves better than anyone else can. The idea that we need less doctor and more patient involvement certainly is beginning to have more appeal. The inner doctor plays a vital role.

That is not to downplay the importance of outside agency. We do not heal alone. The compassion and wisdom and skillful means of a health practitioner empower a patient's self-actualization. They are an indispensable complement to self-care in stimulating and guiding the healing process. The language of genuine friendship and concern that develops between a patient and health practitioners is fundamental to creating an outcome of cure. Regrettably, technology often distances doctors and nurses from patients. The experience of being cared for, listened to, of knowing that your suffering is seen and understood by others, is quintessential to healing.

Medical physicians are able to offer highly specialized knowledge and expert skills to help their patients find health solutions. Doctors also need to take an active role in the advocacy of self-healing. A pioneer thinker in the philosophy of medicine, Bernie Siegel, notes in *Love, Medicine & Miracles* that exceptional patients want to learn and become the doctors of their own cases. Medical practitioners, as teachers, ought to offer their patients sound training in how the body functions and how healing proceeds.

Health is an achievement of consciousness that develops out of a desire for wellness. Cures are sourced from a hunger for wholeness deep within ourselves. Though we have grown up with an exaggerated faith in medication, surgery, and technical know-how, we are coming to better understand the importance of self-intervention. We are newly challenged to undo our habits of powerlessness, to become our own primary doctor, and to create informed strategies for personal health.

the summons of symptoms

Pain has a way of commanding attention. It creates different measures of distress to summon a response to the trouble it signals. Symptoms act themselves out in bodily and behavioural pathologies until we are ready to be attentive to our health needs. In listening to the purely physical aches we suffer, we come to understand the language of the body. However, "total pain" refers to affliction that is felt on all levels, body-mind-spirit. It issues a call not only to physical transfiguration, but also to psychic and spiritual transformation.

It is true that we can ignore our bodies for a time, neglect their care, and be in denial. However, we pay a big price for avoidance, and our inattention only feeds a further spiral of disease. In *The Body Has Its Reasons*, we read, "They'll say they have fallen ill. But you don't fall ill; you slide. Sometimes very slowly, over a long period of abuse and lack of awareness."[62] Though nature does not endow us with a full measure of health, nevertheless, through the nurture we bestow on our bodies, our wellness is constituted. We do indeed inherit misfortune, germs, and bad genes, but getting sick is more than bad luck. There are many decisions we make about our lifestyle and behaviours. Heredity and environment are certainly not the only factors constitutive of disease. Our illnesses are as much a matter of poor awareness, steady abuse, and the neglect of nurture and self-care.

No matter what my health track record, I need not come down on myself. Self-blame runs interference on getting a healing process started, and only makes matters worse. Health begins in a single moment of intention. Though better sooner than later, it is never too late to choose health. As my inborn desire for wellness becomes more conscious, I am ever more responsive to the summons of symptoms. Symbols of health begin to catch my attention, inviting me to reimagine my physicality. In responding to the body's needs for nurture, rest, and sound knowledge, I keep discovering its powerful regenerative capability.

As a healing journey gets underway, symptoms sometimes seem to get worse before they get better. At the outset, a lot of pain can be experienced. Symptoms often intensify as physical and psychic poisons are stirred up, creating a down cycle in the body before an eventual benefit is felt. The healing process can be experienced as two steps forward and one step back. Healing contains an implied invitation to change, and change is never easy. It is good often to remind myself to be on a best-friend basis with my body.

comprehensive healing

The diagnostic process builds insight upon insight, a cumulative understanding that emerges as we search for a new balance of health. The task of healing follows the same pattern that we have seen before, a path of sound discernment and decisive response. The body throws out symptoms in declaring its desire for wholeness. We need to listen vigilantly to the data of physical and emotional experience, monitoring symptoms with inner attention and medical biofeedback.

Sound diagnostic investigation is the outcome of thorough inquiry. Any misinterpretation of illness limits the realization of cure. Misdiagnosis reflects fast conclusions, simplistic answers, quick reductive explanations, and incomplete understanding. With inaccurate insight come ineffectual choices. In order to eliminate guesswork and self-deception, we need sound test results and hard evidence to support our conclusions. Diagnostic discernment requires a commitment of time to avoid deficient assessment, and we must keep asking more questions to avoid the narrow perspectives. The integrity of any healing process demands that we learn as much as we can about our bodies and their connection to mind and spirit. It takes effort to uncover the gaps in our self-understanding.

The Ayurvedic tradition, a philosophy of medicine on the Indian subcontinent, is a patient-focused approach to illness. Western medicine looks more at effects using the linear causation of scientific inquiry. However, the Eastern traditions include other modes of diagnostic investigation, going beyond a strictly scientific method. They do not place exclusive attention on the disease itself, but rather explore a wide background of personal experience. Ayurvedic investigation examines attitudinal profiles, psychological factors, the quality of relationships, lifestyle choices, emotional patterns, and moral inventory. Each person is an indissoluble unity, and tracing symptoms to their true source creates the integrity of the healing journey. The diagnostic process is an open questioning – itself the treatment.

The Ayurvedic practitioner probes the history as well as the immediate experience of an individual, family life and friendships, thinking patterns, attitudes, emotional habits, memories, dreams, frustrations and failures, meanings, events of trauma and loss, diet, peak experiences, out-of-touchness, guilt complexes, and the like. In this way, the practitioner attempts to identify what is throwing the organism off balance and blocking vitality, and tries to get a grasp on the whole flow of an individual's personal story. All life experience is factored into the health equation. In *Quantum Healing*, Deepak Chopra, an acclaimed author in body-mind-spirit medicine, states that an Ayurvedic physician

> … recognizes that what makes up the person is experience – sorrows, joys, fleeting seconds of trauma, long hours of nothing special at all. The minutes of life silently accumulate, and like grains of sand deposited by a river, the minutes can eventually pile up into a hidden formation that crops above the surface as a disease … my body is metabolizing everything I see, hear, smell, and touch and turning it into me, just as surely as it ingests my orange juice.[63]

Whatever tradition of healing is followed, our return to wholeness rests on the holistic understanding that mind, metabolism, memory, matter, and meaning all intersect within. Our wellness is realized on many different levels. Health is a dance of consciousness and energy. To heal essentially is to let life bring you something new.

The final focus in the healing process turns to treatment in order to map out a path of remedy. Addressing both symptoms and root causes, a treatment plan proposes a tentative blueprint for cure. Comprehensive healing asks for a quality of data, deliberation, and decision-making in acting towards the good. The better my understanding of the origins of illness, the likelier I am to find true remedy. Successful treatment hinges on answering to the deep underlying roots of a malaise, and on my bold readiness to replace unhealthy patterns of living with wholesome behaviours and lifestyles.

At a farmers' market in southern Ontario, I approached a table laden with containers of wild blueberries. "How much for that 3-litre basket?" I inquired. "Twenty-two dollars," was the vendor's reply. I turned away, thinking the price prohibitive. I walked about ten paces, then stopped and said to myself, "Hold on a minute. I just spent more than that on an oil change for my car. What about my own body maintenance?" Then I thought, "Blueberries are a perfect medicine." I went back to the market stall and handed over the $22, feeling very grateful for the basketful of phytonutrients.

Part 3

Mud Path: Darkness

11
Desolation ...
Evil and Impermanence

The violence of evil threatens every type of human good. It threatens the grace and strength of the body, the virtues of character and intellect, the kindness and compassion of the human heart. It threatens the love within families, the intimacy of friendship, political solidarity, economic justice, peace between nations. It threatens our cities, towns and rural hamlets, as well as the extraordinary world that human hands have built and cared for. It threatens the natural universe itself, water, air, earth, and sky, the ozone layer above our heads.

Michael McCarthy, *The Mystery of Evil*

The thought of death, its universality, its inevitability, its indifference, shoots a cold current into our vision of a meaningful cosmos.

Sebastian Moore, *Dying, and Behold, We Live*

The decisive question for man is: Is he related to something infinite or not? That is the telling question of his life. Only if we know that the thing which truly matters is the infinite can we avoid fixing our interest upon futilities, and upon all kinds of goals which are not of real importance.

Carl Jung, *Memories, Dreams, Reflections*

shattered adventure

A couple of hundred metres below the rapids, I spotted a paddle floating in the water. Minutes later we came across a waterlogged canoe pack, and just a little further downstream a shipwrecked canoe. As we undid the straps of the soggy pack, we found camp gear, some neatly arranged clothing, and six containers of food carefully packaged for the ill-fated journey. We presumed that the canoeists had been rescued. A deep sadness overcame me as I watched my rivermates tidy up the remains of an adventure that had lost its way. Struck by a sense of tragedy, I pondered the shatterings we all experience on the river of life, and how so many of our best-planned schemes and noble dreams are confounded as awareness and meaning and love falter. Indeed, the river is treacherous, and we become vulnerable to the same fate as the capsized canoeists – all the more so when sound judgment is lacking. In the deficits of ignorance or indecisiveness, of chronic illusion and cramped intention, so many mishaps arise. A misguided step, a single lapse in attention, or a reckless reaction can lead to a quick demise. As I beheld the aftermath of that unfortunate river misadventure, I thought about the times when I myself had lacked the needed wisdom of life to negotiate the waters of change and challenge.

Perhaps these poignant feelings were a concurrent part of my experience of mid-life, at which time I was getting a personal taste of the shattering that comes with aging. I had felt more or less indestructible until my 40th year, but then, as I came face to face with my mortal nature, a bitter grief washed over me. Out of the blue, I experienced some cartilage disintegration in my feet, which left me unable to run, ski, or hike, let alone walk easily. This loss of bone health put my athletic ambition suddenly into reverse, much like the abrupt ending to the canoe trip that hit the rocks. My diminished mobility brought feelings of deep desolation.

Other aspects of my life also felt threatened. My dad had passed away, and my mom was growing more enfeebled with age. My roles as teacher and community worker were to be turned inside out – it seemed that now I was the one who needed to receive. As youthful dreams lost their power, my idealism and hero images of self took a beating. Highlighting these mid-life woes, a hot water tank in my home burst – a rude sign of the waters of uncertainty, frustration, anxiety, loneliness, and anger that were flooding through my psyche.

At that time a spiritual mentor introduced me to the term "black gold," an image found in the world of alchemy and symbolizing the archetype of transformation. Alchemical processes involve the transmutation of base substances into precious metals. Crude ingredients are placed in a sealed container, heat is applied, and a series of operations are conducted to change their nature. In such manner, lead turns into gold. Metaphorically, goodness can likewise be extracted out of baseness through a miracle of transformation. I often rely on this image to appreciate the notion of tragedy disguised as potential blessing.

I knew that if I tried to sidestep my mid-life grief, I would only lock into more pain. My mentor assured me that things would work out in a way I could not then imagine, and this gave me the courage to move forward. She recounted the story of her own night journey, and how she had found unsuspected treasure at the end of a hard struggle. This led me to recall the turmoil I had experienced at the age of 22, when giving birth to young adult identity. In that earlier passage, I received a clear message in the eye of my dark desolation, and was able to clarify the next steps on my path. Now, nearly 20 years later, again in a black hole of emptiness, I hung onto the hope of finding a way through. Listening to me with compassionate sensitivity, my mentor simply exhorted me to "stick with it." She assured me that, in the mire, I would find gold.

"At the bottom of the abyss is heard the voice of salvation."[64] I find much encouragement in this refrain at those times when I experience my world falling apart – a dread of annihilation arises whenever I have intimations that life will no longer be more of the same. With each ending comes a sadness for what must be left behind, and the fear of the unknown that lies ahead. I have been introduced, over and over, to the law of impermanence, only to learn that every grief masks a fresh beginning.

grip of darkness

None would deny that human existence has a very harsh side. Much of our way through life follows along a muddy path. Who among us has not experienced a measure of hardship and suffering? Our aching bodies, troubled psyches, and broken hearts tell the tale of our trials. In the long shadows of our nights, each of us has felt the grip of darkness alienating us from the grandeur of life. I frequently find myself struggling to comprehend why things sometimes go so terribly wrong.

Throughout the ages, through diverse philosophical frameworks of meaning, humankind has sought deliverance. During the Seder supper, Jewish people eat bitter herbs to remember the anguish of their ancestors, and dip these herbs in a mixture of honey, apples, walnuts, and cinnamon to sweeten their bitter sorrows. The Buddhists teach that life is full of suffering that stems from the craving for pleasure and the avoidance of pain. They recommend an Eightfold Path of right living to remedy this unrest. The central prayer in the Christian tradition likewise contains the plea to "deliver us from evil." All religious and wisdom traditions address the problem of evil in one way or another, seeking to liberate the goodness and beauty of life.

At seventeen, when I left home to take on my first summer job, I began to be aware of the problem of evil. I recall telling my parents in a letter how brutal my new world was. In this rude awakening, I was exposed anew to different forms of human greed and violence. I felt a burden of disillusionment and a fresh loss of innocence. As I encountered deception, discord, and more sinister sides to life, it seemed I was being asked to surrender my belief in human goodness.

In *The Mystery of Evil*, Michael McCarthy suggests that evil emerges when good fails to be actualized. In the neglect of freedom, evil gets its power, and

> ... begins in thoughtlessness, inattention and insensitivity;
> it spreads through culpable ignorance and intellectual sloth;
> it is solidified through rash and presumptive judgments;

it is most conspicuous in the weakness of the will, in the failure to do what we have reasonably decided is right and good. It is most frightening in hardness of heart, in deliberate malice, in the cold resolve to inflict pain and suffering on other people.[65]

Many long years since that first letter home, now with less innocence, I continue to negotiate a darkness I meet both inside myself and in the world. I clearly see how all forms of evil have their foothold in the refusal of self-knowledge, critical reflection, and moral virtue.

Between noble and negative inclinations, I find myself tossed about in the wind. In thought and actions, I do both the right and the wrong thing; others witness, better than I can, the ambivalence of my own back-and-forth motivations. An inner tug-of-war, at times dramatic, plays out between fear and love, aggression and gentleness, spitefulness and kindness. I find in myself primitive vengeance meeting inner longings for reconciliation. I experience sexual lust and the urge to possess pleasure, yet also have a need for detached self-control. At times, I know envy, and it reveals the limits of my gratitude. These ongoing struggles mark a heart divided between the pulls and counterpulls of positive and dark energies. Without a question, the wind blows in opposing directions, and I find myself moving along spectrums between grief and equanimity, between acquisitive grasping and generous giving.

Are not all of us both victims and perpetrators of evil, the offended and the offenders? In the tragic failing of love, not only do we suffer the wrongdoings of others, but we ourselves are doers of wrong. Refusing wakefulness, we wander in the dark, blind to our own motivations and the behaviours they generate. We habitually put ourselves first, and we put others down. Unbridled emotions and impure intentions debase the integrity of our relationships, and self-centred attitudes block expressions of love. The reverse also holds true, and we find ourselves on the receiving end of insult, neglect, cruel judgment, inconsideration, abandonment, betrayal, injustice, and abuse. Whether victim or victimizer, through selfishness of thought and action, we become the thieves of one another's freedom.

Deep down, though, we long for an original purity of heart where goodness issues forth. I often go back to Sebastian Moore's definition of human alienation as the radical distrust in our own goodness. The Lebanese poet Kahlil Gibran puts this same idea a different way. He speaks of the human experience as a divided house, where we are both one-with and not-one-with ourselves. And when we are not our true selves, we are not evil, just not yet truly actualized: a rudderless ship, a root that clings to the earth, asleep, limping. Both Moore and Gibran suggest that the truth of being lies in goodness; the adventure of personal authenticity entails learning a confidence in our true worth. Through using our freedom to cultivate a power of determination towards goodness, the human spirit becomes truly heroic. Beyond the world of the profane lies profound beauty – an integral love that teaches us to become thoughtful, sensitive, vigorous in our pursuit of insight, bold in action, deeply compassionate. In this light, life then becomes a quest to awaken such beauty – to find gentleness, to do justice, and to bear light.

demon of impermanence

Our human sojourn on earth is but for a short time, and mortality gnaws in our bones. Though dreaded, and to a great extent denied, disintegration and decay are ever in process. A fear of death ever haunts us. For a time, we may be able to keep death out of sight and go along feeling more or less indestructible. But when denial fades, the primal terror of death surfaces. It carries with it an apprehension of annihilation, the fear that life comes to a sudden and senseless end. This terror of nothingness fills us with trepidation and forces us to ask: is this all there is? Much like Macbeth, we taste the void: "Out, out, brief candle, life is but a walking shadow; a poor player who struts and frets his hour upon the stage, and then is heard no more. It is the tale told by an idiot, full of sound and fury, signifying nothing."[66] In these poignant moments of meaninglessness, we long for enduring significance, and wonder if the meanings we have made have been all in vain. Understandably, as we become aware of our finite limits, we long to know that our lives count for something of lasting value.

Our earthbound existence seems caught somewhere between time and timelessness, between impermanence and eternity, between certainty and mystery. Enclosed between birth and death, our imagination is forced to stretch beyond temporal existence. Certainly, the way we image the interplay between finite and infinite dimensions of reality serves to define the nature of our fears, as well as the various attitudes played out in our living and dying. Through reflections on impermanence, we come more readily to an acceptance of death, perhaps awakening the sense that death is not the final word, but rather passage into greater freedom. The "demon of impermanence" is highlighted in the Buddhist tradition, whose teachings focus on the fact of death. The Buddha speaks of decay as inherent in all things, and exhorts us to work out our salvation with diligence. We pass through many lifetimes of sorrow and suffering, striving after the peace of perfection. The Buddhist task of immortality is to break out of the wheel of rebirth by putting an end to the craving of transient pleasures, and climbing the eternal ladder of love. The Christian goal is likewise a transformation of consciousness that restores us to the perfection of love.

the cost of denial

The fear that human existence is absurd impels us to reach for the heroic, and thereby find a way to preserve life's essential value. In *The Denial of Death*, Ernest Becker describes the universal human longing to appropriate lasting meaning in order to "... outlive or outshine death and decay."[67] He suggests that, as a defence against death, we compress our lives into small, manageable pieces and create a momentum of activity around narrowed-down meaning. Though decay and death haunt us, we shrink from opening ourselves up to larger realities, only to live a kind of grim existence. As we repress ambiguity in order to find security, we create an illusion of control, and attempt to bury ourselves in the power of others and the values of our culture. Failing to draw on the real energies of life, we forfeit our potential creativity and abandon ecstasy.

The more we create a fiction of permanence, materialistic striving replaces the search for ultimate meanings. Perhaps, as Becker suggests, it is because we are out of touch with our deepest longings that death becomes so alien. If we treat fleeting reality as if it is all that is real, death becomes the absolute end. Once ruled out, there can be no regard for a future ever after. Without a notion of immortality, our strategy for happiness holds its gaze on short-term matters – keeping temporal life intact becomes the pivotal concern. This traps us in the tyranny of the ego and the pursuit of immediate temporal gratifications. The view of mortal life as a final horizon limits any reach for ultimate purpose. When we lack a sense of transcendent meaning, all attention turns to the here and now and tends to feed a quiet despair.

As the transitory values of secular living become more emphasized, the terror of death grips us even more tightly, and we become somewhat obsessed with security. When our fears of annihilation and insignificance become amplified, we grab onto this life for all our worth. We chase after material ambitions, build elaborate defence networks, and pervert our talents and the earth's bounty in order to protect our "hour upon the stage." Based on the limited consciousness of the separate self, false meaning becomes tied up with short-term self-protection and self-interest. We plunder the planet and destroy one another, desperate to secure temporal existence, an existence that is a mere breath.

In rejecting transcendence, we truly get caught up in the banal world. We are then inclined to put our faith in materialism and secular purposes, our confidence in the achievements of science and technology, and our trust in intellectual talent and human knowledge. In the will to power, many define a matrix of political ideologies as an answer to life. Even those who put their faith in an afterlife look for security in dogmatic creeds and fundamentalisms to provide certainty against chaos and contingency. Spiritual systems themselves are often tainted with fear and egoism. As such, they shrink from the mystery of the transcendent unknown, and create closed belief systems geared to guarantee salvation.

Beyond our primal anxieties of death, however, we are captivated by intimations of eternity, and turn our attention to the mysteries of non-finite time. In rejecting ideas of finality, we yearn for a sense of meaning that stretches beyond temporal reality. Though we experience the forces of disintegration and fear the loss of vital meanings, we nonetheless feel the desire to outlive death. The antidote to the terror that death instils in us is found, essentially, on the level of meaning. Because the locus of fear centres around the shattering of significance, Sebastian Moore suggests that our release from terror comes with "the death of meaning exploding into the meaning of death."[68] The spiritual quest does not end the terror, but rather, takes us head on into and through it. Through discovering our true significance, we are liberated from our existential anxieties, and empowered to surrender to a mystery of life bigger than our ability to comprehend. With hearts aching for enduring meaning, we point ourselves in faith and hope to the unknowable. Aware of the brevity of our moment in time, the archetype of eternal life awakens.

the passages of time

There are different seasons in a human lifetime, requiring us to go through a sequence of transformations. We pass through many deaths, each a rebirth, a threshold to the expansion of existence, rather than a loss of being. Our very birth is the first death we undergo, and in that initial separation from the mother, we lose the security and safety of the womb, and enter into a new life of dynamic interaction. Through childhood years, we develop as autonomous subjects and slowly come into the possession of basic life skills. At adolescence, another reconstruction takes place. The child dies, and with it, a sweet innocence; from then on life is never quite the same. Adolescent self-assertion and powerful new hormonal drives push us away from parental security in a thrust towards independence and new experiences of intimacy.

As we surrender adolescence, we turn our attention to the formation of young adult identity. At this threshold the tasks are threefold: separating from our family of origin, finding an intimate mate, and choosing a career track. This is the age for becoming fully self-responsible. For many, parenting becomes the focal task of meaning. Some call this stage the prime of life, yet as always, a momentum of longing pushes us forward.

Mid-life, sometimes referred to as our second adolescence, arrives in our late 30s or early 40s. It has been described by the poets as a journey out to sea, alone, at night. It is a time when our youthful dreams are modified, and old self-images and roles are again relinquished. The task of individuation that begins in mid-life demands a new attention to the inner self. Its twofold imperative is to discover our unique innermost being and our deepest creativity. Then, as we continue to grow older, the youth, beauty, and strength of the outer being gradually die along the way, and our bodies undergo a marked decline in power. Our roles are redefined many times over. We age, and become elders and grandparents, and in time, must let go of the body as the final curtain falls.

death of the ego

In the dance of change, there is endless disruption, chaos, and stress. Ever vulnerable, our passions rise and fall, our interests wax and wane, and we are constantly on the move. To embrace the flux is to live inside the tension of a treacherous adventure. The Buddha said that living in a mortal body is like living in a house on fire.

The spiritual thrust of human development pushes in the direction of relatedness. Our deepest longing, it seems, is to discover unbounded love as the ultimate mystery of being. However, the strivings of the ego interrupt that momentum, and constrain growth into a larger love. The ego's focus on comfort, survival, and keeping things the same represses our desire for greater possibilities, and thereby inhibits the excitement of expanding the story of our lives. Dying to the small ego self then becomes requisite for our entrance into freedom. The human journey is marked by continuous change that demands that we die over and over.

As the movement of life propels us into the mysterious unknown, we suffer the collapse of many identities. Each identity we form is but for a time, and then left behind. There is much grief work to do in learning to let go of an old self. A greater suffering, however, arises when we resist traversing the thresholds that maturation demands of us. The slogan "no pain, no gain" reflects the cost of growth, and heroic courage empowers ongoing transformation. Each leap of faith dives into the mystery of being – the practice of letting go enables us to continue our river journey oceanwards.

The death of the body is sometimes referred to as a second death. The death of the ego – the dying to the me of ego-consciousness – precedes it. After this first death, what is born anew is the self on its journey to love. Fear tends to rule much of our lives, and we are chronically on edge, at times in pure panic. A steady self-preoccupation traps us in distress and dread: worrying about pain, loneliness, sexuality, the negative judgments of others, injury and illness, the loss of autonomy, survival, debt, death, and meaninglessness. This self-consciousness locks us into prisons of self-concern and isolates us one from another. But what most threatens our ego standpoint is the death of the body, challenging the separate self that lives in a narcissistic world centred on its own ambitions and futile striving. The bias of self-interest, the suffering that arises from egocentricity, engenders an indifference towards others. Only through the surrender of this bias do we find that there are ultimate meanings bigger than life and death, and bigger than the ego's concerns. Our task, then, is to cross the span between time and timelessness. Fear is a voice that challenges us to make that leap.

Seen in this light, the ego is only the beginning self, and must be dropped to make way for enlarged consciousness. Our task is to undergo this transformation, the death of the absolute ego bent on holding and defending its pose. The real significance of death then becomes the end of egocentricity, the self as the centre of things. It is the beginning of a new world of love. We are called to suffer the transformation of the finite into the infinite, an ordeal inviting a huge leap of meaning. Moore suggests that, in an uprush of Spirit, the fear-of-the-end is transmuted into the end-of-fear. Likewise, the Christian mystic Gerald Heard describes the ego as an unstable state of consciousness, "a degenerative process."[69] The determination to be separate, and not for others, is born of greed, fear, and ignorance. Heard suggests that what must die is pretentiousness (the love of fame), possessiveness (the love of gain), and addictiveness (the love of pleasure). In this dying, self-seeking then yields to God-providing. We are to remember that the body is not for keeps.

The Buddhists describe this process as the Eightfold Path. According to their teaching, there are four noble truths: life is full of suffering; this suffering stems from our craving of pleasure and aversion to pain; we can end suffering by ending attachment; and the way of ending attachment lies in the Eightfold Path. This path consists of right views, right resolve, right speech, right conduct, right livelihood, right effort, right mindfulness, and right concentration. Existence as we know it is profane and must be left behind. *Nirvana*, which means "to blow out," is a state of perfection achieved by blowing out the flame of wrong desire and climbing the ladder of love. Extinguishing craving, we escape the wheel of rebirth and achieve a state of bliss beyond temporal existence.

Buddhist teacher Sogyal Rinpoche, in *The Tibetan Book of Living and Dying*, proposes the practice of meditation to undo our ordinary ways of thinking, and to purify the mind of its delusions and its tendency to distraction. Meditation is a journey of discovering our true nature, developing an attitude of non-grasping, and dissolving negativity. It is "the supreme antidote to distraction."[70] Stephen Cope, a yoga instructor, describes meditation as a boat to help us cross the river of delusion. The Benedictine monk John Main similarly advocated meditation to encourage an inner death that dismantles egoism and gives birth to love. The sense of self as separate, the ego's perspective that divides us from ourselves and others and God, is brought to an end. For John Main, the repetition of a mantra was a way to stop the mind from endlessly thinking about ourselves. In learning to overcome self-preoccupation, we achieve a new liberty of love and awaken into a new wonder of being. Through a process that involves continuous dying to ego-striving, "the goal or destination is nothing less than an infinite expansion of being."[71]

beyond desolation

We travel many rivers of disappointment, for not a single dream ever finds complete fulfillment. The many deaths we have been reflecting upon – the shatterings of significance, of innocence and identity and idealism, of the ego and its strivings, of the body and time and our fictions of permanence – serve as an initiation into a new dance of consciousness.

This is not to romanticize the tragic mistakes and mishaps that weave into the tapestry of our lives, but rather to recognize the potential creativity that can be born in the gaps where lack and limitation play out. We pay for what is missing in our consciousness, but have only to learn and move forward. As we journey, the river is constantly being left behind, as are our disappointments and our dreams. We have only to go forward in the direction the river is taking us, ready to be surprised by the truth of life.

In the experience of any setback lies a test of acceptance, the trial of letting go of resistance to what has or has not happened, the challenge of embracing a river of change from moment to moment. This is not easy, and we become caught in fear and lament. But a river must be met as it presents itself, whether it conforms to our wishes or not, and learning is wrested in each moment. Beyond each grief, we find new waters; beyond each death, rebirth. The river follows an unknown trajectory, and what makes a canoe unstable is trying to hold on. When we stop holding on, we discover a new world.

Without love, life is totally desolate. As our hearts open to wisdom and compassion, we awaken vigour and zeal to constitute our world anew. The freedom we gradually discover in life is the fruit of growing intellectual and spiritual light that alters the entire horizon of our learning and living and loving. Our striving consists in the effort to identify and implement the human good, to find solutions to evil. We seek that law of harmony where greed transmutes into generosity and gratitude, where ignorance leads to insight, and where fear turns into a freedom to love. Sound spiritual endeavour builds, breakthrough by breakthrough, a rich framework of values and meaning. Any true awakening is marked by a beautiful transformation of consciousness: love pouring in and pouring out. The love of family, the delight of friendship, the beauty of the natural world, and a growing sense of solidarity with all humankind bring us to full aliveness.

The whole effort towards integral life lies in finding a unity of love. Evil introduces itself when our intention to love falters. In ceaseless spiritual yearning, we reach for illumination, for luminosity, for a light to dispel the darkness. All religious traditions affirm the quest for goodness. Most spiritual practices point to radical self-knowledge as the sure means to redeem us from a bondage to dark inner demons. Different wisdom traditions put forth the teaching that love casts out fear and enables us to find an authentic way that yields joyous light.

I recall a beautiful morning one springtime many years ago. I felt joyous as I soaked up the hot April sunshine after a long snowbound winter. I had been reading for quite some time before I put down my book, and became aware of the song of a hundred birds singing – they, too, were celebrating the return of spring. It was only when I tuned into their presence that I was able to enjoy the benefit of their song. A thought then arose: the gift of love is always present to me, yet it becomes my delight only when I recognize and receive it. The journey of my spirit is a process of attunement to a song of freedom that I long both to hear and to sing.

12
Guilt and Amendment ...
Scapegoating

Evil originates not in the absence of guilt, but in the effort to escape it.
M. Scott Peck, *The Road Less Traveled*

A soldier asked Abba Mius if God accepted repentance. After the old man had taught him many things he said, 'Tell me my dear friend, if your cloak is torn, do you throw it away?' He replied, 'No, I mend it and use it again.' The old man said to him, 'If you are so careful about your cloak, will not God be equally careful of his creatures?'
Roberta C. Bondi, *To Love as God Loves*

God is not needed to create guilt or to punish. Our fellow-men suffice, aided by ourselves. You were speaking of the last Judgment. Allow me to laugh respectfully. I shall wait for it resolutely, for I have known what is worse, the judgment of men.
Albert Camus, *The Fall*

self-contradiction

"Has anyone here ever felt guilty?" I sensed an atmosphere of sudden uneasiness, and could tell that the group had been caught a little off guard by my unexpected question. The responses were revealing: "That's a tough one!" "Oh, man! Where do you want to start?" "Guilt is a bad feeling that goes away with time." "Useless, it ran my life for seventeen years." "Guilt is self-disappointment." "I block it out as much as I can. I can't take the pain." "Guilt makes my stomach hurt." "I don't want to go there." "It's a tight feeling." "Guilt is necessary, it educates us, guards our integrity."

Thinking back to my first days on assignment in northern India, I recall a drama of guilt that played out in my psyche.

When I arrived from Canada two weeks earlier, I was sent to take up temporary residence at Gayaganga on the Terai plains at the foothills of the Himalayas. It was the tail end of the monsoon season, and I had been assigned to evaluate an adult literacy program for the Adivasis (tribal people) sponsored by the Canadian International Development Agency. The project, set up on a food-for-learning basis, had become dysfunctional; my mandate was to find out why.

I drove by jeep from village to village, and in each location met the elders and teachers. Through a translator, they described their situation. While the small schools had been set up and classes had begun, the food that had been promised had not been delivered. Not only were the new students angry, they were also very hungry. As it turned out, the food relief was being pilfered in Calcutta.

Each morning at my Gayaganga residence, a handful of half-starved children would gather outside our dining area and stare at the small group of us eating a hearty bowl of bulgur wheat for breakfast. My encounter with these youngsters, as well as with the hungry villagers, left me with pangs of guilt. I did not know how to sort out my uncomfortable feelings. On the one hand, I argued that for my work to be effective I must take care of myself; on the other hand, the integrity of relationship I would create with the tribal people could not be based on my having a wealth advantage. The affluent West was meeting the poverty of the Third World inside my conscience.

Some weeks later, after I had gone up to the mountains, I was working on my report. Late one afternoon, I headed off in the direction of the Darjeeling bazaar looking for a market stall where I could buy some *bedees* (rolled tobacco leaves). I met several beggars along the way, and my guilt feelings were reignited, and this time were all the more poignant. Strong self-reproach came with the thought that my tobacco was being bought at the expense of both hungry persons as well as my own health.

I sought to resolve the tension by making a deal with myself. I would give an amount of money to the beggars equal to the cost of my tobacco. But in the end, this did not resolve the matter, for my discomfort remained. In time, I came to learn that this guilt was not there to torment me but to instruct my heart.

Authentic guilt reveals inner contradiction, the betrayal of personal meanings. It is a signal that something is amiss. Values are recognized, but not realized. To be guided by our conscience, from the Latin *cum* (with) and *scio* (to know), is to obey our own truth, to be consistent with what we know. In other words, it is to choose to live according to our truest values. A guilty conscience creates tension, a tight feeling that sets in when we breach personal integrity. Perhaps we have mistreated our bodies, wasted our talents, mismanaged a relationship, badmouthed a friend, ignored the suffering of others, or harmed the earth – feelings of guilt arise to announce the malaise.

Guilt is a message from within, and a very healthy emotion when properly discerned. However, if misunderstood and mismanaged, guilt destroys psychological and spiritual health. It can be legitimate or false, healthy or pathological, appropriate or unfounded. As guilt feelings surface, they must be identified and interpreted, and then acted upon. Often their messages are misread or completely neglected. Guilt is frequently pushed out of awareness, denied, and commonly projected outward. We can either benefit from guilt or drag it around as a heavy burden. It is a question of how well we recognize, translate, and respond to the messages guilt sends.

a good guest

A drug addict in recovery once made a remorseful confession to me of some serious crimes of his past. He ended by asking, "The only problem is, can I get out of it, that's the thing. Like I think I can accept responsibility, but can I get out of the guilt?" At a loss about what to do when we fall, all of us, no doubt, have asked this same question. Ideally, guilt is a temporary visitor, and never meant to stay for long. It is a good guest when it comes as a messenger of truth and alerts us to something wrong, something in need of correction. Guilt asks us to confront self-deception and our untamed egotism, to unmask our narcissistic illusions, to rehabilitate our negative behaviours. Guilt, when it is well founded, proposes purification. It urges us to become responsive to love and attuned to our true values.

If a guilt feeling is not acknowledged, the message is missed. Feelings, like our five senses, are wonderful avenues of awareness. The lepers I encountered in India made me aware that a large part of their suffering results from external injuries. Because this disease causes nerve endings to die, lepers lose sensation in the extremities of their bodies. Without signals from the sense of touch, they do not feel their pain. So when, for instance, they walk on a sharp piece of glass or put their hand on a burning coal, they do not have any physical recognition. Sense perception is vital, both in becoming alert to danger and in being aware of an injury once sustained. Just as sight, sound, smell, touch, and taste keep us attuned to our environment, and vigilant regarding potential hazards, so, too, guilt sends out warnings. Author André Guindon sums it up: "Guilt is a sort of alarm signal. It should be heeded, not silenced."[72]

Ideally, guilt serves to kick-start a fourfold process of re-visioning, which includes acknowledgment, regret, amendment, and reform. The initial step involves simply admitting and re-specting our mistakes. A genuine determination to turn things around builds a sound correction process. Remorse, the painful remembrance of past wrongs, arises as we become aware of how our misdeeds have adversely affected the lives of others or our own personal well-being. Authentic remorse inspires a humble acknowledgment of error. It acts as a catalyst prompting apology, as well as atonement and restitution whenever possible. True reconciliation expresses such remorse and aims towards reparation. The resolve to correct past error becomes clearly evident.

unfounded guilt

Guilt is an unwelcome guest if it sends false signals to create a distorted sense of wrong. All too easily we can become misguided in our moral assessments, and let ourselves get hooked into destructive blame manipulations. Guilt springs from exaggerated ideals of perfection, or through absorbing the guilt projections of others. Only through honest self-evaluation am I able to clarify whether my guilt is, in fact, unfounded. At times, it becomes apparent that I am not truly culpable, that the harm I think I have created is not caused by my own neglect, selfishness, or willful malice. As we come to understand where our involvement with and responsibility to others starts and stops, then we are able to reject false accusations and the guilt trips others impose on us. Once these are unmasked and recognized as inappropriate, we can then give the boot to mistaken guilt. As the abusive guest takes leave, body and spirit are released from an unpleasant and unnecessary burden.

I once counselled a woman who had carried a very heavy load of guilt over a long period of time. Forty years earlier, Peggy recalled, her mother had said, "If you don't behave, we'll lose him. And then we'll really be in duck soup." Peggy spoke of the burden of responsibility she felt for her mother's well-being, and how she thought it would be her fault if her stepfather walked away from his relationship with her mother. Peggy continued, "I've been trying to behave ever since! All these 40 years, I have been in the habit of blaming myself for things that go wrong around me. I have let myself become a scapegoat for others. Now that I see this, a burden seems to have lifted from me, and I actually feel lighter in my body." A series of such interactions with her mother created a groove of guilt in Peggy's psyche, causing her to suffer long years of destructive self-blame. Peggy finally found some liberating insight.

beyond repression

Repressed guilt blocks the flow of vital energy, and it can literally run a person's life for years. Rather than acting as a signal to alert us to moral malaise, it stays lodged in the psyche, exacting a painful toll on body and spirit. The ancient psalmist highlights the cost of repressed guilt: physical wasting, mental moaning, the collapse of energy.

> I kept it secret and my frame was wasted.
> I groaned all day long, for night and day your hand was
> heavy upon me.
> Indeed my strength was dried up as by the summer's heat. [73]
> (Psalm 32.3-4)

By attending to my personal mistakes through careful observation and assessment, I find myself guided to questions that help me identify my true values. When I remain open to the disturbing questions that conscience raises, I indicate my readiness to confront self-deception. I think that the amount of freedom I gain is a function of the thoroughness of my questioning, and of my determination to live in accordance with the values I discover. In this way, guilt guards my integrity and sets me free.

A middle-aged man had been in counselling for a year, and was trying to come to terms with some turbulent emotions. The following dream, narrated in his own words, reveals how he was able to undo repression and get in touch with buried guilt feelings:

> I felt betrayed. I didn't get the job promotion I had been promised. Someone with far less experience than me was chosen. I was very disappointed, and really angry at the people who were deceiving me. They were hiding something from me. It was the deception that I most resented. Because they had distanced themselves from

me, I couldn't communicate my resentment. The dream was mostly about how frustrated I felt that they wouldn't let me communicate my feelings of anger. My supervisor didn't tell me he had changed his mind. He had created a false expectation. Why didn't he tell me? I wasted my time while I could have been looking for another job.

Then, all of a sudden, it hit me. I'm the one who's done that! In my multiple relationships with women, I never let myself feel my guilt and was always able to justify my behaviour. In the dream, I came to recognize what all those women had felt. My pattern was always the same. I withdrew, put a lid on the guilt I felt, and slammed the door on each relationship. When I blocked all emotional intimacy, the women I abused had no way to express their feelings of betrayal. The dream allowed my guilt to come through, and I stared my lust in the face. Without the dream I would have just kept going on. It helped me see how I had violated the meaning of friendship.

Through his dream, this man had found a window into a world of unconscious feeling. By choosing to go into counselling, he revealed a willingness to open himself to self-critique, to struggle with his moral confusion, and to come to terms with the demands of his conscience.

Apart from our dreams, what helps us take the lid off repressed guilt? Making an examination of conscience or taking a moral inventory are examples of spiritual practices designed to monitor personal moral performance. Followers of Ignatian spirituality pray for a sense of sin, and thereby challenge themselves to form a strong conscience. The fourth step in Alcoholics Anonymous focuses on taking a fearless and searching look at oneself. An inventory of ethical behaviour taken regularly keeps one's moral awareness razor-sharp, and serves to protect sobriety. All moral workouts in one way or another help us examine personal motivations and meanings, and critique our behaviours and biases. Lama Surya Das, a well-known spokesperson for

Buddhism in the West, suggests that this process allows for greater authenticity. He asks,

> Or is it not most transformative, most earthshaking, to pierce the veils of self-deception and illusion, and crack the eggshell of ignorance, to most intimately encounter oneself? Through honest self-inquiry and honest no-holds-barred meditative introspection over a sustained period of time, one can take apart and deconstruct the hut that ego built, thus entering the mansion of authentic being. This may seem challenging, but it is actually easier than you think.[74]

projecting mud

Not long after John began his drug rehabilitation program, it became apparent that he was carrying the brunt of his family guilt. Issues involving the sexual abuse of other members in the family were kept hidden from view, while his abuse of drugs occupied the limelight. John was identified as the bad guy who brought disrepute and disruption to the family – his drug behaviour became a scapegoat to camouflage the real problem. In its avoidance of honest awareness, the family created a semblance of healing, but refused to delve into the true underlying causes of its disordered interpersonal dynamics. In targeting John's drug abuse, they chose to address a single symptom of family dysfunction. In flight from the truth, more serious issues were covered up. Seven months after John began his program, his sister committed suicide, thereby revealing the earlier scapegoating deception.

In the delusion of our own innocence, we dupe ourselves – we disidentify with evil and tend to locate the base world outside ourselves. The roots of violence stem from this denial of our own complicity with evil. Christ asked, "Why do you observe the splinter in your brother's eye and never notice the plank in your own?" (Matthew 7.3) Admittedly, it is often harder to critique oneself than to criticize others, because I dread answering to evil within myself. The guilt trips I put onto others consist in throwing blame outward in order to avoid shameful self-knowledge. An old proverb points out that the kettle likes to call the pot black. Inasmuch as we cannot bear to acknowledge our dark deeds, even to ourselves, any unowned guilt becomes twisted into the moral reproach of others. We prefer walking on the high ground of moral blamelessness.

An addiction to perfection can certainly put us at huge odds with ourselves. When I demand of myself an impossible moral faultlessness, I become prone to hide my flaws along with my own self-intolerance, setting the way for dangerous self-inflation. This feeds self-destructive false pride. If I cannot possibly see myself in the wrong, infatuated as I am by images of my own perfection, my ability to be self-critical shuts down. Then, I readily deny the part I play in evil-doing. Author Jerome Miller writes, "The reason one cannot stand to be evil is because one is still in love with the dream of one's perfection."[75] Our false pride eventually cracks with the inability to measure up to the aspiration of moral uprightness.

Most of the time, we do not realize what we are doing when we proclaim our innocence and insist on being right. Scripture is filled with notorious stories of those who try to justify their actions. Without mincing words, Jesus confronts the spiritual elite and calls them to task on their bogus religious practices: "Alas for you, scribes and Pharisees, you hypocrites! You who clean the outside of the cup and dish and leave the inside full of extortion and intemperance! ... you are like whitewashed tombs that look handsome on the outside, but inside are full of dead men's bones and every kind of corruption. In the same way you appear to people from the outside like good honest men, but inside you are full of hypocrisy and lawlessness." (Matthew 23.25, 27-28) Oblivious to their own guilt, they transfer their failings onto others, and refuse to acknowledge their own participation in violence. Yet their guilt remains.

To project literally means "to throw." Projections generally refer to any unowned psychic content that, as it becomes discharged from the unconscious, flies outwards. Projected guilt finds many varied targets to blame: the devil-who-made-me-do-it, other people, a rotten childhood, the conditions of life, the weather, uncontrollable events, alcohol and drugs, undesirable circumstances, the unconscious itself. It looks for outside causes on which to attribute the agency of evil. The burden of guilt transposed to a scapegoat becomes a poisoned arrow of accusation. These arrows hold the dark shadow content of that which has been banished from awareness. Withdrawing such projections means pulling the guilt back and owning it as our own. This is a challenging growth, but ultimately leads to interpersonal freedom. This freedom is seriously compromised when projections are left out there and accusations continue to abound.

The word "accuse" is derived from the Latin *ad causam*, which points "towards the cause." When things go wrong, we seek out who or what is at fault. Our accusations name reasons, trace cause and effect, and assign blame. Conversely, the word "excuse," which is derived from *ex causam*, means "to rule out as cause." I grew up in the French-speaking city of Montreal, and one of the first phrases I quickly learned in that language was "*ce n'est pas ma faute*" (it is not my fault). At times we may need to fend off unjust accusations that fly in our direction, but more often we avoid responsibility for things going wrong. All of us have been well schooled in playing the blame game, and know the debilitating consequences it engenders. As we fail to address our own failures, we become hung up on guilt, and this leads us to find fault with others. Offence becomes our first line of denial; by going on the attack, we attempt to get ourselves off the hook. Pointing the finger becomes a way to justify ourselves and camouflage personal guilt. Blame, condemnation, and name-calling serve only to create friction, breed malice, and feed interpersonal antagonisms.

The lies of our guilt projections ultimately give way under the strain of their own inherent falsity. Sooner or later our dark deeds become unmasked, and we are called to be accountable for the exposed misdeeds. Our displaced shadow contents, having taken a rather circuitous route through others, return to their proper owner. The key to a healthy relationship lies in an ability to delineate personal boundaries and to know where culpability starts and stops. When I withdraw guilt targeted onto others, I accept responsibility for my own task of transformation. Ideally, I want to catch myself sooner rather than later in my accusation of others, to enable me to withdraw my projections before they do too much damage. Unfortunately, the cover-up in Johnny's situation was exposed all too late. The family was afraid and ashamed, and the projection of its shadow impaired their ability to face the truth. Unfortunately, it took his sister's suicide to expose the wrongdoings of the past.

scapegoat mechanism

A story in the New Testament tells of a woman caught in adultery. Her accusers intended to stone her. Targeted as their scapegoat, she was condemned; in fact, she was cast out by their own unrecognized guilt. When Jesus said to them, "If there is one of you who has not sinned, let him be the first to throw a stone at her" (John 8.8), they withdrew from the scene. The term "scapegoat" originated in ancient times when atonement practices included a goat ceremony. The high priest laid both hands upon the head of a live goat, symbolically transferring to it all the faults and violations of the people. The goat would then be led deep into the desert, and left there to die or be killed. In some cases, the goat would be driven off a cliff to ensure its death. The goat would thereby rid the community of its burden of sin.

Here we see how the resolution of violence is sought by means of violence. This consists in the sacrifice of an arbitrary victim held responsible for defilements within a political, religious, or social community. But any community founded on violence against a scapegoat fails to come to terms with its own dark side. It seeks to cover up its own participation in violence, and the knowledge of its own dark guilt becomes intolerable. Scapegoating happens at the collective as well as the individual levels.

In this scapegoating process, a community gangs up on an individual or a particular group and identifies him/her/them as the one and only cause of the trouble. Ethnic groups, women, gays, blacks, immigrants, and entire races or nations have been accused of the evils within human societies. In placing the burden of blame for error onto an accused, the community exempts itself from culpability. Previously divided by conflict and destructive rivalry, the community overcomes chaotic discord by uniting against a common enemy. A case of all-against-one effects new cohesion within its members. Newly reconciled to itself through its unanimous verdict, harmony returns to the community at the expense of the accused individual or targeted group.

As this mechanism has been exposed through time, the innocence of surrogate victims of collective violence has become better recognized. The prophets of the Old Testament sought to unmask the scapegoating mechanism and progressively introduce a God of non-violence. Jesus came to reveal the truth about violence, but himself fell victim to the violence he decried. He taught his message of peace by refusing to meet violence with violence.

The deconstruction of systems of violence requires that individuals and communities be willing to explore their own basis in violence. They must withdraw transferences onto scapegoats, and come to terms with their own blindness and hardness of heart. Jewish thinker and mystic Etty Hillesum emphasizes that the real work of transformation begins with ourselves: "The rottenness of others is in us too ... I see no other solution, I really see no other solution than to turn inwards and to root out all the rottenness there. I no longer believe that we can change anything in the world until we have first changed ourselves. And that seems to me to be the only lesson to be learned from this war."[76]

To get beyond self-deception, I must first remove the plank from my own eye. This requires a commitment to vigilance and ongoing honest self-critique. It is humility's challenging task to examine personal experience, to be alert to guilt. Attentiveness to conscience allows me to identify and withdraw harmful projections, and to find genuine growth in the very mud of owned imperfection. Indeed, the beginning of virtue lies in my capacity to acknowledge the ever-present threat of violence within myself. Humility never discounts the forces of evil that can hold me captive.

gentle correction

A correction process entails the threefold task of acknowledgment, apology, and amendment. The confession of sin is an integral spiritual practice in the Christian community. In ancient times, one put on sackcloth and ashes and did public penance. The Roman church sealed the confessional in the eleventh century, and wrongdoings were acknowledged in a more private manner, one-on-one to a confessor. In Christian scripture, one of John's letters states, "If we acknowledge our sins, then God who is faithful and just, will forgive our sins and purify us from everything that is wrong." (1 John 1.9) Here it is suggested that the essence of correction lies in acknowledgment, while God does the actual perfecting.

Likewise, the need to admit error is proposed in the Alcoholics Anonymous program. The fifth step in their recovery process reads, "Admitted to our higher power, to ourselves, and to another human being the exact nature of our wrongs." And a later step adds, "... and when we were wrong promptly admitted it."[77] Speakers at AA meetings, as they testify to the misdeeds of their past, are eating their shadows. Therapeutic communities of modern times afford opportunities for intimate contact that allow individuals to drop their masks and reveal their dark, hidden secrets. In healing circles, within an atmosphere of understanding and acceptance, participants may confront their inner darkness, acknowledge shameful conduct, and thereby discharge their guilt. All such acts of acknowledgment, whether within a group or to a therapist, minister, or friend, mark a threshold of conversion. As we root out guilt, and declare our remorse for the past, we find the resolve to monitor our mistakes more closely.

In the matter of self-forgiving, I find beautiful encouragement in the writings of Saint Francis de Sales who, 600 years ago, proposed that amendment ought to know a gentleness transcending angry self-reproach:

> One of the excellent practices of gentleness that we could learn has to do with ourselves: never to be provoked at ourselves or our imperfections. Even though it is reasonable that we must be sorry and displeased when we commit some fault, yet we must refrain from a harsh, vexed, gloomy and angry displeasure. Many make a great mistake in this regard. ... Believe me, Philothea, the correction made by a father gently and with love has much more power to correct the child than one made with anger and fury. So too when our heart has committed some fault, we must correct it with gentle, calm remonstrances, with more compassion for it than anger against it, encouraging it to amendment. Thus the repentance it will form will sink in much more and penetrate more deeply than a fretful angry, stormy repentance.[78]

An act of self-pardon serves as a good starting point to help us reconcile with those we have wronged. In this way, we learn to affirm the basic goodness within ourselves despite our falls into error. Humility helps us learn the importance of respecting the difficulties we encounter in moral living. I have often heard it said that it is better to light a candle than curse the darkness. To say this is not to condone wrongdoing, but rather to engage the contents of our shadows creatively. By cultivating an attitude that is self-forgiving, we learn to accept what we have done or failed to do. This frees us to make amends and choose new courses of action, both for ourselves and with others.

13
Moral Breakthrough ...
Beyond Blame

Ethics is about the good that we build and sustain in common with others. ... We must take responsibility for developing character in our own lives and in the lives of others, transcending self-interest, nurturing social order, but also transforming social order towards the longest ranging flourishing of humanity and society.

Kenneth R. Melchin, *Living with Other People*

An error doesn't become a mistake until you refuse to correct it.

Anonymous

A sudden rebellious sense of injustice caused the region of her eyes to swell with the rush of hot tears ... never in her life – she could swear it from the bottom of her soul – had she ever intended to do wrong; yet these hard judgments had come. Whatever her sins, they were not sins of intention, but of inadvertence, and why should she have been punished so persistently?

Thomas Hardy, *Tess of the D'Urbervilles*

victim or victimizer?

Mary Jane spoke softly, sometimes sobbing, as she told her tragic tale to the alcohol recovery circle. "I had been drinking all day, and I was quite loaded when I stepped into my mother's car and took off down the highway. I did not get very far before I sideswiped another automobile, sending both vehicles careening off the road. The driver of the other vehicle sustained serious injury, was hospitalized for two months, and left with a chronic disability. I myself escaped with only minor injuries. I feel so guilty, and filled with remorse at the thought of the long-term harm I have inflicted." Mary Jane paused a moment, and then exclaimed, "I don't know whether I'm a victim or a victimizer."

She was not only wrestling with deep feelings of guilt, but also with the angry resentment she felt towards her family. "I guess I'm both innocent and to blame," she added.

In the days that followed, Mary Jane painted a picture of her home situation and how she had begun drinking at the age of twelve. Now, six years later, she was dependent on alcohol as a way of coping with her problems. As long as she could remember, her parents had had bitter arguments, often ending in outbursts of violence, and when Mary Jane tried to protect her mother, she, too, was frequently slapped around. Her father had never been able to hold down a regular job, and the family was poor. Eventually, the parents divorced, and Mary Jane felt somehow to blame for things falling apart. She spoke of being unwanted most of the time, of being in the way. That sense of not belonging was also experienced at school, and Mary Jane described herself as feeling different from her peers. She was unpopular, unattractive, and unable to perform well academically. Mary Jane suffered a strong sense of isolation and inadequacy. She talked of her deep feelings of loneliness.

It is easy to see that Mary Jane's childhood was broken to an extreme. Her inner world was tumultuous, defined by a pattern of emotional chaos and painful rejection. The more she had become afraid and isolated, the more she was inclined to drink. Mary Jane received few rewards in her day-to-day living, and she sought the gratification of alcohol as a way to placate negative emotions. "My life has been unfair," she would say, expressing her deep resentment. "Everyone else has been a lot luckier than me." Mary Jane, though, is guilty of drunk driving, and her inability to deal with her own feelings has left someone else to suffer. Is it her fault? Is she to blame? Should she be held responsible for her actions? Is there a way for Mary Jane to come to terms with what has happened?

culpability and capability

The appraisal of moral fitness raises many questions with regards to the matter of culpability. At what point do we become accountable for our misdeeds? How much guilt is to be assigned, and to what extent should we be punished? Growing up, I was taught that we become responsible for our actions at seven, the so-called age of reason, and that a final leap into moral maturity takes place when we reach adult status at eighteen, Mary Jane's age at the time of the accident. It is clear that maturation can be stunted by many factors, and that response-ability does not develop simply with the passage of linear time.

More often than not, it is assumed that we are capable of choosing our behaviours. We hear the common refrain, "They should have known better." Rarely does one hear, "They know not what they have done." Though we tend to carry heavy judgments with respect to moral failing, both our own and that of others, perhaps we are not in the driver's seat to the extent we believe. Are we more captive to our wounded biographies than we think? We grow up within particular physical and psychological milieus, subject to certain cultural and spiritual influences. Context plays into character; conditions and conditioning configure behaviours. Though no one has ever been loved perfectly, some suffer extreme deprivations of care and nurture. Such experiences raise the question of culpability, and how we factor mitigating circumstances into our equations of moral accountability. To what extent are we determined by external factors, patterned emotion, malnurture, social injustice, disordered family relationships, and degenerative environments? Do these past influences dictate the present? Are we thereby exempt from personal responsibility?

The courts use terms such as "temporary insanity" and "crimes of passion" to apply their judgments and to attest to the inability of persons to control behaviour. We echo the same feelings of powerlessness and non-culpability in phrases such as "I didn't mean to," "I didn't know any better," "I couldn't help it," "Why didn't anybody tell me?" or "If I had only known." Certainly our actions do not always line up with our intentions – when blind to truth, we embrace illusion or simply fail to recognize the right thing to do. Maladaptive behaviours, narcissistic impulsivity, addictions, and patterns of social withdrawal define a wide range of moral poverty. The freedom to choose the ways we act is somewhat more restricted than we deem it to be. It would follow that there is no reliable claim we can make on virtue.

To whatever extent we are culpable, I would suggest that we need to focus more on amendment than accusation, and to think in terms of fostering moral capability. A good part of the time we seem to get hung up on questions of blame and punishment, and thereby fail to take a look at the things that actually have gone wrong. The Buddhist monk Thich Nhat Hanh, in *Being Peace*, advocates using insight meditation to move beyond blame towards an understanding of the real nature of moral failure:

> Suppose we have a son who becomes an unbearable young man. It may be hard for us to love him. That is natural. In order to be loved, a person should be lovable. If our son has become difficult to love, we will be very unhappy. We wish we could love him, but the only way we can is to understand him, to understand his situation. We have to take our son as the subject of our meditation. ... With that power of concentration, we can look deeply into the problem. This is insight meditation.

> First we are aware of the problem, focusing all our attention on the problem, and then we look deeply into it in order to understand its real nature, in this case the nature of our son's unhappiness.

> We don't blame our son. We just want to understand why he has become like that. Through this method of meditation, we find out all the causes, near and far, that have led to

our son's present state of being. The more we see, the more we understand. The more we understand, the easier it is for us to have compassion and love. Understanding is the source of love. Understanding is love itself. Understanding is another name for love; love is another name for understanding. When we practice Buddhism, it is helpful to practice in this way.

When you grow a tree, if it does not grow well, you don't blame the tree. You look into the reasons it is not doing well. You may need fertilizer, or more water, or less sun. You never blame the tree, yet we blame our son. If we know how to take care of him, he will grow well, like a tree. Blaming has no effect at all.[79]

When accusation stops, we can begin to backtrack along our paths of folly and to focus on making things right. In this manner, we avoid the repetition of mistakes. I love the story in the New Testament of the prodigal son who had completely squandered the gifts he had received. It was only when his life turned into complete disaster that this lad was able to come to terms with the illusions that had gripped him. Upon returning home, there was no "I told you so." In fact, the son was celebrated rather than scolded. His father's delight came from knowing that his son's shattered illusions had led him into noble awareness. I take more and more comfort in the realization that my past errors offer some of life's most valuable lessons, affording me opportunities to stop and ask myself what I did not know that I needed to know, or what I did not do that I needed to do. The failed way points to the true good, and indeed, some of the best clues to help me discern my vision and values have grown in the mud of my mistakes.

reframing failure

Beyond judgment and punishment, and the badness we usually ascribe to human error, we can empower healing and begin to make things right. The wrongs of the past are not neglected, but attended to and mended. To reframe wrongdoing entails coming to know the complex motivations that undermine moral performance. The reframing process moves towards understanding the whole ground of our mistakes in order to learn whatever lessons are required to help us break out of debilitating moral confinements.

Reframing is not to condone or excuse evil, or claim it as a fact. Nor is it a justification for bad behaviour. It is not to refuse guilt, nor to disclaim moral responsibility by scapegoating drugs, our childhood, parental failure, anybody or anything under the sun. The true task of correction lies in examining what has motivated the misdeeds in order to identify the root causes of maladaptive behaviour. Moral ineptitude reflects a failure to recognize and act towards the good, and calls us, with the support of the entire community, to the task of learning and restitution. Through acknowledging those factors limiting moral capacity, remedial effort is able to get underway. The reframing process examines the outlook and attitudes of the wrongdoer, and the extent of desperation and damaged personality that have contributed to faulty patterns of behaviour. Knowing the concrete historical background of the wrongdoer allows the corrective process to be seen in a new light: that is, as an opportunity for compassionate understanding, instrumental to healing the past and liberating the future. Moral failings are best reversed in an atmosphere of rehabilitative justice.

Moral capability is cultivated somewhat like a garden. The soil for some has been fertile, yielding sound insight, right judgment, and responsible deeds. For others, the soil quality has been deficient, and the flowers have not grown very well. In the latter instance, exiled from awareness and love, moral development has been impoverished. Many individuals are raised in milieus where manipulation replaces the language of love, where education is lacking, and where injustice abounds. In this way, goodness becomes warped and bent out of shape. This does not represent badness as such, but rather points to deficient development. Failed human beings come from failed families and failed societies.

It might be said that Mary Jane, though physically driving the car, was herself "being driven." As we have seen, disordered conduct grows where development has been wanting. Mary Jane's alcoholic behaviour was bred in her gross lack of adequate parenting. But then, her parents were products of their own broken lives as well. These failed people are in as much need of reparation as the tragic victim of the auto accident. The remedy is not simple, and challenges all parties to a long healing journey. Mary Jane is required to come to terms with her concrete history, to own it as her own. For moral impotence reflects limited moral capability together with the failure of personal courage. She is challenged to break out of the confinements of her past, and dare a healing journey. There is always hope for flowers to grow, and a beautiful and sensitive heart can open up out of Mary Jane's deep suffering.

river of integrity

I like to imagine that moral maturation can be seen as a river of meaning, small and dynamic at source, expanding as tributaries feed into it, and gathering volume and velocity in its downriver thrust. As the river quickens, we cross new moral thresholds to discern a wider truth of value.

Let me tell you another story that elucidates the way a moral sense develops over time. Peter was expelled from his high school after being caught stealing money from the lockers of his fellow students. Whatever his motivation, he could offer no justification for his misdeeds. He seemed absorbed in a world of his own personal needs, and disconnected from his peer group. Though Peter seemed to profit from his stealing, he had put himself at odds not only with his peers but also with himself. His horizon of meaning had been limited to an egocentric goal – he was not yet aware that his happiness could not be purchased at the expense of others. The victims that Peter hit on, as well as the wider circle of students, felt vulnerable and betrayed. His parents were perplexed about how to respond to their son's moral failure.

The looting of his peers did violence to the meaning of human relatedness. Peter had contributed not to the good, but to a widespread mistrust affecting the integrity of the entire school community. Only in time, through a restorative justice process, did Peter begin to fathom just how much he had violated his fellow students. The victims were invited to share the feelings of betrayal and vulnerability they had undergone. As each one spoke in turn, Peter came face to face with the tangible harm that his thievery had caused. Peter braved the healing shame of confessing his "self-centred stupid stealing" to his peers with heartfelt contrite emotion. He wrote a letter of apology to his victims, asking for their pardon and another chance, and he agreed to pay back what he had stolen. Tears filled Peter's eyes when his fellow students asked the principal if she would let him back into the school. The encounter had elicited his remorse, and allowed Peter to release his guilt. He was readmitted to the school the following morning – a happy ending to a hard lesson.

It seems to me that the essential focus of moral life lies in creating harmonious relationship with others, and with the natural world. I think it is essential to discover our place in the web of life and find a part to play in shaping the common good. Moral development centres on working out patterns of relationship that benefit the whole, not only in the present, but in consideration for the future. The moral task is propelled by a desire for value, which finds expression in the nurture of self and the care of others, in social justice and human generosity, and in the effort to live with ecological integrity.

Moral meaning gives momentum to one's quest for happiness. It responds to our deep desire to find what is really worthwhile in life. Canadian ethicist Kenneth Melchin, in *Living with Other People*, discusses the process of moral maturation, and outlines three horizons of meaning: the good that is personal, social, and historical. A horizon indicates a reach of vision; a moral horizon marks the reach of our grasp of insight and value. On the first level of meaning, moral striving searches for what best serves the individual good, demonstrated by a willingness to confront personal failure. By entering into the restorative justice process, Peter put his own behaviour and motives under scrutiny. In doing so, his notion of the good underwent revision, and he was able to bring closure on the matter of his delinquent behaviour. Peter was learning to care for himself in a new way.

On the next level, the field of concern encompasses empathy and a sense of social obligation. Identifying with others, we come to better recognize the value of co-operation and working together. The notion of interdependence is appropriated. From the error of his ways, Peter learned the vital meaning of relationship and how to be more considerate of others. In moving from a private to a social ethos, Peter clearly understood that his wrongdoing had been an injury to himself and to his peers, a theft of the good of both.

A commitment to a broader notion of the common good represents the third horizon of moral meaning. Here, moral deliberations transcend self-interest and are guided by a momentum of widening consciousness and compassion. The moral task now reaches into the public realm and into the future. Several months after the locker incident, Peter talked about a breakthrough of insight he had experienced. What had dawned on him was an awareness that, just as his theft had harmed others, nations also steal the goods of the Earth from one another and from future generations. This was a big moral leap, and clearly demonstrated Peter's expanding horizon of sensitivity.

The achievement of moral maturation is marked by a concern for true value on all three levels: the care of self, a concern for others, and a sense of responsibility to the future.

sexual meaning

A focal point in personal moral development centres around human sexuality, and our quest for satisfying fulfillment and loving relationship. The definition of a sexual ethic is the task of each individual, a challenge of self-knowledge and moral courage. Each of us initiates unique sexual meaning that builds on our subjective understanding and intentions, and the personal decisions we make. In our sexual exchanges, moral meaning is realized progressively as we move from seeking short-sighted self-gratification into expressing profound respect for the well-being of the other. In sexual experience, the challenge lies in creating an ethos that honours the truth of love through sexual expression.

We are a bundle of raw drives and rich meanings. Biological dynamism meets spiritual delight, and they play in tandem. The sheer pleasure of sexual expression shares fully in the significance of human love. The other person is treasured; as an ethic of love is developed, pleasure intensifies. Sexual excitement is tied into the meaningfulness of soulful encounter.

Most of all, it seems to me, sexual integrity celebrates friendship. Its achievement rests on the quality of love brought forth in relationship. Sexual fulfillment knows affection, empathy, honesty, gentleness, intimate communication, deep caring, and sacredness. Sexual partners bestow dignity on one another by honouring each other's subjective meanings and creativity. Ultimately, it is the quality of mutual concern within a relationship that supports sexual integrity. On the other hand, when genuine friendship is lacking and noble intention absent, there is a deficit of meaning. The pursuit of short-sighted gratification focuses on having the other person more than being for the other. If not oriented to mutual enjoyment and care, sex becomes meaningless, and inevitably leads to disintegration on many levels. Negative outcomes always ensue when persons are exploited and dominated. Expendable sex, functional pleasure, mutual narcissism, and attitudes of transitory possession lead us into an emotional wasteland.

Relationship is the adventure of cultivating authentic friendship. Full sexual encounter is person-centred, and builds a body-mind-spirit intimacy that is directed to the well-being of the other. Healthy relationship celebrates the mutual enjoyment of valuing the other and of being valued. In the interplay of love, each person becomes a gift to the other. As a love story develops, the roots of commitment go deeper into a soil of trust. As authentic sexual encounter engenders a growing depth of love, a shared joy finds outward expression in new circles of friendship, and gives rise to varied kinds of creative energy. A focal point of creativity is childbirth and the parenting of offspring. As a love story gathers momentum, it stretches into the future. Sexual expression involves more than transitory encounter; it is a project that forwards history. It has an ongoing quality, promotes stable direction, celebrates expectation. It creates the journey of true love.

As we grasp authentic sexual meaning, and come into an experience of genuine happiness, we experience profound value. There is no limit in our learning to be for others. The integrity of friendship in sexual encounter is realized as a function of developing a language of relationship whose poetry is the joy of learning a larger love.

genuine value

The quest for the good life has a dynamic quality – it is ongoing and entails continuous change. Human development is driven by questions that reach for creative solutions to the conditions and challenges of modern life. In my search for personal integrity and the meaning of happiness, I need to discern wherein genuine value lies, and then dare to act courageously on the truth I discover. Finding right direction involves more than private inquiry; our best moral insights are born out of collaborative reflection. Traditions of moral knowing serve to guide subjective insight and provide frameworks of wisdom from which our explorations take place – they help us pose the right questions. However inspired by the moral accomplishment, insight, and virtue of others, it is still up to me as an individual to question the whole ground of personal experience in search of authentic value.

Knowledge cannot be value-free, but must be aligned with the truth of life; that is, it must serve the well-being of all. Terry Tekippe, who wrote a Lonergan primer, suggests that value-free science is not the final word on human knowing: "Indeed, that is often the problem of the contemporary world, in which the physical and the human sciences reveal possibilities without being able to say whether they are good or not; technical possibility becomes the law of action, from atom bombs and gene manipulation to brainwashing and psychological torture."[80] However, moral knowledge points to the wisdom of love, identifies the true good, and awakens creativity and compassion.

Love, says Thomas Merton, is a movement of the will towards what intelligence – emotional, rational, artistic, spiritual – identifies as the good. In order to initiate the good, it first must be clearly defined. Merton suggests that intelligence and will are our two key spiritual faculties, and that accurate insight and decisive action must work together. The good we desire is knowable and asks to be discovered. Our moral poverty results more from a lack of knowing what is good for us than from refusing the good once it has been identified. It was the other way around for the apostle Paul, who saw the good, but admitted he could not always embrace it: "I cannot understand my own behaviour. I fail to carry out the things I want to do, and I find myself doing the very things I hate." (Romans 7.15) What happens, says the apostle, is that he does not do the good he wills to do, but the evil he does not intend. Frustrated by his lack of self-control, Paul describes his personal liberation as the outcome of divine gift, the love of God poured into his heart. The moral task, he suggested, is more than a purely human effort towards perfection; he had to rely on divine assistance to make hard moral choices.

The call to moral maturation dares me to discard what I come to know as contrary to the good, and to integrate true value into my life. Popular morality seems more bent on pleasure and the avoidance of pain. Based on easy compromise, it seems to follow the rule of "if it feels good." To choose value, however, means that at times I must forgo immediate satisfactions and sacrifice my comfort. Sound moral choices express a commitment to value in every situation. In this way, I ultimately win my freedom and move towards genuine happiness.

Insight meditation, intellectual endeavour, emotional and ecological literacy, and artistic sensitivity enable us to distinguish clearly what is worthwhile from that which devalues life; they also point to how such value is to be realized. Through the ages, a variety of spiritual practices have helped cultivate those habits of virtue that strengthen our commitment to value. Melchin points out that "… just as the musician continually reinforces and develops her skills in specific directions through normal performance, so too, our daily operations of moral meaning continually and subtly form our capacities, skills, and virtue in the same direction."[81] Moral progress then results from a persistent discipline of discernment and from a steady commitment towards the realization of meaning. When we lack routines of attention, our moral achievement becomes lacklustre and compromises our contribution to social progress. On the other hand, diligent inquiry, skillful deliberation, and decisive daring enable us to counter the dynamics of decline. The thrust of human development rests on the moral breakthroughs of individuals.

begetting the good

We sabotage human goodness by getting caught up in endless dramas of accusation and blame, self-reproach, suspicion, and condemnation. All too often we place heavy burdens of negative judgment on others as well as on ourselves. Judgmentalism, associated with self-righteous authority, expresses disgust and outrage at imperfection, and gossips about the moral failings of others. This, perhaps, suggests how much we are at odds with ourselves. Christian scripture reminds us that, as the rain falls on the just and the unjust, love transcends both virtue and vice. Human goodness is not based on moral performance, not built on appearances of virtue, and not won by ego-striving.

Authentic moral development reflects a growing ability to live from love. Moral endeavour seeks to distinguish true light from false, to find ethical clarity through discerning what adds value to or devalues life in each moment. It claims a personal ethos that guides us into a generous expression of love, and unmasks all the lies told about our true goodness. It does not deny evil, but knows that goodness dispels darkness as the sun melts a morning mist.

The goodness I bring forth saves me, and the goodness I do not bring forth destroys me, suggests Jesus in the gospel of Thomas. As I learn to break my identification with that which negates goodness – fear, ignorance, greed – I come into a recognition of the true good that enables me to appreciate my life as a work of art. Through learning to cherish myself, I come into a profound respect for others, or vice versa. Goodness begets goodness, and leads towards a sound social ethos that reveals our interdependent goodness. The private and common good are one and the same, and lead to higher achievements in social co-operation.

14
The Practice of Forgiveness ...
Justice-making

Yes, wonderfully, exhilaratingly, we have this extraordinary capacity for good. Fundamentally, we are good; we are made for love, for compassion, for caring, for sharing, for peace and reconciliation, for transcendence, for the beautiful, for the true and the good.

Archbishop Desmond Tutu

The lover of justice is possessed by justice and inherits its strength.

Meister Eckhart

But if you do not clear a decent shelter for your sorrow, and instead reserve most of the space inside you for hatred and thoughts of revenge – from which new sorrows will be born for others – then sorrow will never cease in this world and will multiply.

Etty Hillesum, *An Interrupted Life*

sweating it out

Nine of us crawled into the sweat lodge and sat on cedar boughs around the perimeter of this low, circular tent-like structure. Dazaunggee, the Aboriginal elder who led this special healing ceremony, welcomed us and asked his assistant to bring seven "grandfather" rocks symbolizing ancestral spirits. In the centre of our tight-knit circle was a small pit dug into the earth, where these red-hot rocks of granite, extracted from a bonfire where they had been heating up for several hours, were placed. The flap was closed, and we sat in pitch blackness. Dazaunggee splashed water onto the rocks, which sizzled and hissed out steam. As the heat intensified, the sweat poured out of our bodies.

Dazaunggee spoke softly: "Let us learn to forgive our parents. My parents weren't very good parents; I grew up with a lot of pain and shame. I am slowly rediscovering the little boy that lives inside me, and my life is becoming sacred again. It was only after I started healing that I began to understand where my father was coming from. He actually had a harder time than I did, especially expressing himself emotionally." More water was splashed on the rocks, and he continued: "Our mothers and fathers may not have been the best. They did what they could. We have to learn from them, and go further than they were able to go. Instead of being angry with them not giving us what we needed or resentful about their lack of affection, we have to learn to understand that they were what they were able to be."

We were invited to tell our own parent stories, if we wished. Much self-expression followed: we sweated out some bitter poisons of the past, and shared some beautiful enunciations of gratitude. During the four hours, we were introduced to Aboriginal symbols: the sacred medicines, drums and rattles, the pipe, and 21 more "grandfathers." The intense heat and the darkness brought us into an altered state of consciousness, attuning us to memory and spirit worlds. This ritual of forgiveness helped us to learn that wounded relationships with family members and friends can come back together, healthier in the end because of honest accountability and the confrontation of past suffering. One of my sacred memories is the warm hug my mom gave me during the last week of her life, and her accompanying words: "Forgive me, I am old." Experiences of genuine forgiveness bring relationships into a new beauty of intimacy. Likewise, we can enjoy this freedom of forgiveness with deceased persons when love is reborn in the silence of our hearts.

"Please hurry up and finish your book," my 95-year-old host for tea exhorted. "I don't have much time left to live, and I want to learn how to forgive my father before I die." Previously I had told Lara that I was writing about forgiveness. Her brother

Thomas, who had four young children, had committed suicide in his 40s. "I loved him very, very much. I have always felt that it was because of the way my father treated him that my brother killed himself," recounted Lara. "Thomas could never measure up to my father's expectations, and my father never stopped letting him know how disappointed he felt." Now, 50 years later, Lara longed to find a way to forgive her father, but it still felt like trying to pardon the unforgivable. As she was telling me this, I wondered if our desire to forgive others reflects the wish to have our own mistakes forgiven. How do we find a way out of our own confinements of hurt and hate? What must we do to get beyond regret and resentment and revenge in order to restore failed love? How can we find a new way of forgiving?

the forgiveness process

To forgive is neither to escape evil nor to excuse it. An initial step in a pardoning process is to recall the wrongdoings of the past and repudiate their violence. Full attention is directed to the particular injuries or injustices that have occurred. The ethic of forgiveness never puts up with further abuse, but acts first and foremost to safeguard an individual from being reoffended.

Put another way, forgiveness neither forgets the past nor is blind to evil. It does not overlook corruption or condone cruelty. On the contrary, it requires us to act vigorously against evil. I visited the ovens at the Dachau concentration camp where the extermination of Jews took place during the Second World War, and was filled with horror. Yet staring into stark images of such brutality opened my eyes wide to the reality of evil. Forgiveness cannot deny the power of darkness. Truth demands a full hearing, and the first intent of the process is to bring truth to light, to take moral issue with evil. The retelling of former wrongs unmasks evil and engenders a new moral sensitivity. Ultimately, what is sought is to liberate the future rather than punish the past.

Through acts of pardon, victims help to set themselves free from hate and the lust for revenge. In forgiving, they hope to bring to an end the repetitious replay of negative emotions, and set their focus on a new future. However, growing into pardon can be a slow and lengthy process, for it takes time for pain to recede. Many experiences of victimization involve deep loss, and, as a consequence, involve a long grief workout. Good counsel supports victims in learning how to be present to their pain as waves of emotion wash over them, and how to vent their rage creatively and let go of bitterness.

no peace without justice

It was the prophet Isaiah who proclaimed that we can have no peace without justice (see Isaiah 32.17). The breakdown of interpersonal relations and the disintegration of social order are clearly outcomes of injustice. It is then the task of justice to restore the health and harmony of relationships that have been injured by wrongdoing. True justice transcends the punitive notion of returning evil deed for evil deed, yet at the same time confronts evil and holds those who do it to account. The power of darkness is broken by rebuilding broken trust and lost integrity. Justice-makers work to re-establish the good and create new accord. Their effort to overcome alienation is through showing mercy, teaching truth, and expressing love.

Nelson Mandela, South Africa's hero, was exemplary in justice-making. No doubt, the outer reconciliation Mandela promoted was the result of a victory won within his own heart. As he healed his own victim experience, he made the vital link between justice and forgiveness. South Africa set up the Truth and Reconciliation Commission (TRC), which sought to tell the truth about the past, and to forgive it. The world anticipated that the black population would engage in an orgy of bitter revenge against whites; rather, they began the brave work of reconciliation with a focus on restorative justice. The TRC, writes New

Zealand author Chris Marshall, "… sought to restore dignity and personhood to victims and to offer a fresh start to offenders by making room for truth in place of silence, repentance in place of denial, mercy instead of retribution, and forgiveness instead of hatred."[82] Nelson Mandela emerged from 27 years of imprisonment, and instead of pursuing a path of retribution, began the vigorous task of liberating the past through confession and pardon. Though some took revenge into their own hands and refused the path of forgiveness, there followed a miracle of truth-telling rather than a bloodletting.

South Africa's agenda for restorative justice was a spiritual scheme to rebuild a new social order with forgiveness as its underpinning. It sought to cure the nightmare of the past by truthfully acknowledging the facts of what actually did take place. As well, it sought to care for the future, by healing and letting go of the anguished memories of the past. Desmond Tutu, at an international symposium in Toronto, illustrated the importance of storytelling:

> We discovered that people experienced healing through telling their stories. The process opened wounds that were festering. We cleansed them, poured ointment on them, and knew they would heal. A young man who had been blinded by police action in his township came to tell us the story of that event. When he finished he was asked how he felt now, and he said, "You have given me back my eyes."[83]

Rather than a blanket amnesty that did not confront past evils, pardon was bestowed only on individuals who owned up to former crimes and atrocities. In this way, the past was faced and its evils confronted. The outcome of the truth process was, again to quote Tutu, "… a spectacular victory over the awfulness of apartheid's injustice and oppression."[84] Indeed, history is best healed by remembering it in a truthful way.

beyond vengeance

The desire for retaliation expresses a longing to get even, and argues that those who have injured us must be dealt with, paid back, punished in kind. "It serves them right," we so often say. "Give them what they deserve." This lust to even the score is a natural reflex; it is normal to feel vengeful when one has been wronged. Retribution seeks equal recompense: an eye for an eye, suffering that matches suffering. Should not the wrongdoer compensate for wrongs done, by suffering the same measure of affliction as that meted out? The law of vengeance dictates that offenders ought to bear pain equivalent to that borne by the victim who has been violated. Is it not only fair that offenders get a "taste of their own medicine"?

An old Chinese proverb says that if you are going to take revenge, dig two graves. For vengeance, history readily attests, only makes matters worse; getting even inevitably becomes a lose-lose situation. Inasmuch as it proposes a counter-provocation, vengeance re-enacts the initial evil, which serves to breed further injury. Retaliation locks the evil into a cycle of crime and punishment. It plays into violence, and creates a downward spiral of reprisal and counter-reprisal. There is enough evidence to suggest that vindictiveness and the refusal to forgive are futile means to compensate a victim's affliction. Victims remain mired in resentment, bound up in revenge fantasies, and in the shackles of a seemingly incurable rage. Any personal satisfaction victims derive from seeing a wrongdoer punished proves to be a temporary and illusory balm. Resentment and revenge serve instead to freeze the past.

Vindictive desires are sometimes covert, and hidden hate often lurks in our hearts. Vengeful feelings can be truly dangerous when covered up, and if the venom of internalized rage becomes trapped within the psyche, it can bring about much inner disturbance. Until hate is rooted out, its poison robs the victim of vitality and causes endless grief. Hate is a prison that always seems to do more damage to the "hater" than to the "hated." Repressed hate reveals a hurt that refuses to heal. The victim remains controlled by the past, and caught in its pain.

Whenever violation takes place, our lives become intensified to some degree. What has happened can never be deleted, nor our affliction undone. Whatever our pain or trauma, we are faced with having to embrace an unwanted experience. Anger, resentment, and bitterness are the poisons that claim our psyche. Ultimately, we have only a single real choice – to heal our horrible experience. Ironically, because hurting victims cannot find justice and remedy without somehow coming to terms with their perpetrators, the lives of both victim and victimizer become bound together by a wounding experience.

Injured parties tend to dwell on thoughts of beating-up-the-bad-guy more than on imagining a task of forgiveness. Stories of pardon are rare, and, when reported, leave us in disbelief – in fact, sometimes aghast that forgiveness can be shown to villains. Beyond retaliation, nevertheless, lies a justice-making of compassion that wants the offence, more than the offender, dealt with. True reconciliation enables us to let go of the past, and releases us from vengeful attitudes and actions. Even after atrocity and abuse, the tall moral challenge lies in finding a healthy way to forgive. Legitimate anger demands the confrontation and correction of evil. But true justice knows a gentle mercy, even as it rages and seeks to right past wrongs.

compassionate justice

As a rule, greater emphasis is put on retribution than reparation, on the notion of punitive rather than compassionate justice. The present criminal justice system establishes legal guilt, and thus sets up a rationale for punishment. Punitive justice is an adversarial approach, somewhat bent on getting tough. On the other hand, a restorative approach is a proactive form of justice-making that focuses on truth-telling to elicit healing. A former Attorney-General in Australia stated that the choice for justice-making for a society boiled down to getting tough with crime, or getting smart with crime. The getting-smart approach involved looking at the legacy of anguish left in crime's aftermath, and endeavouring to make right what had gone wrong.

In short, restorative justice deconstructs the ethos of retribution. Rehabilitation becomes the focus, and its driving intent is to redress injuries and find comprehensive remedies. Restorative justice prescribes innovative ways of doing restitution; offenders are punished with a view to integrating the penalty into a repentance process. This approach avoids treating perpetrators as social outcasts, and highlights a shift from punishment to prevention.

A restorative conference creates a context for truthful confession, apology, forgiveness, victim restitution, and offender rehabilitation. Such circles elicit awareness and foster mutual empathy, thereby healing memory for both victim and victimizer alike. The full accountability a healing circle encourages has been shown to dramatically reduce incidences of reoffending. Acknowledgment and amendment seem to run on parallel tracks.

Victims are given a voice and the opportunity to portray their personal pain. In this way, offenders find out how the lives of others have been impacted by the violation. The practice of restorative justice aims to return harmony and a sense of safety to injured individuals and vulnerable communities. Through being listened to, it becomes easier for victims to recover personal dignity and bring closure to their experience. They themselves help work out a way where the harm done can be mended. The conference format also affords a victim the opportunity to offer pardon to a victimizer.

Wrongdoers also need to have their stories listened to with care. As they give an account of the past, they come to better understand their own maladaptive behaviours and misguided motivations. Their stories allow their victims to make better sense of what happened. Studies reveal that criminal behaviour has roots in social injustices. The foundations of violence grow out of the inequities within a society, and disparities in access to wealth, education, and employment. A society's inequities are revealed in the makeup of prison populations. A larger justice aims to right these very imbalances, and undo the vicious cycle of crime and punishment.

Offenders, when they come face to face with those who have suffered hurt and see the harm their misdeeds have done, are called to apology and reparation. In this encounter with their victims, offenders frequently undergo an agony of shame said to be harder than going to jail. Such shame and contrition work positively to prompt true remorse, often evoking spontaneous acts of compassionate forgiveness. When the urge to vengeance loses its grip, all parties are able to renew their hope for the future. In this hands-on model of justice, the circle defines, out of its own sense of fairness, a just agreement with respect to penalty, reparation, and rehabilitation.

insight mediation

Mediation is a co-operative process. It looks upon the experience of discord as a conflict to be resolved rather than a contest to be won. Such a process of conciliation seeks to empower rather than overpower. Conversely, the adversarial approach is a form of power bargaining that pays attention to matters of dispute and controversy without dealing with their emotional issues. Insight mediation is a non-adversarial model for resolving conflict worked out by Kenneth Melchin and Cheryl Picard of Ottawa. It involves five stages: introducing the process, defining a path of inquiry, probing for deep feelings and concerns that underlie conflict, generating solutions, and reaching an agreement. Insight mediation sets up a format for conversing about contentious matters – it marks out a path of inquiry in search of insight, emotional healing, and effective settlement. The disputants themselves, facilitated through a mediator, probe to understand the inner working of conflict, and to achieve their own accord. In this way, those who created a problem are asked to take responsibility for finding its real solutions.

The focus of this mediation process lies in uncovering the deeper forces that drive and sustain a conflict. To do this, awareness must be brought to the feelings under the surface issues that point to the things that really matter to the disputing parties. A breakthrough between conflicting parties is usually experienced when both sides move out of the distress of deep vulnerability and begin to feel safe. When the disputants no longer fear that what they value is threatened, they begin to trust the mediation process and to recognize each other's concerns. Melchin and Picard call this "de-linking." It is effected by digging deeper into the underlying feelings, which they emphasize is "the key to unlocking the secrets of the conflict."[85] It is vital to get in touch with the emotional aspects of the conflict, inasmuch as feelings point towards the core values that are threatened. Where there is a precise understanding of the existing discord, new directions can be formulated.

Thich Nhat Hanh speaks of a tradition of dialogue that has been used to settle disputes in Buddhist monasteries for the past 2,500 years. It is a system of seven practices of reconciliation, somewhat similar to the restorative justice model: sitting face to face, remembrance, non-stubbornness, covering mud with straw, voluntary confession, decision by consensus, and accepting the verdict. Any monks in conflict with one another are brought before the entire monastic community, where an effort is made through dialogue to understand the conflict as much as possible. Facing each other, the disputing monks recall as much detail as they can about the whole history of the conflict. The community expects them to demonstrate a willingness for reconciliation, and to do their best to let go of any stubbornness. Elder monks in the community advocate on behalf of the monks in discord by "putting straw on mud," that is, loving-kindness on the friction. The conflicting monks each confess their own shortcomings, the community takes a decision by consensus to resolve the matter, and everyone is expected to live with the verdict. This format for conflict resolution presents a model of justice-making that sets a true healing intent for the disputants as well as the wider community.

the law of mercy

The law of mercy reaches towards a justice that is not based upon what we deserve, but upon our deep desire to be forgiven. Who would not love to have all their past misdeeds blotted out of memory? All of us long for forgiveness, and stand in need of it. It is sweet consolation to be sensitively understood in times of moral weakness. Only gentle understanding liberates our guilt; the justice of compassion knows a mercy without limits.

The law of mercy proposes that nothing we have ever done makes us unworthy of love. There is no derision or damnation in mercy. Retaliation towards others or punishing ourselves does not break the power of evil, and mercy is an integral part of forgiveness. In the scriptures, the good is defined this way: "To do justice, to love kindness, and to walk humbly with your God." (Micah 6.8, Revised Standard Version) To love kindness is to encourage a direction and decision towards just and humble living. The voice of mercy does not mock our mistakes, but asks us to begin with them and to be willing to grow. Love asks us to forgive ourselves and then proceed in truth.

As we learn to pardon ourselves, we become empowered to forgive others. Conversely, in extending pardon to others, we learn to be self-forgiving. True mercy does not draw a line with respect to choosing to whom we bestow mercy. It does not depend on the merit or demerit of offenders, nor ask whether they deserve to be forgiven. Thomas Merton suggests that God never makes distinctions between those worthy of love and those unworthy. In matters of love, such classifications are without significance. While we might want to avoid wasting our love on an unworthy object, in truth, love can never be wasted. Love offers itself to the lovable and the unlovable alike, as the lilac tree offers its sweet perfume to all. It does not discriminate with respect to whom it is given. Unconditional forgiveness even offers itself to an unremorseful wrongdoer whose intent remains mean and malicious. Mercy is for everyone, and, paradoxically, for those who stand most in need of forgiveness. The physician comes not for the healthy, but for the sick.

In *The Therapy of Desire*, American philosopher Martha Nussbaum suggests that we need to understand with empathy our own motivations and those of others to help us cultivate an attitude of mercy towards imperfection. She proposes the telling of stories to help us find comprehension and compassion:

> In mercy, the soul turns itself away from strict punishment of each defect, even where a fault is present, understanding the difficulties the person faced in his or her efforts to live well ... here we have a source of gentleness to both self and other that can modify one's passions even where there is wrongdoing and even where there is both anger and ill-wishing. Nikidion our pupil will be urged to assume this merciful attitude toward the lover who has wronged her – imagining patiently and vividly (in the manner of one watching a play) the difficulties and obstacles, both social and psychological, that contributed to his wrongdoing, until rage gives way to narrative understanding. She will also, and just as urgently, be urged to take up this attitude toward herself, understanding the reasons for her resentments and her evil impulses, and relaxing the harsh punishments she is inclined to mete out to her own soul, seeing in the nature of human life itself grounds for mitigation. The attitude that engenders mercy is, I argued, an empathetic narrative attitude .... [86]

Earlier in this chapter, we met in Lara that longing to forgive. The challenge she faces is to transcend the deep affliction of losing a brother she loved so dearly; the challenge is to find that heroic love that will take Lara beyond her own long grief into an empathetic embrace of the wounded humanity of her father. In letting go of a burden of judgment, Lara must attempt not to justify, but rather to understand the failed goodness that caused much family suffering. She will need to listen in silence to the stories that Thomas and her father could never tell.

Darkness encloses the worlds of both those who do wrong and those who are wronged. Both worlds are full of pain, and acts of mercy help release victim and victimizer alike, permitting a leap into a larger freedom for both. Forgiveness heals past memory, unbinds present pain, and liberates the future. When a victim becomes capable of offering authentic forgiveness, that victim ceases to be a victim. An act of pardon awakens a depth of love that goes beyond normal understanding and expected responses; the victim's natural reactions are composted into a response of love. I recall the story of a Tibetan monk held prisoner for eighteen years. When he was released, he fled to India, and reported that he was at times in great danger. When asked what kind of danger, he remarked that he was in danger of losing compassion towards his captors.

In its fullest expression, forgiveness learns to be for the enemy. By harnessing forces of love against hatred, the enemy become other than enemy. Genuine reconciliation heals every form of crime or cruelty; indeed, it puts evil to rout. To hold a wrongdoer's happiness in our heart is to bless that enemy with an extraordinary gift of love. To pardon one's victimizers, for the very sake of their well-being, enables them to rediscover their authentic goodness. Condemnation hardens hearts, while pardon heals and brings hope. Indeed, forgiveness lies at the heart of compassion.

song of forgiveness

It is unnerving on wilderness outings – I speak from repeated experience – to wake up from deep sleep to the sound of raccoons fighting viciously among themselves for rights of access to our food packs. Waking up to human violence in the dark stillness of night is, however, all the more disturbing. We once took a few of the street guys for an overnight camping trip in Mont Tremblant Park north of Montreal. The weather was beautiful, and the colourful autumn leaves were at their peak of brilliance. At three o'clock in the morning, two of the men got into a fierce brawl inside their tent, over what will never be told. The rest of us had to scramble out of our sleeping bags and pull the two apart, and the opponents were reassigned to separate tents. I think we scared away the raccoons that night.

The next morning, we had breakfast in an atmosphere of relative calm, and afterwards took a two-hour hike up a mountain trail to a scenic lookout. At lunchtime, all eight of us gathered into a circle overlooking the lake below to offer a prayer of thanksgiving before our meal. The two men stared across at each other, and spontaneously crossed into the circle. They shook hands and apologized to each another, and to the rest of us. It was a heartwarming moment of reconciliation with a spiritual beauty equal to the autumn grandeur all around us. There was much joy in our camp after that.

15
Mud and Mystery ...
The Deathdance

I think love – deep human love – does not know death. ... Love will always reach out toward the eternal. Love comes from that place within us where death cannot enter. Love does not accept the limits of hours, days, weeks, months, years, or centuries. Love is not willing to be imprisoned in time.

Henri Nouwen, *Seeds of Hope*

It is born out of a paradox: that we deal most fruitfully with loss by accepting the fact that we will one day lose everything. When we learn to fall, we learn that only by letting go our grip on all that we ordinarily find most precious – our achievements, our plans, our loved ones, our very selves – can we find, ultimately, the most profound freedom. In the act of letting go of our lives, we return more fully to them.

Philip Simmons, *Learning to Fall*

Shiva's dance is the universe. In his hair is a skull and a new moon, death and rebirth at the same moment, the moment of becoming. In one hand he has a little drum that goes tick-tick-tick. That is the drum of time, the tick of time which shuts out knowledge of eternity. We are enclosed in time. But in Shiva's opposite hand there is a flame which burns away the veil of time and opens our minds to eternity.

Joseph Campbell, *The Power of Myth*

death row

I had been to the Québec Ministry of Justice headquarters in Montreal many times before. The top floors of this twelve-storey structure serve as a jail where those recently arrested are detained; I had often gone there to interview prisoners asking admittance into our drug rehabilitation program. But this time was different. I was being led to the sub-basement that housed the city morgue to identify a nameless body. I remember the layered rows of frozen corpses and the overpowering smell of formaldehyde. A drawer was pulled open, and there lay Nan, as naked in death as she had been in life. "Yes," I told the morgue official, confirming the body's identity.

Several years earlier, some university students came to my door in Griffintown, an inner-city neighbourhood. They were conducting surveys for their studies in social work, and I asked them what they were finding. They described a number of individuals they had encountered living in abject poverty, in isolation, in sickness. I asked for addresses, went and knocked on several doors, and jumped into a lion's den. My work with the dying in India had prepared me for the challenge that now faced me.

Nan was one of seven persons whom I accompanied over the next few years; each found death in their own unique way. Nan was a chronic alcoholic who had spent her life at sea, working as a chambermaid in the bowels of several ocean-going vessels. She had had polio as a child, lost her twins at birth, and was repeatedly raped by captains and crew members while at sea. Carrying huge burdens of grief, shame, and hopelessness, she drank to kill the pain. I visited her weekly over a four-year period, offering my friendship and a listening ear. It was thus that I became keenly aware of the extraordinary power of human presence, of the dignity one bestows on another by witnessing their life journey for better or worse. Nan would often say to me, "I spend three and a half days each week anticipating your coming, and the other three and a half days remembering our time together."

From visit to visit, as Nan spun the tale of a very difficult life, she regained a measure of health and composure. She had some very good moments, though would relapse into alcoholic binges, and we went through a lot of ups and downs together. Then one day she did not answer the doorbell or telephone. I waited a couple of days before calling the police. They broke down the door to her apartment, and found Nan's overdosed body on the floor. At face value, Nan did not die well. Her inner woundings had metastasized like a wild cancer. But I know that the friendship she and I shared transcended her time-bound sufferings, and taught us both to hope.

Through contact with the destitute and dying in India, and the experience of my palliative care apprenticeship in the streets of Griffintown, I was brought face to face with death. This set the later stage for involvement in hospital cancer wards. Frequently I have been asked if working with the dying is depressing. To be sure, it has had its gut-wrenching moments, but in actual fact, has amplified my energy. Those I have met on "death row" have taught me a profound reverence for death's mystery. It is wondrous to witness the grandeur of love exploding into the middle of the tumultuous commotion of dying. In those very special moments, one touches what seems to be truly real. To be with the dying, as they tell their stories and share their life meanings, has been for me a privileged intimacy.

Being where dying and living intersect, I have witnessed the chaos and beauty revealed at the end of life, and the dramatic interplay of the profane and the profound. The more I have stood before the mystery of death's paradox, the more my wonder of it has gone unanswered; yet that wonder seems to act as an antidote to worry. In my interactions with individuals right at the edge of life, I have vicariously tasted the experience of being at my own brink. It is there, to my surprise, that I find my centre. The more attuned to death I become, the stronger I seem to feel the pulse of life.

the truth of death

Existence undergoes a momentum of change marked by repeated disintegrations and constant re-creation. We are immersed in an evolutionary process perhaps best described as an unrelenting cycle of life-death-rebirth. The sun rises, circles the sky in daytime, and sets in the west. Through night-time it goes on an underground journey and is reborn each morning in the womb of the east. We see this continuous process of rising and falling in all things under the sun. Seeds are planted in the fields, signifying birth, followed by growth and a harvest, the matura-tion of life. Later the fields are ploughed under, signalling death and the decay that ushers in a new cycle. The wind blows north, then south, and back again. Circling round and round we cannot know the wind's ways. The seasons come and go, and the flowers blossom and fall away only to bloom again.

Distinct rhythms mark the change of the seasons. Winter has a feel of dormant beauty and rest, while spring speaks its poetry of rebirth and resurgence. Summer gifts us with an abundance of nurture and lush resplendence. Parker Palmer describes autumn as "... a season of great beauty, but it is also a season of decline: the days grow shorter, the light is suffused, and summer's abun-dance decays towards winter's death. Faced with this inevitable winter, what does nature do in autumn? It scatters the seeds that will bring new growth in the spring – and scatters them with amazing abandon."[87] On canoe trips through Algonquin Park, I am always struck by the powerful image of the fertility of death. The spectacular beauty of tall great-grandparent trees compen-sates for the toil of long portages. These trees, with splendid arching limbs and thick trunks, are wrapped in aged bark, and in their midst are even more ancient stumps. It is out of the very rot of these relics of the past that vibrant young trees begin their long life journey, ready to take their turn in the forest's proces-sion. Life and death are starkly juxtaposed, yet joined in full embrace. It seems so very matter of fact that life and death in the forest are not separate, but belong together as a whole.

Dark death haunts and finds each of us. Though we run from death, it is simply a matter of time before we get to meet it firsthand. And though we know full well that we are going to die, we sometimes have trouble believing it. Try as we might to deny the inevitable, the fleeting world keeps reminding us that it is not for keeps. I remember Sue, the very first patient I encountered in palliative care, who, in each of five consecutive visits, momentarily opened her eyes; all she ever said was, "I don't believe this is happening to me." The paralysis of her disbelief was making the dying process unbearable. Sue's non-acceptance fed her anguish.

Death, as a rude awakener, calls us from slumber and invites us to deepen our dialogue with the mystery of our uncertain being. Does life at some point just vanish? Or do we move towards an infinite horizon? Is there another world beyond? The death of someone we love intrudes, often quite unexpectedly, into our own denial. Like a thunderbolt, this intrusion disrupts everydayness and can give us a real jolt. As we stand at the gravesites of those whose love we have known, the forward momentum of our own lives is brought to a halt. It is then that we find ourselves at a vulnerable edge, where feelings of terror, puzzlement, and loss wash over us. In such poignant moments, time is partially frozen, and our place under the sun appears more tentative. The sorrow that accompanies our expanding awareness of transitory existence introduces us to deep inner loneliness, and sets us to wonder if life goes on and on and on. We grope to comprehend the mysterious conjunction of the finite and the infinite.

The truth of impermanence can also be experienced as a great freedom. In meeting death, I have often experienced an inexplicable undercurrent of joy amid sorrow, a mysterious stirring of hope. Dutch writer and priest Henri Nouwen describes the privilege of being close to his mother's last suffering, and of accompanying her in the agony of her dying: "I was blessed to be part of a moment of truth. Everything was truthful, there was no lie. Mother was dying and nobody denied it."[88]

Likewise, Joseph Campbell points out the significance of coming face to face with mortality:

In meeting the fear of death, one paradoxically can affirm all of life, for death is a part of life … The conquest of the fear of death is the recovery of life's joy. One can experience an unconditional affirmation of life only when one has accepted death, not as contrary to life but as an aspect of life. Life in its becoming is always shedding death, and on the point of death. The conquest of fear yields the courage of life. That is the cardinal initiation of every heroic adventure – fearlessness and achievement.[89]

In death, the mystery and meaning of a particular life are returned to the larger whole. Even as we experience loss at the very heart of lamentation, death is no longer seen as an enemy. A sense of mystery frees us from the prison of temporality and terror, and allows ongoing life to unfold. To know life and death as one totality reveals the dance of larger life.

the task of grief

In the dance of change, we go on dying over and over again. We experience separations continuously: a good friend moving away, job transitions, injury and illness, the loss of autonomy, the death of a pet, the sale of a cottage, retirement, the end of a romance, the divorce of parents, environmental deterioration, or the death of a beloved one. Relationships ebb, identity devolves, and things keep falling apart. Life keeps moving on with a rhythm of gain and loss. Grief is the emotional pain associated with loss, and knows a whole gamut of feeling: numbness, anger, loneliness, desperation, and much sadness. We always seem to be in departure mode, and our never-ending separations leave us feeling deeply mournful. "I spend my whole life saying goodbye" was my mother's refrain over and over again, as she bid farewell at the end of sojourns with her children. I used to try to talk her out of her sadness, not realizing the value of being present to it.

In the mournful aftermath of deep personal loss, we frequently feel bereft to the point where it is hard to believe that our emptiness will ever go away and that we shall ever be happy again. When a relationship comes to an end, through death or separation, we not only grieve our happy memory of the past, but also lament the forfeited future, the shattered hopes and unfulfilled dreams we shared with that person. Grief also takes us down long corridors of buried sorrow to meet the ungrieved losses of our past.

The task for survivors is to learn to accept bitter loss, to relinquish what went before, and to open up to a new moment in time. However, I know from experience that, if I suppress my pain, it only haunts me. Denying my feelings does not make them go away; I do not escape grief by refusing to talk about loss. In fact, when I avoid going down into grief with my heart open to pain, intensified feelings of hopelessness and sadness become buried inside me.

Telling our stories and experiencing our mournfulness ultimately brings us to the point where we can remember the past without pain. As we accept the irreversibility of loss, sorrow is transfigured into joyful memory, and absence turns into presence. Then we are empowered to move forward. The depth of our grieving is a function of the degree of loss and the extent of our attachment. Grief work takes time, longer than we would wish, but slowly and progressively, acceptance and emotional detachment are realized. For survivors, significant identity changes are involved, and the uncertainty and confusion about new roles must gradually work itself out. A patient attitude honours the time it takes to adjust to change, to discard a former living situation, and to reorganize life into a new configuration.

The youth circle was closing its evening meeting when Monica complained of a severe headache. Within days the diagnosis revealed that a brain tumour was exploding inside her skull. Three weeks later, it ended her sixteen-year-old life. Her sister, Samantha, was a good friend of mine. She was devastated, but put on a brave front and held together through the funeral process. I sang Samantha's praise for being so strong, telling others how well she had handled her sister's sudden death. Three years later I realized how much of a disservice I had done to Samantha. I had not been able to let her express her sadness, to work through her grief, and to explore a framework of personal meaning. In my applauding her stoic quality, the poignant sorrow she experienced could only be internalized. Eventually, the dam burst and Samantha poured out the buried grief that she had dragged around for so long.

A listening ear and calm manner invite stories of loss to be told. If a warm openness and receptivity are indicated, those in grief welcome the opportunity to tell their tales of sorrow and be given permission to express painful emotions. A friend's silent presence, loving touch, and gentle humour act as a balm to those bereft after loss. It would have been better for Samantha to let go rather than hold on to her sadness, and even better if I had been able to give her permission to do so.

preparing to die

On hospital rounds one morning, I encountered Martha, a 96-year-old woman who was fit to be tied. As I entered her room, she said, "You don't want to talk to me today. I'm in the worst mood I've been in in 96 years." Martha needed little encouragement to continue. She had a 40-year-old granddaughter who, more than ever, wanted her to live to be one hundred. Martha complained that her granddaughter did not want to hear her talk about being ready to die and about the suffering she was going through. Martha, in her anguish, scoffed at the idea of living another four years. With angry emotion she continued, "She just does the telling it, I have to do the living it!" We conversed a while longer, and as we concluded our visit Martha said, "Now, don't you pray that I go on living."

"Don't worry," I replied, "I'll only pray that God-speed-the-light."

"You've got it right!" she said.

Martha's granddaughter was unable to accept her grandmother's impending death and to help her prepare to die. Rather, she focused on encouraging her grandmother to live another four years. But Martha was in so much pain that she really did not want to live even another four days. She needed more to express her anguish and grief, and to indicate her readiness to die. Her granddaughter's denial made it impossible for Martha to share all this with her granddaughter and to say a loving goodbye.

For the most part, our biomedical models of health care attempt to prolong life as long as possible. Spiritual care, on the other hand, focuses on helping people prepare to die. Those at the edge of life need companionship, hope, spiritual insight, and a great deal of emotional support to negotiate death's dark unknown. Life's thresholds are much more easily traversed with accompaniment. A presence of love to the dying, to their misery and mystery, engenders immeasurable comfort. Compassionate friendship empowers those who are undergoing an ordeal of transformation to better interpret and bear their suffering, to find courage and confidence, and to abide in hope. To companion another's affliction is to offer a true gift of consolation.

Serenity is the sense of profound connection that arises when we belong to ourselves, to others, to meanings of suffering and joy, and to love itself. It is deep-felt as we learn to respect the mystery of our personal life journey, including the experience of dying. We cultivate that serenity through spiritual practices of wisdom, awareness, beauty, reaching out, forgiveness, prayer, gratitude, and letting go. The fruit of these practices allows us to become mindful of our true nature – that is, to awaken goodness and gentleness and generosity.

To conclude life well is to find a meaning that makes death itself a fulfillment. Over and above attending to unfinished practical matters, peace is experienced in that conscious process that allows our spiritual values to come through. This involves the effort to reconcile the past: releasing regret, attending to our afflicted emotions, and moving through bitter memory. True healing occurs through focusing on the expression of love and forgiveness in significant relationships. To live until we die is to come into possession of our sacred potential through recognizing what is best in us, and then choosing a further direction of growth. Most importantly, we ask what remains to be lived and what we can still give to life. We are simply invited to take the next step, to deepen consciousness, to seek a larger love. It takes heroic courage to stay with the process and trust life's final mystery.

In fact, at any stage in life, the finest way to prepare for death is to die over and over, to live at the edge. It is to practise an attitude of non-grasping. It is to suffer the chaos of things falling apart, to go down into hopelessness and grief, to let go of control – ultimately, to learn to relax into trust. The practice of death invites us to move forward from identity to identity, from each season of life to the next, experiencing the sting of continual goodbyes. Spiritual practice involves holding the tension of our impermanence, working with the turmoil of change, feeling chronic vulnerability, and experiencing continual dislocation and emptiness.

river beyond time

Like a river, the story of life keeps rolling on and on. The river we travel today is left behind, and gone tomorrow. I sometimes link my image of death to a set of river rapids. The archetype of rebirth suggests that death always yields to more life. While river rapids mark the end of one stretch of river, they mark a passage to more river. In this way, I think of death as one aspect of a riverscape with no bounds.

An awareness of death begs the essential questions of existence. Meeting the destructible aspects of life over and over again brings us to the indestructible truth of love. As things fall apart and come back together and fall apart again, we realize that attachment is our greatest source of suffering. The self that grasps at delusions of pleasure and self-protection needs to learn to cherish others and let go. The way of non-attachment brings us to essential meaning – that is, to a focus on learning to love. Love unbinds us and sets our stories free.

I remember hearing someone say that there are two main jobs in old age: loving and dying well. It was further suggested that the first is the best preparation for the second. Love cannot be a prisoner of time, and there is much joy in reclaiming an adventure that takes us beyond immediate time horizons to the far reaches of being. We cannot run from death nor overcome mortality, but only grow to trust our intuition of unending life. Though our bodies become exhausted, our spirits cry out for the inexhaustible. Love itself stretches beyond time because it belongs to the transcendent unknown. It links time and the time-less. Nouwen writes, "Eternity is born in time, and every time someone dies whom we have loved dearly, eternity can break into our mortal existence a little bit more."[90]

completing the circle

My mom died in the month of December, on the night of the winter solstice. The autumn season had marked for her a descent into physical discomfort and enfeeblement. She had a sense that no further horizons lay ahead, and her loneliness grew thick under death's lengthening shadow. In Canada, the long nights of the northern winter render us prisoners of darkness, often stirring poignant feelings of our own inner night. As dark winter yearns for the summer sun, we, too, feel a spiritual ache for the dawn of new light. Mom's dying amplified the December gloom and intensified our winter longing for joyous light.

At her funeral liturgy, I was comforted by an image of death as the completion of the circle of finite life in its return to the source of infinite love. I quote the words of Paul Geraghty, a hospital chaplain and friend, who gave the homily:

> … death is no longer the final word of our story. Birth and death are no longer separate points at either end of a straight line that seems to come to an abrupt and absurd end, but rather they are points on a circle that flows out of and returns back to the same source… . As you gather as a family to surround Pat with your love, as her life passes through this particular point on that circle, the point we call death, you gather to celebrate not the end of her life, but its completion. The completion of the circle of life in its return to the One who is its source and its goal – the God who is love. In our return to that God, we celebrate our release from all that has limited us and perhaps prevented us from fully experiencing the depth of life for which we were created.[91]

Five months later, on a beautiful day in May, when the green grandeur of fertile spring had transfigured the barren winter, we buried Mom's ashes near the family cottage at Cedar Point. We sang to the eagles, asking them to bear her up on the breath of dawn.

The primitives were not so primitive after all, points out Ernest Becker. They were much more in touch with the primal world and deeply attuned to death seen as "the ultimate promotion."[92] Tibetan masters do not celebrate their birthdays, but rather their death-day. Elisabeth Kübler-Ross describes death as the final stage of growth. I like the word "deathdance," which presents for me a picture of death yielding to timeless beauty and bliss. My father died of Alzheimer's disease. As I watched the disintegration of his mind and body, I found great consolation in the New Testament story of Lazarus dying. When Jesus was pressed to do something, he responded: "This sickness will end not in death, but in God's glory… . (John 11.4)

There seems to be a moment when dying patients leap from the finite world and touch a new reality. As physical and emotional discomfort intensifies, the body itself becomes a burden too great to bear. The dying often express in different ways their desire to get out of the desert of arid human suffering. Some are blessed with a vision of bliss, and fresh spiritual energy emerges in the midst of waning physical strength.

Mike was a cancer patient who came from rural Québec, where he had lived for 20 years on a property treed with hardwood maples. Each spring when the sap began to stir, Mike would tap the runoff and boil down the sweet tree water into thick syrup. Now it was March, and Mike lay dying, filled with sad lament that he was not able to return to the forest to greet the spring and tap the flow of liquid gold. On one visit we were talking about the marvel of running sap as it releases out of the dead of frozen winter. An image started to dance in Mike's mind, and he became very enlivened. The sap had taken on a symbolic quality. I could feel his excitement when he said, "I guess the sap inside me also will one day run again."

We dream of ourselves in terms of unboundedness. Though the endpoint of the journey is unseen, life invites us to abandon ourselves to awe and mystery. A profound longing motivates the perennial quest for an invisible yonder, a lost paradise. We strain after true liberty, a stable centre, lasting meaning. As we engage our hope, we learn to trust that the dawn ever follows our dark nights, even those that are darkest. Though death is often a difficult song to sing, its deep notes sound the call of the eternal. An Okanagan Indian woman chose to sing at her former teacher's gravesite a sad song of lamentation that she said her Creator had given her as a child. Afterwards, she recounted that she had once been asked, by that same teacher, when he was alive and she was young, "Why are you crying?" She had responded, "I am not crying, I am singing."

We die but to live. The resurrection motif can be seen threading itself through the spiritual traditions of all ages, echoing a cry for the eternal. The moment of death in its awesome mystery ushers in a secret new adventure. Death deconstructs the protective shell of human existence to bring about a mystery of transformation. The archetype of rebirth expresses the universal hope captured in the lyrics of Mahler's *Resurrection Symphony*:

> What has come into being must perish. What perished must rise again. Cease from trembling, prepare thyself to live. O Pain, thou piercer of all things, from thee have I been wrested. O Death, thou masterer of all things, now art thou mastered. With wings which I have won me, in love's fierce striving, I shall soar upwards to the light to which no eye has soared. I shall die, to live![93]

Deep within, I think we all long to hear, when earthly life is silenced, a song of immortality whose lyrics echo the sentiment of Julian of Norwich that "all will be well, and every kind of thing will be well."[94]

Part 4

Sacred Fire: Compassion

16
Inner Connection ...
The Silent River

Ultimately, we have just one moral duty: to reclaim large areas of peace in ourselves, more and more peace and to reflect it towards others. And the more peace there is in us, the more peace there will also be in our troubled world.

Etty Hillesum, *An Interrupted Life*

The hero goes inward, to be born again.

Joseph Campbell, *The Hero with a Thousand Faces*

Somewhere we know that without a lonely place our lives are in danger. Somewhere we know that without silence our words lose their meaning, that without listening speaking no longer heals, that without distance closeness cannot cure. Somewhere we know that without a lonely place our actions quickly become empty gestures.

Henri Nouwen, *Out of Solitude*

doing time

"Thap, thap ... thap, thap," sounded the red-hooded woodpecker, piercing the pure silence of a winter morning. The frozen lake and woods lay perfectly still. As I sipped a cup of lemon-ginger tea, I felt myself drawn into a deep, timeless world. I felt safe, connected, alert, calm. The repetitious pecking became a mantra to dispel my scattered thoughts. I had lived alone in a forest for the past five months, "doing time" and writing this book. I had experienced some very lonely times, yet the prolonged silence drew me into a zone where I was discovering a deeper truth of meaning. That morning, as I listened to the woodpecker labour at its tireless task, peck by peck, I realized that *River of Awareness* could be written only word by word by word. I finished my tea, then sat down at my computer to put into print my telephone conversation with Jean-Paul the night before.

One might say that Jean-Paul was a very successful bank robber, inasmuch as he had never been caught in seventeen hold-ups. As I came to know him, it became apparent that he carried overwhelming guilt about all the fear he had left in his wake. He was continuously haunted by the faces of the terrified bank tellers he had victimized, imprints of anguish he now carried in his own heart. Furthermore, Jean-Paul felt aggrieved about messing up his own life "after having been given so much." He also spoke about feeling tormented because other perpetrators of lesser crimes had received jail sentences, while he got off the hook. "I want to go to the pen. That's where I deserve to be." Eventually, Jean-Paul acted out this wish, and found himself doing time in a maximum security prison, but still he carried an agony of guilt. Jean-Paul described some of his prison experience in this way:

> One thing about being in the pen is that there is an unspoken understanding by the inmates that, behind their defences and bravado, everybody is very lonesome and very scared. We know that we all cry alone at night in our cells. And there is an extraordinary tenderness we feel towards one another knowing that we share that deep pain in common.

The focal experience of his time in prison was a three-month stretch spent in solitary confinement where "I was alone as never before, and also alive as never before." Jean-Paul relates the story of having a profound encounter with himself in the midst of his silent squalor:

> The conditions were an indescribable filth and misery, and I felt pathetic that my whole life had come to this. I said to myself you've got to stop destroying yourself. If I were God I would be very sad. That's when I became conscious of divinity. I felt God's sadness. I felt I was brought back to the very core of myself. From there on I didn't have the luxury of hating myself anymore. I had carried around this

habit of guilt and of beating up on myself. Being in solitary confinement, with nobody there, I started to make wordless gestures of compassion to the outside world. I started to feel connected to others and really close to people.

An agony or an ecstasy brings us into contact with the most intimate part of ourselves. In our bitter weeping, as well as in our deepest joys, we discover some of our most hidden inner depths. When we leave behind our ordinary routines, our emotional habits, and outward distractions, we often receive intimations of a deeper truth about life. Letting his inner anguish speak, Jean-Paul saw that the life that he was living was absurd, and that that same life wanted to be lived in obedience to a richer meaning. A profound longing for love broke through in the ordeal of his dark suffering.

Years later, in search of a new experience of inwardness, Jean-Paul found himself in a monastic cell rather than a jail cell. He had chosen to do a 22-day retreat with a group of Trappist monks at Oka. He recounts, "In jail we had eight head-counts a day. Here the monks have seven prayer times. The monks, very much like prisoners, are silent watchers. They, too, are marginal. But they share a deep joy with their fellow monks in the solidarity of their longing for real freedom." The archetype of renewal that Jean-Paul had experienced years earlier in solitary confinement was reactivated at Oka. "I can certainly relate to the monks," he concluded. "They say that your cell will teach you everything."

inwardness

Though solitary confinement is not the recommendation here, the cultivation of intimacy with oneself is vital to happiness. I rejoice to be on silent waters where I can listen to the rhythms of life deep within. When I take time to hang out with myself, I always hear a call to greater authenticity. This is the voice Jean-Paul heard inviting him to create a new integrity of relationship, and his subsequent healing was born out of an intimate encounter with self. The word "intimacy" derives from the Latin *timere*, which means "to fear." To be timid is to be shy, fearful. To intimidate another is to instil fear. The word "intimate" indicates the negation of fear, and thus, as intimacy grows, fear diminishes. Without a doubt, I know that a vibrant inner connection enhances my capacity for interpersonal intimacy.

When we become too extroverted, most of our interest is directed towards the external world. Only when the outward flow of psychic energy reverses direction does the inner world become the focus of attention. Jungian author Esther Harding suggests that, if we resist this natural reversal and the need of introversion when it is called for, much unhappiness ensues. If we become concerned exclusively with outer interests, we will experience difficulties, even disaster, in our lives. As we begin to negotiate our resistance to introversion, we sometimes enter into a wilderness of emptiness and depression. Initially, the distress of guilt surfaces, and we must discover what exactly we are feeling and why. Guilt results from not being right with our most fundamental values. Our guilt feelings become buried deep within, later manifesting in feelings of uneasiness or inferiority, in physical symptoms, and in states of depression. Often we must come to terms with an overly materialistic outlook on life and a lack of meaningful direction.

When Emma came to see me she reported, "I feel totally messed up. All my motivation is gone. I have never felt so down in all my life." In time it became apparent that the meaning of Emma's depression lay in the avoidance of her world of inner feeling. She had gone through a very painful divorce, but had never come to terms with the loss of her spouse, who meant the whole world to her. Emma continued to push herself to perform in the outer world, but dragging herself out of bed each morning became harder and harder. Eventually, her energy collapsed, and Emma faced the depth of her pain. She would later report,

"I was hurting so much. The grief in me was deep, but I never let myself feel it." Emma had needed to become intimate with her sadness and work it through. But she had been preoccupied with extraneous matters, and so avoided spending time with herself. I encouraged Emma to develop habits of inner attention and to set aside time on a regular basis to be with herself.

The journey into self is a long pilgrimage to the heart. Harding speaks of the unknowing that is present at the outset. We do not really know what we are getting ourselves into, yet we feel compelled to dive into the process. She comments on Bunyan's classic *Pilgrim's Progress*,

> ... the man, Christian, is, indeed, on the threshold of such an adventure, but at the beginning he did not understand anything of its real nature, neither its arduousness nor its lifelong duration nor its dangers nor its goal. These things were hidden from him; he only knew that he was driven by fear. In just such a fashion, many people today are driven to embark on the journey of the soul not on account of any conscious desire for inner development, but because they are hounded by some neurotic symptom or inexplicable depression.[95]

During mid-adolescence, Brendan's family fell apart, and his entire world was turned upside down. As he tried to come to grips with a serious psychological crisis that followed, he found some unexpected solitude and inner healing. After a 52-mile hike, Brendan reflected, "I have always loved wilderness canoeing. But hiking is even better. In a canoe I was always with a mate, but when I was hiking, I would spend hours trekking by myself. That gave me a chance to meet myself in a way I had never done before. The solo time helped me to get connected to the me inside me." I recall another hiker once saying, "With all that time on the trail alone with yourself, you can sure burn off a lot of emotional junk."

There are times when I have a certain amount of resistance to being alone. With never-ending distractions, I let myself get hooked on the outside world. Nevertheless, I realize that inner experience shapes the true story of my life more than the outer situations in which I am bound up. To a certain extent, I am constituted by what happens to me, but even more so by how I am with myself in response to the flow and flux of external life. Spiritual guides and gurus through the ages speak of the prime importance of getting to know ourselves. They seem unanimous in pointing to self-knowledge as the essential challenge of human development. We bring on a good deal of distress by getting swept up in the busyness of the world. Our avoidance costs us the opportunity to encounter ourselves intimately, and so we forfeit much inner vitality. When Jean-Paul dealt with the guilt dominant in his psyche, and Emma faced her sadness, they were both able to reclaim their vital life energy.

In the grip of attachment, we cling to people, to our emotional routines, to ideas and possessions, and we preoccupy ourselves with trivial reality. Modern culture tends to focus on security and satisfactions that effectively drown out our deeper longings. The terror of meeting our inner loneliness drives us into busy activity, and alienates us from deeper layers of meaning and mystery. This leaves us radically at odds with our true personhood. The Christian-Hindu mystic Bede Griffiths emphasizes the need to attend to the inner reaches of being. He exhorts us not to wander in a world of shadows, and not to mistake the world of outward appearances for reality. Muslim writer Muhammed Iqbal likewise speaks of the paralysis of energy that comes when we lose contact with our inner depths. He warns that our ruthless egoism and infinite gold-hunger bring us nothing but life weariness. The Trappist Thomas Merton interprets why some have chosen the monastic path:

> … there is something in their hearts that tells them they cannot be happy in an atmosphere where people are look-

ing for nothing but their own pleasure and advantage and comfort and success. They have not come to the monastery to escape from the realities of life but to find those realities: they have felt the terrible insufficiency of life in a civilization that is entirely dedicated to the pursuit of shadows.[96]

Whether we are monks or mystics, or neither, the challenge that faces all of us is to go beyond that false self that chases after security, affection, and pleasure. Our real quest is the true, wise self that reveals a deeper law of harmony. When we avoid intimate self-encounter, we remain slaves to our needs and fears, and continue to chase after shadows. But when such avoidance comes to an end, we discover a new language of intimacy, and touch a deeper inner centre. As self-understanding develops, we are able to befriend past, present, and future: we learn forgiveness, find new equanimity, and open up in trust to the path of our becoming.

the task of individuation

Individuation, a term coined by psychologist Carl Jung, depicts the process through which our personal integration is achieved. It is the journey of finding authentic and original identity, the task of becoming our own person. The urge to individuation pushes in the direction of particular meaning, challenging us to find our own specific purpose and possibilities. The individuation process brings us into our hidden depths to discover our own truly unique potential, which can never be matched or repeated by anyone else. As we brave our own deeds, it becomes imperative to define ourselves from the inside out, not the outside in. Each of us is called to make an unprecedented contribution to life.

This entails standing out, going it alone, fashioning one's unique meaning. An individuated person abandons safety and rejects conformity in order to blaze a path of new creative endeavour. The path we must follow is sometimes very lonely, often requiring us to leave collective society and break away from established patterns of value. To be innovative is to dare being original, and to go out on a limb.

We live soullessly, however, if we act simply in blind obedience to social norms. Authenticity demands that we refuse to let our values and meanings be dictated by an impersonal culture. Pushing towards the goal of self-realization, the individuation process entails discarding our persona, the external social mask that generally describes young adult identity. As we individuate, old images of self are dropped, allowing us to take possession of our truer path. Many refuse individuation, holding onto habitual self-images and social identity, and so restrict their self-discovery. The consequences of either relinquishing or retaining our personas are contrasted by Hall and Nordby in *A Primer of Jungian Psychology*:

> An individual overdevelops his persona to such a degree that he is little more than a robot acting in conformity with social convention and tradition. As a consequence, he becomes listless, bored, irritable, dissatisfied, and depressed. Finally, he feels the need of getting away from his mundane life, and goes off by himself. He sheds the rigid mask of conformity and discovers the hidden riches in the unconscious. He returns to his everyday life refreshed and invigorated, more of a spontaneous, creative person and less of a puppet of the environment... . Most people who find themselves imprisoned by convention resort to diversions such as drinking, gambling, fighting, and sensuality, from which they learn nothing.[97]

Through this process of shedding the persona, we forge indivisible personhood; we become less divided and more individual. The Jungian understanding of human personality depicts a tense showdown between ego and the Self. As we mature, the narrow ego is called upon to step aside to make room for the Self, which is the totality of personhood. A whole world of creativity and

meaning opens up beyond the scope of the ambitious, self-pro-
tecting ego. But as long as we maintain an egocentric pose, the
Self remains stifled, which puts a great strain on relationships.
Eventually, the ego standpoint is challenged by a mutiny from
within – the hidden Self demands recognition and development.
Individuation is about moving beyond the ego into a larger story;
it is the process of realizing authentic being.

still waters

The movement of life has its roots in stillness. Love springs
from a receptive silence. Love means concentration. In solitude,
the heart knows rest and becomes full. The Dutch author A.
D. Sertillanges, in *The Intellectual Life*, writes, "Rest cannot
be found in scattering one's energies. ... Rest is a return to our
origins: the origins of life, of strength, of inspiration."[98] Outside
our normal routines of activity and achievement, above the noise
and nuisance of every day, beyond our many plans and projects,
we meet a part of ourselves that belongs to no one else. We
discover a silent river that words never touch. This silence leads
us to our own truth.

Tranquil concentration involves bringing all our attention to
a single point. It does not come easily. Saying this brings to mind
a teaching about focused attention. Upon entering the dining
hall, I saw my friend Mark off in the corner eating breakfast and
reading. Having just listened to the above teaching story, I said
to him, "Mark, this is poor eating. This is poor reading. When
you eat, eat; and when you read, read."

Mark glanced up and retorted, "Sure, I know ... and when
you eat and read, eat and read!"

Roberta, sitting in earshot at a nearby table, piped up: "I
used to always be doing seven things at the same time. It took
me a long while to discover the wisdom of doing one thing at a
time. Now," she mused, "I am trying to do just half a thing at
a time."

I used to get myself into a real tailspin trying to reach the meditation centre on time. I would set out late, fight the traffic, and fret at every red light. Finally arriving, frantic and out of breath, I would run into the meditation room, and spend the next half hour recovering, only to rush back to work. It gradually occurred to me that my meditation had become just another activity in the breathtaking frenzy of my days.

Time often seems so much like an enemy. I am always fighting it, losing it, running out of it. I remember seeing a slogan painted on a street in Mumbai (India) that read: "He speeded to his grave never to use the time he saved." Even as I complain about the busyness of my life and never having enough time, all the same, I am addicted to my routines of activity. Hooked on external stimuli, my habitual pace of interaction leaves little time to listen to the songs within myself – they tend to get drowned out by the constant commotion I have built into my life. The widespread addiction to activity in modern culture seems to indicate the common avoidance of self-encounter.

In *The Tibetan Book of Living and Dying*, Sogyal Rinpoche makes this same point: "Generally we waste our lives, distracted from our true selves, in endless activity.... Our lives are lived in intense and anxious struggle, in a swirl of speed and aggression, in competing, grasping, possessing, and achieving, forever burdening ourselves with extraneous activities and preoccupations."[99] Philp Simmons, in *Learning to Fall*, writes of his spiritual journey after being diagnosed with a terminal illness at age 35. He advocates finding a still point in life's downhill rush:

> ... our busyness is often a distraction, a way of avoiding others, avoiding intimacy, avoiding ourselves. We keep busy to push back our fears, our loneliness, our self-doubt, our questions about purposes and ends. We want to know we matter, we want to know our lives are worthwhile. And when we're not sure, we work that much harder, we worry that much more. In the face of our uncertainty, we keep busy.[100]

Still waters run deep. When we let water stand, it becomes more and more transparent; we are then able to look right through it and see into great depth. Just as a calm surface allows us to see a mirror reflection, so, too, the still mind sees more. But the restless mind is like wind-driven waves that prevent depth perception. Only when we let the turbulent mind settle do we acquire calming perspectives in the flux of day-to-day living. The practice of stillness allows us to become attuned to the silent river within ourselves.

the truth of silence

What we most fear, perhaps, is the encounter with our deep inner loneliness. However, the refusal to enter into our solitary depths prevents us from knowing ourselves. This, in turn, impairs our intimacy with others. The primal anxiety arising from our inherent loneliness, in fact, gives birth to our desire to transform a consciousness of separateness into an experience of intimate communion. In *Markings*, Dag Hammarskjöld, a former Secretary-General of the United Nations, wrote, "Pray that your loneliness may spur you into finding something to live for, great enough to die for."[101]

To meet ourselves as lonely is to know this longing for love. Solitude cures loneliness when we meet within ourselves a desire for friendship, and find that same desire in others. We fashion solidarity with others out of the very need we have to find a way out of loneliness. Our deep urge to belong inspires us to reach out to other persons where they are most alone, in confusion and conflict, in fear and inner darkness. The early monks presented an image of their monastic life as a journey to centre, as a movement from the circumference of a circle towards a God-centre – as each monk moved along a particular radius towards the centre they would draw ever closer to one another.

In solitude we cannot hide. There the truth of silence is experienced and the truth of self exposed. As words are left behind we undergo rejuvenation, much like the springtime that incubates in the dead of winter. When we become still, we touch an inner emptiness from which an extraordinary source of hidden vitality arises. Silence leads to the death of the self, and that is when love is born.

Contemplation is far from an idle pastime. It is a vigorous engagement with ourselves. As we cultivate a steady centre of awareness and seek a deeper knowledge of the heart, we get in touch with our inner rhythms. Solitude moves us towards simplicity, and does away with the unnecessary and the unreal. In times of silence, we are able to meet our mistakes, as well as atone for them. Silence creates a true context for rigorous purification. Solitude also affords us the opportunity to imagine possibility, to be innovative, to become attuned to vision. Jung wrote that "the years when I was pursuing my inner image were the most important in my life – in them everything essential was decided."[102]

When we enter into solitude, ordinary consciousness takes a back seat. What normally lies outside our field of vision comes to the foreground, enabling us to witness the extraordinary forces guiding our lives. Depths of beauty, love, and pain, ordinarily out of the range of everyday awareness, visit us. Beyond the noise of our surface emotions and the mist of habitual thought, we come into contact with a deeper spiritual stratum: there we discover the essential self. True self-knowledge replaces a more vagrant self-attention. The archetype of desert spirituality suggests going into an empty place to court a vast silence where only the voice of God is heard. In the desert, we come face to face with life and death, our inner poverty, with the essential questions about life meanings. The desert becomes the symbol of purification, a time of testing, a place of formation to prepare for our missions in the world.

inner workout

Striking the right balance between inwardness and outgoing activity is different for everyone. It seems to be the rule, though, that most of us are somewhat addicted to activity and overextended in outer social commitments. We find ourselves entangled in a complex mesh of obligations, and perceive ourselves to be the victims of time. But when we learn to pay tribute to silence, we undergo surprising renewal. Wisdom is bestowed on us in solitude, along with new sources of inspiration and insight. The quality of our inner attention allows us to be attentive in a new way to the world around us. When motivated by right intention, interiority is not a self-indulgent navel-gazing exercise; in truth, it guides us into an expression of greater love for others.

On the solo path, inwardness can be practised in many ways. In addition to different techniques of prayer and meditation, active imagination allows us to witness inner consciousness. In this manner, we are able to observe ideas and images that arise spontaneously into waking consciousness, similar to our dreams that intrude into sleep. In active imagination, our conscious and unconscious worlds meet and work together. Esther Harding talks of the "inner guide" and the imperative to find a guiding spirit deep within oneself. The inner voice is heard in dreams and in active imagination. We must find our own inner law and obey it. The inner guide "… is the first carrier of the individual's own law, a guiding spirit who speaks with an inner voice to those in great need and distress. This helpful voice is particularly liable to be heard in dreams or in active imagination when the conscious personality has been thoroughly aroused to its helpless condition."[103]

Andrew says of his practice of meditation, "It is the best way to go that I know. I feel pulled in that direction. Meditation attracts me as an image of health, and awakens in me a memory of calm." He paused, and then continued, "Calm, it's waiting there for you." Ellen, another long-term practitioner, describes meditation as "... somehow reconnecting you with yourself. It provides a stable centre, a focal point where your vital energy is. It is like the calm in the centre of a storm. A lot of activity needs a still point. Everything moves around a still point." The practice of meditation, found in many spiritual traditions, is oriented to attaining the state of non-distraction. It is going inside to get control of our mental processes, ultimately to quiet the mind and find a peaceful centre beyond the world of conceptual thinking. It is a continuous letting go of thoughts and habitual worrying, and aims to find a calm detachment from our normal anxious reactions. Beyond the noise of the psyche, meditation helps us to recollect our fractious desires and scattered attention. Meditation draws us away from ego-striving into the heart of love.

A daily practice of meditation involves a departure from our ordinary routines onto a river of silence. The habit of stillness follows the hero motif: when we break the momentum of our physical and intellectual activities, we disappear alone into the "deep" to transform consciousness, later returning to the world to shine new light. Great discipline and courage are needed to remain faithful to this process of finding the essential self. Some say they haven't the time, but meditation can be viewed as an investment in love. Though it costs a practitioner perhaps an hour a day, with a recollected mind, life is met with a much better quality of attention – and so the meditator might save six hours, translating into a net gain of time. Wherever meditation is taught, newcomers inevitably want to know how long it takes to still the mind. "The first 20 years are the hardest" is the customary response.

17
Born in the Encounter ...
Belonging and Wholeness

Community is not only where we give back; it is also where we learn to receive, learn to trust, learn to allow ourselves to be loved and cared for. No one grows up alone. No one is healed in isolation.

Robert Jingen Gunn, *Journeys into Emptiness*

To reach out for truth is to reach out with our whole person for relationships which can reform us and the world in the image of love.

Parker Palmer, *To Know As We Are Known*

In the presence of some people, we immediately come to life, leaping forth as who we truly are. Such people enable our truest personality to blaze forth. ... Suddenly, we meet someone; suddenly, we find some community; suddenly, we discover friendship, and in that instant our self blazes into existence.

Brian Swimme, *Earth Fire*

authentic belonging

For the most part, the men who came to our hospitality house were socially withdrawn. Some were completely isolated, never having anyone call them by name from one end of the day to the other. It was apparent that Mario, one of our regular drop-ins, had been seriously traumatized and had retreated into himself. He always sat to the side, too afraid to express himself. Whatever his hurt and fears, we knew that Mario felt very alone in his suffering. But he would show delight when I greeted him by name, and I learned to feel comfortable talking to him without expecting a response. Whenever I invited Mario to help with a chore, he was more than eager to pitch in. Trust slowly developed, and one day three months later, Mario surprised me with "Hi, Steve." Afterwards, bits of self-expression followed as Mario gradually healed his deeply wounded sense of belonging.

The primacy of the need for relatedness is clearly revealed in those who are most marginalized. Street people, many of whom have a history of mental illness, suffer extreme loneliness. Though they lack food and shelter, their condition of isolation defines a more acute poverty. I have recognized this also with inner-city youth who join gangs to find identity and establish bonds of friendship. "This is where I feel connected. These are the people who really look after me," said one nineteen-year-old gang member. The question of identity answers to the human longing for love.

Many individuals lack a core identity because they have no primary belonging. Family breakdown accounts for much of this paucity, and leaves a young generation struggling to find a sense of connection. Because of the gap in family identity, many youth depend on surrogate mothers and fathers. Away from home one Christmas, I returned to find that my Montreal home had been broken into during my absence. It turned out I knew the person responsible. "I had nowhere else to go; I hope you'll forgive me," said the fourteen-year-old lad I had met at camp the summer before. "I thought of suicide. I cried for months when I came back from camp. It's the only place I ever had a sense of belonging, of people really caring."

All forms of identity – family, social and cultural, work, spiritual – seem threatened in an age of rapid upheaval and change. We hunger for vital human connection, and find belonging in different patterns of relationships. We are born into a family clan, join groups or gangs, enter into special love relationships, and seek out kindred spirits. Obeying a law of inexplicable attractions, particular friendships are mysteriously discovered. We are most drawn to those with whom we share a mutuality of interests, experiences, and values. A great amplification of creativity comes about as we band together with those whose passions are similar to our own. In any pattern of relationship, we hope to trade our isolation for intimacy, our loneliness for love. I have boundless gratitude for family and friends with whom I have shared much delight. I bow before the mystery of how our lives have come together, standing in awe of the meanings hidden within each encounter. Conversely, I experience a sadness inside myself when I think of those to whom I remain a stranger, especially in the experience of unresolved discord.

Beyond all else, what we truly desire is to enjoy others and to have others enjoy us. I sense my friends are happy when they know that I am enjoying them. Taken further, I enjoy others enjoying me enjoy them – so forth goes the dance of delight. The sum and substance of relatedness is well described as the experience of that reciprocity of enjoyment. The happiness we feel in belonging to others reveals the deepest longings of the heart. This is how Sebastian Moore puts it: "I show that I love myself by the fact that I want this self that I love to be important to another. Experience testifies that there is no greater satisfaction than that of knowing that you count in the eyes of someone special, that that person's life is different because of you and happy because you're around."[104]

To belong, then, is to enjoy connection and companionship. Our search for intimacy responds to the crucial human need to belong, and indeed, zest of living arises from interpersonal communion. Special friendships create a vital rapport that lets us live, laugh, worry, weep, play, and pray together. Through learning to let go of fear, trust develops and empowers our capacity to respect one another. Even in the midst of deep affliction, authentic encounter brings great solace to suffering. It seems ever true that the bliss of belonging springs forth in relationships characterized by genuine engagement and profound presence.

beyond isolation

Intimate encounter was very much the hallmark of our drug rehabilitation process. Within our healing circles, we had the opportunity to become sensitively involved with each other. As the roots of trust went deeper, a special bond was created, allowing us to drop our masks and open up to one another. This experience of compassionate intimacy enabled profound healing. As our capacity for honest self-expression expanded, we marked the extent to which we were learning to negotiate our fears. One of our participants put it quite simply: "We discovered how to be real, and to find real friends."

It became apparent to me that we grow especially well in the soil of appreciation. In the experience of mutual trust, we learn to believe in ourselves. Over time, in the recovery process, we cut through negativity and found a language of affirmation that enabled us to value self and each other. This inner and outer befriending taught us to appeal to the best rather than find the worst in each other. Conversely, we came to realize that, as much as encouragement engenders confidence, ridicule erodes self-esteem. Insensitive criticism and admonitions go nowhere, and telling others what we do not accept about them hardly supports change. Not only do our overt putdowns block growth, so do our lack of reassurances. The poverty of much human interaction reflects a deficit of positive affirmation; all too often we hold back kind words of acknowledgment. In our healing circles, this did not mean that we did not voice sharp criticism. But we aimed at positive criticism, and experienced firsthand that it goes a long way in sparking the transformative process. When a vibrant rapport has been created, guidance and correction are readily accepted.

We seek intimacy because we are looking for a way out of fear. Intimate relationship allows us to feel at home with one another – that is, not to feel afraid. Fear is the enemy of belonging, and results in deep loneliness. Fear inhibits the generous giving of ourselves. Not to belong is to withdraw from others into insular and lonely worlds of self-concern where we become preoccupied with self-protection. The illusion of the separate self is a grave distortion that gives rise to the pride of self-sufficiency. Our efforts to go it alone are indeed misguided.

Much about who we are is discovered through living with others. Deep personal meanings are revealed through our relationships. Cosmologist Brian Swimme suggests that we are "born in the encounter," that when we meet others we ignite unsuspected dimensions of their being that would not have been brought forth had we not come along. Likewise, through interaction, we discover new aspects of ourselves. We exist as a bundle of possibilities, and the infinite depth of each person opens up in the experience of human relatedness. Swimme writes:

> Love ignites being… . What is our fullest destiny? To become love in human form. Yes, we awake to fascination and we strive to fascinate… .

> We work to enchant others. We work to ignite life, to evoke presence, to enhance the unfolding of being. All of this is the actuality of love. We strive to fascinate so that we can bring forth what might otherwise disappear. But that is exactly what love does: Love is the activity of evoking being, of enhancing life.[105]

the jamming factor

In the experience of true intimacy, we cease being strangers to one another. The practice of awareness, the habit of careful communication, and a method for resolving conflict help create deep interpersonal connection. These reflect the need to be continually attuned to oneself and one another, and the importance of addressing interpersonal discord.

The sweet delight of friendship quickly sours when conflict comes into play and is left ignored. When interpersonal conflict arises, we begin to appreciate the large challenge of living with others. Sebastian Moore speaks of "the jamming factor" to describe situations of conflict. The continuity of any relationship hinges on the capacity of individuals to un-jam, that is, to deal with discord when it arises.

> Perhaps what happens when you experience a sharp dislike of someone or a deep misunderstanding is that between you, the shared resonance (primary familiarity) started up as usual, and then was jammed when the other person or yourself, or both, turned in and got caught in some hang-up ... In this interplay (interacting self-awareness), we are not strangers to each other. We become strangers precisely through the above-named jamming of the interplay.[106]

We likely all agree that relationship is always somewhat less than ideal. In every human encounter, a certain amount of tension comes into play in the mix of ideas, beliefs, and values. The radically opposite ways we communicate and behave create significant jamming. Marked differences in temperament exist, and the negative characteristics of our personalities are frequently activated as we relate one to another. Emotional stresses, as well as tensions of competitive self-interest, feed interpersonal conflict. Because we often meet one another in unconscious and insensitive ways, our shadow selves can run much interference on our ability to love. As we move in dissimilar directions, with divergent passions and ambitions, we perturb our interactions.

Unattended conflict undermines the integrity of relationship and threatens existing levels of trust, and the parties at odds with each other find themselves stuck in an enveloping dissonance. Paradoxically, exploring the friction may help strengthen a friendship that feels threatened. Differences often do divide, but, when creatively engaged, can help build true synergy. The practice of awareness is a cornerstone for what Thich Nhat Hanh calls "interbeing." Finding a method of unjamming is crucial in order to achieve new accord.

Authentic friendship begins with a readiness to meet one another "as is," and to be sensitively attentive to the confusion and conflict that arise in the interplay of differences. The fact of dissent itself demands an active and conscious search for common ground, for mutual values and meaning. Through examining and interpreting its own experience, a relationship keeps reconstituting itself and defining an evolving identity. Genuine encounter requires the dynamic involvement of each individual to find a relational path of meaning. Friendship is more than just being together – it requires that we become sensitively attuned to one another. Whether in our living arrangements, at work, or at play, we join together in response to a need to form solidarity in the pursuit of common goals. Friendship often takes a path over very difficult terrain towards an unknown destination. Dialogue that is responsive to the ever-changing needs and challenges along that path enables a relationship to learn where it truly wants to go.

A genuine connection of love takes us out of ourselves and leaves us with enhanced vitality. Living with others teaches us to overcome self-centred motivations, and also to be open to receive from them. True intimacy finds expression in co-operation rather than competition, and dissolves those gaps in our relationships that fill with fear. Fear constricts love and impels us to exert power over others. It does not let us share our mutual vulnerability. Rather than daring to trust, we intimidate one another. Rather than caring for each other, we compete for advantage. In this atmosphere of intimidation, belonging is stifled.

In the exchange of compassion and gratitude, true friends witness the triumphs and defeats of each other's lives. We belong to others not only in their joy, but also in their sorrow. Moments of compassionate intimacy miraculously lift our burden of suffering or grief, and bestow on us extraordinary strengths to face insurmountable challenge. In sharing our deep suffering with others, we give them the courage to meet their inner pain and surrender their own fears. A commitment to the journey of intimate friendship unfolds relationships of great value. At the end of Dostoevsky's *Crime and Punishment*, the narrator recounts the miracle of love experienced by Raskolnikov and Sonia, after a long road of trials, through encounter:

> How it happened he did not know. But all at once something seemed to seize him and fling him at her feet. He wept and threw his arms around her knees. For the first instant she was terribly frightened and she turned pale. She jumped up and looked at him trembling. But at the same moment she understood, and a light of infinite happiness came into her eyes. She knew and had no doubt that he loved her beyond everything, and that at last the moment had come. ... They wanted to speak, but could not; tears stood in their eyes. They were both pale and thin; but those sick pale faces were bright with the dawn of a new future, of a full resurrection into a new life. They were renewed by love; the heart of each held infinite sources of life for the heart of the other.[107]

interplay

Interactive conversation engenders self-discovery, and our thoughts, feelings, and meanings are revealed as much to ourselves as to our listeners. A. D. Sertillanges put it this way: "And then, when an exchange takes place, the concert grows richer: each person speaks and listens, learns and teaches, takes and gives, getting something even as [s]he gives."[108] The circle motif was certainly impressed on my young imagination. As a lad, I spent many summer evenings around a campfire, enjoying the magic of a circle. Transfixed by the dancing flames, we would "sit and spit" for hours, and listen long to one another's tales. In a similar format, our family gathered for daily meals around a table where we exchanged our everyday stories – through self-expression we met each other. I also discovered myself in new ways, for in telling others about myself, I would stretch my self-knowledge. The more I experienced opportunities for conversation, the more I began to sense my connection to a larger whole. The circle became a powerful symbol that indeed was to shape my spiritual outlook.

When we travel the whole circumference of any circle, we learn to hold the many tensions and contradictions and mysteries bound up within it. The further our self-exploration takes us, the more rounded we become. Where there is a spirit of openness, everyone is eager to hear from everyone else; this lends to a rich diversity of expression. A true circle celebrates the back and forth of oppositions that build into a communion experience. Through encounter, within a tension of differences, we discover the unique beauty of each individual, and learn to celebrate diversity. An inclusive circle teaches the language of acceptance, and, as such, offers a place of authentic belonging where trust flourishes.

A compelling image for me is that of a seed holding within itself its own potential of maturation. Yet seeds need rain, soil, and sunshine, and a habitat that enables them to germinate and grow. An acorn becomes a mighty oak tree when it finds fertile soil and the right amount of sunshine and rain. Individuals become truly human in environments that encourage self-discovery and enable love to flourish. A seed of love is within each of us, and the company of inspired others offers that seed the nurture it needs. We inhibit the growth of others when we fail to be a fertile soil of enabling awareness and love.

the great oneness

All circles hold endless tensions of opposites: yin and yang, potential and limitation, instinct and spirit, hope and despair, complaint and gratitude, loneliness and intimacy, error and mercy, hostility and hospitality, silence and activity, vulnerability and protection, consolation and desolation, for better and for worse. The interplay of these opposites constitutes the dynamism of creativity, a dialectic of continuous disjunction and conjunction. In the tension of these dichotomies, truth exposes illusion. The opposites stand as separate radii, and manifest the distinct elements of a situation. As differences interact, they come together to create a surprising revelation of wider meanings.

The greatest dichotomy lies in the co-existence of good and evil; we have pondered through time how to reconcile their tension. Emphasizing that the sun rises on the honest and the dishonest alike, and that rain falls on the just and the unjust, Jesus instructs us to love our enemies and pray for those who persecute us. Here the principle of compassion points to a large love that embraces evildoers in a creative manner. Spiritual luminosity ultimately resolves the problem of evil. We are asked to acknowledge evil, but further invited to trust the power of light to dispel its darkness.

In human endeavour, darkness and light stand both in conjunction and in contradiction, and are held together in paradox. Inclinations to both good and evil are played out in the same ring. We feel both the pull and the counterpull to and from the good. Jesuit writer Robert Doran suggests that the reconciliation of good and evil is achieved beyond the psychological realm through spiritual transformation. He cautions us not to reduce spirituality to psychology, nor to divorce the two. Doran makes it clear that we can flee insight, resist truth, avoid decision, and run from God as passionately as we can pursue insight, intend truth, act towards the good, and be open to the love of God. The resolution of the problem of evil, Doran suggests, is more than a process of the natural reconciliation of tensions within the psyche. Its resolution enters the spiritual realm, requiring the discernment of spirits and God-given love. Doran proposes that we not rely solely on human understanding, for psychological self-knowledge expands in the delight of divine revelations. We are invited to acknowledge our sins and admit evil as a real force. As the forces of good and evil face off, it is the spirit of truth that discriminates between the two attractions, and breaks the power of evil. We conquer evil with good – good summons transformation.

Living the horror of the Holocaust, Etty Hillesum gives us a good example of the power of love to unbind dark hate. She advocates that we bear sorrow from time to time:

> Yes, life is beautiful, and I value it anew at the end of every day, even though I know that the sons of mothers, and you are one such mother, are being murdered in concentration camps. And you must be able to bear your sorrow; even if it seems to crush you, you will be able to stand up again, for human beings are so strong, and your sorrow must become an integral part of yourself, part of your body and your soul, you mustn't run away from it, but bear it like an adult. Do not relieve your feelings through hatred, do not seek to be avenged on all German mothers, for they, too, sorrow at this very moment for their slain and murdered sons. Give your sorrow all the space and shelter in yourself that it is due, for if everyone bears his grief honestly and courageously, the sorrow that now fills this world will abate. But if you do not clear a decent shelter for your sorrow, and instead reserve most of the space inside you for hatred and thoughts of revenge – from which new sorrows will be born for others – then sorrow will never cease in this world and will multiply. And if you have given sorrow the space its gentle origins demand, then you may truly say: life is beautiful and so rich. So beautiful and so rich that it makes you want to believe in God.[109]

The integrated wholeness we seek grasps a unity that transcends, or comes to terms with, opposites. In attempting to balance polarities, we bring oppositions into creative interplay; we hold their tension, and see where they want to go and what they want to reveal. Death and life, for example, are not opposed to each other. The cycle of life, decay, and rebirth describes the restless movement in which all things appear and disappear, yet reappear in a process of continuous becoming. Likewise, we negotiate chaos to discover a deeper order, and move through confusion to find a deeper clarity. We find ourselves frequently at the edge, where we are asked to let go, die, leap into the abyss, trust, find a fuller life. If we deny death, we in fact resist our transformative potential. The sun falls each day from the sky, and we, too, must learn to fall. The moon wanes, the tide ebbs, the sun sinks in the west. Night belongs to the day, and death to life, an endless circle dance.

A wide range of opposites introduces us to a world of paradox and to a wisdom bigger than the sum of their parts. Analytical and intuitive processes each help us to make more complete sense of the unknown, which consists of endless variables. As we have seen, inwardness and outwardness together build a depth of intimacy. Despair recognizes in its anguished cry the poverty of what is lacking, and thereby gives rise to hope. Dependence and independence lead towards healthy interdependence. In the adventure of becoming, a balanced knowledge of possibility and impossibility enables us to actualize potential within a given set of limitations.

The Tao Te Ching suggests that primal virtue leads all things back "towards the great oneness." The wholeness we seek is hidden in a mystery bigger than the grasp of our thin insight and fragmentary meanings. We live in a mystery circle that ultimately transcends dualistic oppositions. The conflicts and contradictions we experience are at length resolved as truth breaks into consciousness, and reveals an unsuspected unity. We are one, but have not imagined ourselves so. As we go round and round the circumference of mystery, attentive to every perspective, we begin to dis-identify with single points of view. As we let go of rigid consciousness, our minds and hearts open to discover that truth is multiple, many-sided, mysterious. The various positions that lay claim to it begin to illuminate each other as we open a space for them to interplay together. New consciousness is evoked through wider interactions, with always more to see and more to imagine. Our discovery, ever reaching towards a higher integrity, keeps expanding the circle, which symbolizes our infinite and hidden wholeness, a mystery that beckons us ever further towards the great oneness.

journey of self-knowledge

The more I recognize that I am in touch with only a tiny part of the circumference of the whole me, the more I become aware of my need to know myself. In ordinary consciousness, I am locked within a narrow set of self-images. This leaves me out of touch with huge pieces of the bigger me, and with the vast expanse of life. Something within is always pushing me to find that bigger me, to befriend my undiscovered self. Though I resist the process, I deeply long to know all of myself and to become fully realized.

The undiscovered self is slowly revealed as we hold the tension between the little self and boundless being. The ego must undergo its progressive dissolution, die to its narrow strivings, and yield a larger love. The journey to wholeness creates a relationship between things seen and unseen, as one-sided consciousness opens itself to listen to the voices of the unconscious. The unconscious includes buried feeling, primal intuition, dark shadow content, and hidden talent largely out of the range of our ordinary recognition. As the contents of the unconscious are made available to consciousness, we invent that bigger me. Nevertheless, all our categories of thought and tools of insight create only partial knowledge, and are not adequate to disclose the full mystery of our being.

Psychological wisdom is attained as we explore more and more of the circumference of the psyche. If we refuse attention to the inner flow of memory and longing, feelings and fantasies, images and intention, we cut off part of the perimeter of ourselves. And if we ignore the sensitive messages of sense and symbol, we lose our full soulfulness. We also must be in touch with the wisdom of our bodies and with the instincts that govern us. The body has its own determinisms, a language difficult to learn, and its needs are dangerous if denied or ignored. Finally, the search of spiritual wisdom teaches the heart to be receptive to the mysterious emergence of truth and love.

To seek wholeness is to penetrate the labyrinth of ourselves. It is to be attentive to all the data of the psyche, the messages of the body, and the whisperings of the spirit. It is to be willing to suffer a transformative process that disrupts the status quo and ushers in the chaos of creativity. We are a complex bundle of energy, and thus our task of awareness is to listen to the music coming from so many different directions. The unrevealed truth of who we are wants to be fully revealed. On the journey towards wholeness, the mystics point to the primacy of self-knowledge. Above all, our real challenge is to awaken that undiscovered love within us that seeks full expression. The path of our becoming involves the daring of love.

18
The Peace Trek ...
Building Synergies

Now that you are an elder, drop your weapons and use your head and wisdom instead.

Eunoto, *Masai Passage to Manhood*

Lord, make me an instrument of your peace.
Where there is hatred, let me sow love;
where there is injury, pardon;
where there is doubt, faith;
where there is despair, hope;
where there is darkness, light;
where there is sadness, joy.

Prayer of Saint Francis

The essence of synergy is to value the differences.

Stephen R. Covey, *The Seven Habits of Highly Effective People*

spilling the wind

I had been trying to quit a nicotine habit for quite some time, without success. Every attempt turned into a huge power struggle with myself and ended in failure. Progressively, I felt more and more down on myself, frustrated that I could never seem to win. Eventually, some insights about resistance in martial arts theory led me to devise a new strategy. I took an advance on the money that I would save if I stopped smoking, and purchased a second-hand windsurfer. The premise of plan B was to give up fighting my "bad" side and befriend health. Not long after, I smoked my last cigarette.

As I began to learn the art of windsurfing, I found a new enemy in the wind – it gave me a hard time, especially when it expressed itself in nasty, unexpected gusts. From the very outset of my apprenticeship, I attempted to muscle the moving air currents, only to become totally exhausted. I found myself more of the time in the water than on my board, again feeling discouraged and humbled. I remember reading at that time what the spiritual writer Ram Dass had to say about the futility of power struggles, which made an impression on me:

> We can't create polarization in our zeal to override the bad guys, or we might create more. As was said in *Be Here Now*, the hippies were creating the police and the police were creating the hippies; it was so obvious in the Haight-Ashbury. The citizens got frightened by the scene, so they demanded their police get more oppressive. The police got more oppressive, and that became a symbol against which the hippies mobilized to fight. The more the hippies mobilized to fight, the more the police got oppressive. Each force was creating the other. And nobody in that space was conscious enough to cut through that polarization, which would have turned it into a whole collaborative dance together.... Every time we're busy struggling against something, we're reinforcing its reality.[110]

No use fighting the wind – it was doing what the wind does, blowing where and how it pleases. Through being brought to my knees, I came to know that there is no stopping the wind. At a later point, I was introduced to the notion of "spilling the wind." This technique, using sail manoeuvres and body movement, deflects the push of the wind's velocity and captures only a small portion of its force to carry the sailboard along. Until that time, I suppose, I had adopted a typical attitude towards all forms of opposition based on the notion that enemies need to be either overpowered or eliminated. Now, after many hours on my sailboard, I recognized the need to let go of combative posturing, and try out the wisdom of befriending the enemy. No longer pitting myself against the wind and attempting to muscle it down, I came to learn how to harness its power. As my skills advanced, I caught a nice tan breezing back and forth across the bay with my friend the wind. And I was now spending more of my time above the water than in it.

Like the motion of rolling waves and wild squalls, life itself knows a lot of unpredictable movement. Through a growing comprehension of wind and sailboard dynamics, I discovered the difference between tack and attack. To tack is to choose a certain direction, alternating between port and starboard, and to position one's sail in such a way as to find an optimal angle to the wind. To try another tack is to look for an alternative, perhaps more desirable course of action. Mastery of the art of wind-surfing entails knowing how to read and dance with the wind. Likewise, in day-to-day living, where everything is in constant motion, wisdom teaches me how to make the right moves and how best to harness the oppositions I meet.

engaging the foe

Enemies draw enormous energy out of us. The way I see it, there are three ways to meet our opponents: annihilate them, avoid them, or answer them imaginatively. The first approach follows the way of a conquering warrior seeking to eliminate all obstacles and oppositions. It is bent on the destruction of enemies. This strategy of might inevitably seems to add fuel to the fire, generating futile cycles of further aggression and counter-aggression. The second response, avoidance, is not really a response at all. It is passive; it refuses to engage the foe, and might well be called the way of the non-warrior. Non-response perhaps has the most dangerous implications, for enemies actually become dangerous when given free rein. The third strategy endeavours to confront oppositions in a positive manner, and to resolve conflict intelligently. The latter way of the creative warrior employs the weapon of truth rather than guns of war.

"What you resist, persists" is an old dictum that I find rings true most of the time. Zero tolerance strategies set up classic power struggles by declaring all-out war on this evil or that enemy. They argue for combat, and set out to crush the foe, or to eliminate all undesirable behaviours and oppositions. Intoxicated with power, might imposes what it thinks is right. In the long term, though, this approach seems no more effective than when I was on my sailboard trying to muscle the wind. The history of war itself gives testimony to the ineffectiveness of armed conflict in securing genuine solutions of peace. A war on crime, drugs, or our own imperfections serves to polarize forces, and to lock us into unproductive struggles. Zero tolerance seems tantamount to that brand of intolerance that breeds only more of what it resists.

An unseen, unacknowledged enemy is perhaps the most dangerous foe of all. If we try to avoid the discomfort of confrontation, hide from the foe, or discount the power of evil, our denial and disregard serve to make matters worse. If friction is ignored, peace can only be pretended. Then poisons fester, dysfunction grows, and antagonisms escalate. Though India's Mahatma Gandhi preached an ethic of non-violence (*ahimsa*), he thought it worse to avoid an enemy. Non-engagement serves to betray truth. Gandhi had a name for shrinking from the enemy: he called it cowardice. Gandhi advocated non-violent resistance to evil – that is, engaging the enemy creatively. He urged us to disarm and to confront our foes with spiritual force.

noble enemy

At the end of a long portage, a strong onshore wind was blowing smack into our faces. Chris cursed the wind and complained about having to paddle "against" the wind. His canoe partner suggested that they rather paddle *into* it. She quipped, "It's not the latitude, but the attitude that makes the difference."

Our enemies are both within and without, and to be found everywhere: our afflicted emotions, someone who has broken faith with us, a depression, the loss of control, ignorance, the collapse of meaning, our own inertia, confusion, sickness or a mental breakdown, another's violent abuse, or an acquaintance who has mocked us. Consciousness and courage empower us best to face our inner and outer foes. Marilyn Ferguson writes, "Conflict, pain, tension, fear, paradox ... are transformations trying to happen. Once we confront them, the transformative process begins."[111]

An enemy becomes "noble" when viewed in its potential to call forth blessing. Examples of such beneficence are found in the natural world. Forest fires, commonly thought to be destructive, actually renew life in the forest. As flames burn away ground debris in white pine stands, they create a new bed for seeds and a canopy that allows sunlight in. Jack pine cones, tightly glued by gum, open up with extreme heat to release new seeds.

Our worst mistakes, in fact, are the enemies that teach us some of our most valuable lessons. We learn the right path after taking the wrong turn. Through confronting the negative consequences that follow our poor choices, we are better able to discern right action. This notion of a blessing in disguise can also be seen within psychological frameworks. A depression, for example, invites an inner journey that can be instrumental in opening up new horizons of meaning. Or, in their struggle to come to grips with deep wounding, individuals who have suffered physical abuse or disability often develop exceptional spiritual qualities. The noble way is found as they move from violence to peace, from division and strife to freedom.

Perhaps it would be too bold to say that undesirable circumstances, difficult conditions, and bitter rivalries are what we "need." In truth, there seems no end to the trials we meet, and we are continuously faced with the challenge of transforming adversity. As we develop wisdom and spiritual ingenuity, we learn how to embrace the "enemy" creatively, turning defeat into opportunity, and antagonism into accord. Respectful confrontation creates that spiritual akido that allows us to flow with the energy of opposition and spark positive outcomes.

negotiating conflict

The avoidance of conflict certainly undermines the integrity of relationship. Difficult issues do not go away if we ignore them; in fact, our denied conflicts get buried inside us, and leave damaging consequences. By not dealing with discord, we achieve a false, short-lived peace. Rosemary Haughton suggests that we end up in relationships of "a covered-up kind,"[112] and very much out of touch. Conversely, true peace begins when there is a willingness to face whatever conflictual issues come along. Ultimately, our differences may bring about transformations of understanding that spur new levels of intimacy and co-operation. There is never an end to dissent, and, therefore, no restriction on the possibilities of growth.

The true nature of conflict often lies under surface issues, and outward disharmony is frequently the manifestation of deep, unidentified inner conflicts. Unresolved tensions of fear, guilt, anger, jealousy, hurt, resentment, vengeance, and like negative emotions inside an individual psyche play themselves out in our interactions with others, sometimes with devastating impacts. This explains why "the jamming factor" (described in the last chapter) often kicks in. Our unhealed wounds and personal failures spill into relationship, and spoil the friendships we enjoy. In *The Way to Love*, Anthony de Mello recommends rigorous self-knowledge as the essential antidote to interpersonal discord. He advises us to look inside ourselves rather than at those who irritate us:

> The question to ask is not, "What's wrong with this person?" but "What does this irritation tell me about myself?" Do this right now. Think of some irritating person you know and say this painful but liberating sentence to yourself, "The cause of my irritation is not in this person but in me." Having said that, begin the task of finding out how you are causing the irritation. Firstly look into the very real possibility that the reason why this person's defects or

so-called defects annoy you is that you have them yourself.
But you have repressed them and so are projecting them
unconsciously into the other. This is almost always true
but hardly anyone recognizes it. So search for this person's
defects in your own heart and in your unconscious mind,
and your annoyance will turn to gratitude that his or her
behaviour has led you to self-discovery.[113]

As conflicts arise in our relationships, and they inevitably
do, Haughton suggests that three response options are available.
The first is to address contentious issues, and to try to work out
our difficulties by confronting conflict directly. Be open to reflection, reconciliation, and remedy. The second option prefers to
mask friction and put on a nice facade. In this instance, we skirt
conflict. We somehow pretend it does not exist, but doggedly
go on together. This cover-up leaves growing emotional frustration and fatigue in its wake, and erodes the spiritual integrity of
the relationship. The third and final option is to decide to bail
out of the relationship altogether, which is desirable, Haughton
suggests, when the relational dysfunction points to an unre-
deemable incompatibility.

Successful conflict resolution avoids jumping at instant solutions, but rather persists at the process patiently. Reconciliation
does not entail heavy-handed attempts to manipulate outcomes.
In search of comprehensive understanding, perseverance is
required to explore all conflictual issues with deep care. The
concerns of all parties must be clearly articulated, and core
conflicts precisely delineated. Such a process needs to sustain a
steady momentum of progress, and have a way to revive itself
when it gets bogged down. Genuine dialogue occurs when minds
are open, and when vested interests give way to mutual care and
compassion.

Power struggles are born of the bias of special interests, and
become counterproductive to the building of synergies. They
engender defensive positioning, manipulative manoeuvring, con-

trol bids, aggressive acting out, and attitudes of domination. Adversarial relationship inevitably creates lose-lose outcomes. On the other hand, synergy-building strategies look for win-win results, and for outcomes that add up to more than the sum of the inputs.

the dance of dialogue

Finesse in communication is the key to generating synergy. Being direct, honest, humble, and attentive enables us to become sensitively attuned to others. Cheap talk, fault-finding, bad-mouthing, the making of assumptions, blame, and prejudice all need to be weeded out and discarded. Quality communication builds trust and co-operation, allows feelings to be clearly iden-tified and articulated, and lets everyone's concerns be factored into the finding of solutions. Innovation and creativity are the hallmarks of synergy.

A dialogue is always an adventure, because we never know where it is going to take us. Through dialogue, a relationship comes into being and continues to constitute itself. Dialogue is its lifeblood. Dialogue is a dance of self-expression where experiences and concerns are shared, where ideas and values are explored, and where feelings and meanings are identified. Dialogue holds the tension of common critical reflection and mutual questions that serve to spark new insights. True commu-nication always includes the continuous excitement of learning. As I listen to other persons, I participate in the mystery of their becoming. As I reveal who I am to another, I discover myself in a new way. Dialogue is a two-way flow of energy, a giving and a receiving.

"Self-expression is the primary sacrament of the universe,"[114] exclaims cosmologist Brian Swimme. In the past, I would often complain about not being understood, until I came to appreciate the fact that it was up to me to make myself known. My task of self-expression is only complete when I can be assured that the other person has truly heard my communication. They might not agree with me, like me, or respond the way I want them to, but they do hear me out. I honour others by revealing to them the truth of my experience.

An old Russian proverb states that the wise person has long ears, big eyes, and a short tongue. As much as I want to be understood, I must place equal emphasis on listening with deep sensitivity. Author Stephen Covey writes, "Empathic listening gets inside another person's frame of reference. You look out through it, you see the world the way they see the world, you understand their paradigm, you understand how they feel ... you're listening to understand. You're focused on receiving the deep communication of another human soul."[115]

dumb bombs

The senior elders at the four-day Eunoto initiation ceremony, marking the passage from warriorhood to elderhood, advise us to use wisdom instead of weapons. Brute force forgoes the knowledge of the things that make for peace; in fact, it gives up on intelligence. Bombs are inarticulate and only tell lies about the truth of peace – the detonation of a bomb is never an act of love. History attests that the human good is not supported by acts of violence, which, in fact, intensify conflict, negate co-operation, and sabotage peace efforts. The recourse to arms refuses critical social analysis and noble negotiation, and thus ignores the foundations of true justice. The essence of the Buddhist view of ultimate reality is non-violent behaviour, not harming others. The Dalai Lama, Tibet's spiritual leader, affirms that the choice of negotiation is a spiritual act. Weapons look for a winner, while words seek a way of understanding.

The drama of human hostility on our beautiful planet delivers a horror of misery, and generation after generation must carry unbearable burdens of grief. As hate and violence contaminate the human spirit, countless souls are left bereft, orphaned, and homeless, in exile from love and land. Each act of war, destruction, and human degradation leaves untold suffering in its wake, and our hope for global peace undergoes a new shattering.

Tibetan Buddhists maintain that hatred is our worst enemy. In the words of the Dalai Lama, "It is the enemy of inner peace, friendship, and harmony, three key factors for positive development, for the creation of a better world.... Once hatred is expressed with all its strength and power, it is difficult to find an antidote to it. It is very important, therefore, to prevent and impede anything which can give rise to hatred."[116] Tibetan Buddhism develops a focus on "inner disarmament" based on the notion that outer peace cannot be achieved unless it is found in our own heart. Hence, rather than an external enemy, we must address our own afflicted emotions – anger, hate, confusion, greed, ignorance, intolerance, inner division. The Dalai Lama suggests that the most effective way to build peace is through spiritual practice. This involves training in ethics with a focus on right behaviour, meditation promoting a concentrated mind, and wisdom with the aim of finding a sound view. For Mahatma Gandhi, the real victory comes through soul force, which relies on the speaking of truth. He believed, "There is no such thing as defeat in non-violence,"[117] and taught this message with the sacrifice of his life. His death is widely acknowledged as a victory in terms of historical progress.

True knowledge originates in compassion. In the modern era we have developed remarkable technologies, yet lack an equivalent achievement in the advancement of love. Our smart bombs accentuate our deep ignorance of peace, and highlight our radical incapacity to understand our roots in violence. The truth of the matter is that we are more committed to the acquisition of sophisticated military technique than to the development of wise understanding. In fact, a majority of all the scientists on the planet are linked to military enterprise. Meanwhile, our educational programs make scant reference to the learning of love. Future peace depends on what we do in the present, and our best hope lies in awakening deep cross-cultural compassion. A more complete knowledge of love is needed more urgently than ever. Otherwise, we are doomed to endless repetitions of human folly.

self-sacrifice

The call to self-sacrifice points to an essential aspect of love: the giving to others at a cost to self. The true meaning of sacrifice is generous compassion. The heroic lover exemplifies a readiness to live with an open heart, and to forgo self-interest and even survival itself. In the Gospel of John, we read that a person can have no greater love than to lay down one's life for one's friends (see John 15.13). The meaning of existence lies in the very gift of itself to others.

The idea of sacrifice sometimes simply means accepting an absurd fate, and working creatively to wrest meaning from the difficult givens of our lives. The call to sacrificial love in this sense asks us to embrace a burden of suffering not of our choosing, and to accept the challenges of strenuous life conditions. The widely known Sermon on the Mount proclaims the message "happy are the poor in spirit" (Matthew 5.3), promising a peace that lies beyond our own security and protection and abundance. As we learn to reconcile ourselves to unmerited suffering, we dedicate our life to a good that is not always apparent, but is to be trusted.

Not all self-sacrifice has its roots in charity – the false hero can indeed be misguided about the truth of love. A suicide bomber, for example, brings about a violence which is not love. False martyrs inflict destruction on themselves; the very actions they think noble, in fact, only serve to destroy peace. On the other hand, there are the sacrifices of innocent victims who re-pudiate violence completely, yet accept to be its victim in order to reveal love. In this instance, a victim becomes the victor, since violence itself is the lie. Whereas false sacrifice transmits victim-age and violence, true sacrifice confronts evil fully, yet refuses to return evil for evil.

Only the wisdom of love can teach us to die for the right reason. Mahatma Gandhi promoted confrontation without violence, but, as much as he abhorred violence, he believed cowardice to be an even greater evil. We must stand our ground in non-violent opposition to evil, even unto death. For the sake of human freedom, both Mahatma Gandhi and Martin Luther King demonstrated this kind of heroic courage. The following story of the monk from Hué, related by Jesuit peace activist Dan Berrigan, likewise invites us to confront violence with the truth of love:

> My mind returns often to this – he stayed put. It was not that he hid out, or vegetated, or gave up, or joined the officer's club, or hardened, or softened, or shrugged away his plight or ours. It meant that he had a place, a center, convictions that held, a sense of himself, wary and troubled as he was.
>
> He reminds me of one of the Vietnamese Buddhist monks he so loved and learned from: Say, a monk of Hué drag-ging his altar into the streets and sitting down there to protest the mad war. The tanks arrive; the monk stays put. Because the monk stays put, the tank is confounded. What does a tank do when a monk refuses to "move when so ordered"? The tank has choices, but they are not large. Can we imagine a tank rubbing its iron skull in puzzlement before the immovable monk? The "it" has met the "he." It is a confrontation worth pondering ...
>
> The impasse comes to this: The monk is more ready to die than the tank is to kill. And that is the rub indeed, for the tank is built to kill, only to kill. But the monk is not "built" at all, in order to do anything at all. If he is "for" anything, if he serves any purpose, if he has any goal in life, it quite surpasses the understanding of the tank... .

If he were to put the matter in words (and that also is un-likely), the monk might say something like this: he is called to be a pure and truthful expression of life itself. Of life.

To be. Neither to strive, to gain, to lose, to earn, to spend, to be skilled, to be pro, to ideologize, to make a mark, to be honoured, to be dishonoured, to survive, to perish … it is all beside the point.

But what has all this, this charade of force, this huff and puff, to do with the monk? He has something else to do: to stay put, to be. Especially to be, in places and times where life itself (his gift, his only love, his bride) – where life is endangered, put to naught, despised, obliterated. Then, oh, then he knows what must be done, he does what must be done!

And at that point something akin to the miraculous occurs. This solitary, foolish, exotic one, this silent refuser, this stubborn sitter, brings something to pass. Alive or dead, he brings it to pass. It being a matter of supreme indiffer-ence to him whether the tank stops short of him or rolls over him. He brings something to pass. He does something no other can do, because he stays put when all prudence, all legitimate self-interest, all logic, all casuistry unite in crying, in warning, "Get up, move it, get the hell out, the tanks are coming!"

No, he stays put. He knows what he knows. What he knows is, he is called to stay put – an ecological rightness, nice to the hair's breadth – there in the path of the tank. This is his native ground; dangerous, they cry, they warn, flat out uninhabitable. No matter; where he belongs.[118]

Love is where the monk belongs, no matter. It is ultimately where we all belong, our native ground. As we wonder who we are and where we belong, we discover our place in the intercon-nected web of life, which opens into an ocean of infinite love.

The remedy for evil proposed by theologian Charles Hefling is best exemplified through an understanding of *lex crucis* (the law of the cross). Seen in the Christian perspective, the death of Christ was the divine option for coming to terms with evil, not a remedy by force but a reversing of evil, a turning-it-into-good. Christ did not resist his aggressors with counter-violence, but rather chose to meet evil with good. It was a demonstration of the divine wisdom in overcoming evil "... not by wielding power, not by matching violence with violence, not by retaliation, not by vengeance, not by getting back or getting even, not by combat."[119] The cross mediates the meaning of non-violence. It reveals evil, confronts it, but does not play into it. Christ rises above violence by unmasking it for what it is, by refusing reprisal and further evils. Before the violence that victimizes him, Christ stands with the truth of goodness. By absorbing its injustice he brings violence to an end. His death on a cross, continues Hefling, points to the wisdom of forgiveness, which offers a love without condition or restriction, a love which reaches beyond deserving friends to undeserving enemies.[120]

disavowal of violence

Resist evil – not with evil, but with a large love. The complete disavowal of war and social injustice is, it seems to me, the necessary prerequisite for peace. I believe strongly that we must put behind us the notion of a just war. We cannot simply talk about the ideal of non-violence. We need more than pious thoughts and pious words. What is urgently needed for the very survival of humanity is the definitive renunciation of violence. As storms of destruction loom in every corner of our planet, that renunciation is foundational to our hope for peace. Thomas Merton prayed, "Grant us prudence in proportion to our power, wisdom in proportion to our science, humaneness in proportion to our wealth and might...."[121] He raised the question of what it means to be in our right mind, asking, "... what is the meaning of a concept of sanity that excludes love, considers it irrelevant, and destroys our capacity to love other human beings, to respond to their needs and their sufferings, to recognize them also as persons, to apprehend their pain as one's own?"[122] Authentic compassion reaches out to the enemy and builds a true sanity. Ultimately, love exposes hate, and the enemy is cured by charity. Such noble encounter begins to bring about an otherwise impossible peace.

The hunger for tender kindness in human hearts echoes a universal longing for happiness. An inborn desire for peace pushes against the inhumanity we meet in ourselves and in the world. The global community trembles in feeling its vulnerability to the powers of darkness and the possibility of wider violence. All spiritual traditions point in the same direction: to the summons of love as a means to undo darkness. Wisdom seeks the insights and practices to help usher in a redeeming light. We need only trust that the exercise of our collective spiritual genius will enable us to find creative alternatives to violence.

19
Earth and Fire ... Cosmic Grammar

Do you have a body?
Don't sit on the porch!
Go out and walk in the rain.
    Kabir

Human health is intimately dependent on the health of the Earth.
Ecology is not a part of medicine. Medicine is a part of ecology.
We cannot have well humans on a sick planet.
    Thomas Berry, *Ethics and Ecology*

A seed of God is within us.
A seed of a maple tree grows into a maple tree.
And a seed of God grows into God.
    Meister Eckhart

mountain tales

I parked my small Toyota at the end of an abandoned mining road located within Strathcona Park in the middle of Vancouver Island. I grabbed my daypack and followed a wide trail through the woods for a kilometre or so, before branching off onto a narrow, undefined path to begin my ascent up the mountain. I had set an ambitious goal for myself, and felt exhilarated as I walked over the rugged terrain through an aged forest of tall evergreens and pulsing mountain streams.

I knew exactly when the sun would set, and so allotted just a little more than half my daylight hours for making my return down the mountain. At two o'clock, I calculated, I would have to turn back. Not long after noontime I reached the snow line, and from there pressed forward, sinking ankle-deep at first, then thigh-deep, into the mushy melting snow. It was slow going and exhausting. At a quarter past two, I finally admitted defeat. With just enough time to get back to my car before nightfall, I had no choice but to let go of my goal of reaching Cream Lake, and began my descent.

Nearly three hours had passed when I became aware that I had lost my way – somehow I had wandered off the trail. I felt a moment of panic, of pure vulnerability. The only thing to do, I thought, was to backtrack. Feelings of desperation intensified for the next 20 minutes as I scrambled through the forest looking for clues to find my true bearings. "There is a God," I exclaimed to myself as I came across the original trail. I hastened down the mountain to make up for lost time. The sun was just setting when I reached the path's intersection with the wider trail, and I relaxed, knowing I had just one kilometre to go. My relief was short-lived, for I caught sight of some very fresh bear excrement in the middle of the trail. A little further on there was another pile, and then another. Would I come face to face with a grizzly bear?

I walked my longest kilometre ever, my heart racing all the way. As the trail opened into the clearing, I welcomed the sight of my blue Toyota. I was safe. In the next glance, I spotted the bear 50 metres beyond the car. It sensed me right away, and for a moment we appraised one another. The bear then reared up on its hind legs, turned about, and disappeared into the forest. It was a moment to remember.

The intimacy with this rugged mountain and the close encounter with the bear seemed to draw me into a long-forgotten world. Though a lot of adrenalin had run through me that afternoon, beyond my feelings of vulnerability, I felt a curious kinship with the mountain and the bear. The solo trek had given me a window onto a hidden world, bigger and more primal than I knew. I felt smaller. I had a sense of awakening contact with some lost primordial spirit within myself.

In Sikkim six months earlier, I had embarked on a similar solo mountain trek. I had climbed to close to 3,000 metres, where I encountered a Buddhist hermit monk in his small temple hut. Again, some lost part of me awakened in this meeting, and I felt an inexplicable kinship to this silent watcher over the world. As I sat on a high ledge and breathed in the thin mountain air, my eyes beheld the full beauty of the Himalayan range of mountain peaks, then lifted to the heavens beyond. I experienced a deep sense of interconnectedness with the lone monk and with the entire earth. In that prayerful moment, I felt profoundly in love with the whole world.

back to nature

Some years earlier, during the summer I turned 30, I had set out with three companions on an 83-kilometre hike along the Long Trail in Vermont. We experienced a wonderful exuberance as we trekked through the mountains and breathed in the forest air. It was a vigorous five-day workout engendering new powers of endurance and confidence. I reconnected with the youthful energies of my body, and also created a deep bond with the beauty of nature. Seeds of something new were blowing through the green, magical forest, but at the time I had no way to interpret the callings of the natural world.

Not long afterwards, we formed a small band of outdoor trippers. All of us were keen on adventure – we shared a sense of how urban life had alienated us from the deep rhythms of the natural world. ONEGWA, a Mohawk word for water, was the name we chose for ourselves. We organized trips, and set out to embrace the spirit of the wild country: riding lakes and rivers, dwelling in the woods, trail blazing, making snow shelters, waking with the sunrise, befriending the moon and the stars.

As we reimmersed ourselves in the world of matter, our senses feasted on the beauty of nature, and our spirits soared. We partook of a rich diet of earth, air, water, and fire – the elements we ourselves are made of – and each brought experiences of deep renewal. Deepak Chopra paints the picture well:

If I find a green meadow splashed with daisies and sit down beside a clear-running brook, I have found medicine. It soothes my hurts as well as when I sat in my mother's lap in infancy, because the Earth really is my mother, and the green meadow is her lap. You and I are strangers, but the internal rhythm of our bodies listens to the same ocean tides that cradled us in a time beyond memory. ... There is good reason for all the ancient medicines to say that man is made of earth, air, fire, and water. Because the body is intelligent, it knows this fact, and when it returns home to Nature, it feels free. With overflowing joy it knows its mother. That feeling of freedom and joy is vital – it allows inner and outer nature to blend.[123]

As we shared misty mornings and moonlit evenings, cooked meals on open fires, negotiated bad weather and long portages, and kept track of our common gear, a special bond developed among trip companions; we discovered a spontaneous caring for one another. Our talents and efforts combined in a spirit of co-operative teamwork to create the magic of togetherness. Of course, there were hardships, frictions within the group, and challenging weather conditions. But though tired and frustrated and pushed to our limits, we found an extraordinary resourcefulness and resilience within ourselves. Together we were learning how to be comfortable being uncomfortable.

The birth of ONEGWA became an integral part of my healing journey. Up to that time, my body and soul had not belonged to each other in an integral way. Through this intimate contact with nature, I experienced a marriage of the material and mystical worlds within myself, though I cannot say how this came about. As I became more one with my world of instincts, I entered into a new harmony with my own body and with the earth. Indeed, it was blissful.

Over the years, the idea of a wilderness solo grabbed my imagination, and eventually, I dared a lone adventure. One early September morning, I set off on a canoe-camping circuit in

Algonquin Park. I paddled for eight days, and by night enjoyed a full-sized harvest moon. I became very attached to my narrow seventeen-foot canoe, and delighted in learning the art of solo paddling. As I penetrated deeper into the wilderness, I entered into a grand silence – in the stillness, I became finely attuned to the wind, the waves, and the woods. These solitary days called forth an intimate listening to the world inside myself; I was taken into the inner territory of my fears, where I was surprised to find a new wellspring of confidence. Beyond the reach of culture, it felt invigorating to stand naked in nature. After evening suppers, as the fat September moon flooded the forest landscape, I was filled with the memories of many canoe trips of the past – recollections of our shared communion of wonder and joy. One rainy afternoon, as I worked the canoe through a winding marsh, I suddenly came face to face with a turtle perched on a clump of mud. Motionless, we stared at one another, and, in that mutual gaze, I felt our worlds merge into one. The turtle's shell held a texture of rich colours, creating the image of a mandala that symbolized for me a unified universe, and a call to the journey of wholeness. Then the turtle splashed back into the Little Madawaska River, and I dipped my paddle into the water and continued downstream.

cosmogenesis

Cosmology is the study of the origin, destiny, and development of the universe and the role of humanity within it. Throughout the different civilizations and cultures of earlier times, pre-scientific myths of our origins abounded. The story we tell of the universe reflects a grasp of cumulative insight, which becomes our shared primary source of intelligibility and value. Modern-day cosmologists Thomas Berry and Brian Swimme highlight the urgency of finding a more adequate wisdom to heal our traumatized planet and reinvent what it means to be human. The scientific account of evolution awakens exciting new grounds for awe, curiosity, humility, connectedness, creativity, and responsibility.

The story of the universe is anything but static. It undergoes review again and again, reigniting our imaginations and allowing us novel visions of reality. Our modern story describes an evolutionary process steeped in an extraordinary dynamism of creativity; it identifies the developmental process of the universe as an open-ended "cosmogenesis," rather than a pre-set reality of fixed determinisms. This account of our origin rests on the empirical knowledge that the universe is ever-expanding, and constantly giving expression to what has never before existed. It affirms that life was not simply created at the beginning of time, but is in continuous evolutionary growth. Species come into and out of existence, and consciousness explodes ever anew. Ours is a universe that is going somewhere, on the epic adventure of its own discovery. The new story of the earth and the fireball is the first cross-cultural narration of our origins emerging from the interface of science and mystery.

The cultural pathology of our age, Swimme suggests, is the loss of sensitivity to the sacred dimension of life, the lack of appreciation for the sheer "elegance that pervades everything."[124] Unable to see what is in front of us, we are prisoners of an outdated world view that has defined energy as physicalistic rather than biospiritual, thus degrading matter, the earth, our bodies. Our genuine growth lies in awakening a feeling for the natural world, and in coming to know ourselves as integral to the creativity of the numinous universe. We too, in fact, "come out of the energy that gave birth to the universe."[125]

the intricate web

Nowadays, there is a growing call to ecoliteracy, reflecting our need to appropriate the wisdom of nature in order to build sustainable human communities. For physicist and author Fritjof Capra, this means that the principles of organization found in nature are the same principles we need to apply to our economic models. The biosphere has organized and sustained itself for three billion years to maximize sustainability. Human endeavour must follow the same laws of life.

The key principle is the interdependence of all phenomena. Both the biosphere and human life are woven into an intricate web of mutually dependent relationship to become an integrated whole. The whole depends on each part, and each part on the whole. Capra highlights how the laws that govern the web of ecological relationships vie with our present economic structures: "Economics emphasizes competition, expansion, and domination; ecology emphasizes cooperation, conservation, and partnership."[126] Ecosystems avoid waste through feedback loops that recycle waste as nutrients to other species. Our economic systems are linear and non-cyclical, with energy resources and material goods ending up as pure waste. Human suffering has its ultimate root in acts of egocentric craving that undermine the principle of co-operation. Competing interests breed greed, bitter conflict, mutual antagonisms, war and hostility – an endless genesis of violence. Human misery results from this disregard for the vitality of the whole; it can be remedied only through a sensitivity to the interconnected dynamics of cosmic reality.

By concentrating almost exclusively on human interests, we have found ourselves radically alienated from the natural world. A perception of being put on the planet has left us with a sense of being separate from the whole biosphere of oceans, soil, atmosphere, and all life forms. Such an anthropological outlook assumes a mechanical rather than mystical view of the natural world: it exists simply for human benefit. By perceiving the universe as something separate from ourselves, we have pursued an agenda that has ignored the non-human community. Through this dis-identification, a massive disregard of the Earth has developed. We have considered ourselves above as well as apart from the material world. We have sought to advance our interests at the expense of non-human life. This sense of separateness and superiority has led to compulsive consumerism and ecological devastation.

Swimme highlights the destruction of the Brazilian rainforests as an example of the alienation we are experiencing. Out of dualistic, mechanistic, and egocentric thinking, we have become disconnected from the natural world. We have had the attitude that nature is there to serve us. We have thought that by tearing down the rainforest we are actually benefiting our lives. The truth that the entire earth community needs the oxygen of these forests is now only slowly being grasped. As we come to understand that the universe is a single energy event, we now realize that we are tearing ourselves down in the process. We are the rainforest. The universe is intricately interrelated, and our bodies cannot possibly thrive at the expense of the rest of nature.

The Earth is one vast community. Humans are only one aspect of the complex structure and functioning of life. Beyond advantage and accumulation, human activity must find its place in the larger creative thrust of the universe, and overcome its narrowness of vision. The Great Law of the Iroquois guides their elders not to act in terms of immediate self-interest, and thereby supports the notion of a sustainable future. It requires of them that every decision be made to benefit the seventh generation not yet born. If we followed this rule of thumb, human decisions and actions would find greater congruence with the rhythms and processes of nature.

We are inseparably bound to the entire living and non-living universe. It exists as a mysterious whole – acting as a unity to organize all its various parts. Its coherence is based on a deep, shared longing at the heart of the universe for life to unfold. All creation is kin to us in that desire. Thich Nhat Hanh reflects, "If the Earth were your body, you would be able to feel the many areas where it is suffering."[127] As it suffers, so do we. In a similar vein, Thomas Berry points to the soul damage, the deep grief we now carry in our hearts:

> ... any damage that we did to the outer world of nature would be a damage to our own inner world. The devastation of the forests, the extinction of species, the poisoning of the waters, the pollution of the air, the blocking out of our vision of the stars; we could not understand that this was something more than damage to our physical or economic well-being; it was also soul damage, a ruin within, a degrading of our imagination, our emotional life, even diminishing of our intellectual life, since all these phases of our inner life needed to be activated by our experience of the outer world. We could not understand that the loss of the grandeur of the forests and the rivers was also a loss of grandeur of our souls.[128]

a perfect grammar

Thomas Berry proposes a "cosmic grammar" that depicts the fundamental order and aim of the universe. The cosmos celebrates diversity, interiority or consciousness, and interconnectedness. Berry argues that anything that runs interference on these tendencies violates the true ethics governing the universe – what we might call bad grammar. What is good is that which ignites differentiated creativity, dynamic interiority, and compassion. Evil, in this cosmological perspective, is the imperfect grammar that hinders or denies uniqueness, interior depth, or the quest for the harmony of interbeing within the whole. Brian Swimme suggests that a perfect cosmic grammar reflects "... a fullness of differentiation, the deepest subjectivity, the most intimate communion."[129]

Differentiation is the task of identifying our true selves in order to awaken original creativity. Like the stars and oak trees, we each gift life in a way that no one else can. It takes courage to stand alone and risk novelty. Yet our special creativity is needed to activate certain dimensions of the universe that otherwise could not manifest the full beauty of life. Indeed, each of us receives a unique assignment. Similarly, each particular culture is irreplaceable, and has a unique contribution to pour into the development of the whole. Whether individual or collective, we need to let things be different, and affirm the infinite diversity found in the universe. When we fail to embrace diversity, our actions become a destructive grammar.

Fritjof Capra celebrates biodiversity, which he sees as integral to deep ecology. The multiple interconnections within a diverse ecosystem create resilience, because the many species linked within a complex network can survive various threats to survival, and reorganize more effectively when disturbed. Capra says this same principle applies to ethnic and cultural diversity, and that multiple relationships are better able to adapt to complex challenges. He warns, however,

> ... diversity is a strategic advantage only if there is a truly vibrant community, sustained by a web of relationships. If the community is fragmented into isolated groups and individuals, diversity can easily become a source of prejudice and friction. But if the community is aware of the interdependence of all its members, diversity will enrich all the relationships and thus enrich the community as a whole, as well as each individual member. In such a community information and ideas flow freely through the entire network, and the diversity of interpretations and learning styles – even the diversity of mistakes – will enrich the entire community.[130]

Subjectivity refers to the deep interiority by which we awaken sensitivity to beauty and suffering, and stir affection for all other animate and inanimate beings. It is to develop our inner soulful depths. Responding to our deep allurements, this interiority ignites archetypal and artistic imagination, and opens our hearts to spiritual revelations of love. Jesuit mystic and thinker Teilhard de Chardin speaks of liberating the spirit in oneself "... through an effort (even a purely natural effort) to learn the truth, to live the good, to create the beautiful; through cutting away all inferior and evil energies; through practicing that charity to all beings which alone can gather the multitude into a single soul … ."[131] Without interiority, we lose our attunement to the whole.

Communion highlights the experience of coming to know our vital interdependence with all other beings; this entails an intimate relatedness amongst all human and non-human life. The mystery of our interconnection is echoed in Einstein's quantum theory: when two particles move apart, they will always manifest opposite spins. If one is up, the other is down. If a down particle is turned up, the other particle instantly goes down. This is non-local causality, which reveals that, even though separate in space, we are directly linked. Every being participates with every other being in a hidden web of life. Like an ecosystem, nothing is affected without everything else being affected.

As individuals, our present mandate is to develop an enthusiastic, competent participation in the vision and task of cosmological creativity. Knowing that we are kin to everything brings us into communion with all life. The word "enthusiasm" derives from *en-theos*, the divine within. The earth itself is an elegant design of exuberant generosity and creativity, and we must follow it as a model to discover that wisdom that will help us reimagine our possibilities.

That new imagination calls for green cities, population stability, durable artifacts, sustainable development, and a pollution-free world. It invites a cultural transformation that will replace competitive struggle with co-operative venture. The "Canticle to the Cosmos," in its conclusion, argues that our fundamental understanding of the cosmos needs urgent revision, and proposes a far-reaching education in the new cosmological story. The present pathology derives from increasing population pressure, the idea of anthropocentric dominance, the mindset of more growth and compulsive consumption, and the flow of poisons into the environment. A pledge to radical creativity is needed to confront our planetary crisis. We get a clue to what the new cosmological commitment might look like in listening to the words of Chief Dan George: "Of all the teachings we receive this one is the most important: nothing belongs to you, of what there is; of what you take, you must share."[132]

primal recovery

I was living in "down under" in the late 1960s when Pierre Elliot Trudeau arrived in Australia for his first foreign visit as the newly elected prime minister of Canada. I remember his inaugural speech addressed to young Aussies: he urged those who had turned to psychedelic drugs to go into the Australian Outback or visit the Canadian Arctic if they wanted to get a real high. I was able to verify firsthand the truth of his message; I was fortunate that same year to travel through Australia's barren "back of beyond" interior. Trudeau, an avid outdoorsman, had written years earlier that "what sets a canoeing expedition apart is that it purifies you more rapidly and inescapably than any other. ... paddle a hundred (miles) in a canoe and you are already a child of nature."[133]

The validity of Trudeau's return-to-nature recommendation is also well reflected in the experience of Brent George, a North American Okanagan Indian, who had lived on the streets of Montreal for seven years as a chronic alcoholic, and who felt, in his own words "... very unsure of his place under the sun." Brent came on one of our canoe trips; seven days outbound set off some profound inner healing that seemed to undo his seven long years on the street. Brent said that he recovered the Indian that had been taken out of him at a young age. "What reconnected me was the wind blowing through the pine trees. That brought me back to when I was four or five. I loved that sound as a kid and I loved the smell of the pine."[134] After the trip, Brent found a new footing in the world.

It does seem true that we become strangers to our bodies the more we become estranged from the natural world of which we are an integral part. Dan Juras, a friend of mine, speaks of a Vermont trek as a poetry of personal healing:

> As I walked the length of Vermont on the Long Trail, I felt many emotional hurts begin to heal. The trail reconnected me into a story of my own re-creation. I discovered the many gifts of nature in the forest. The sweet hypnotic spiraling song of the hermit thrush sent its notes drifting and flying like words of balm into my tired body. My body hardened as it came to know what it had been made for, and was calmed by deep respiration from the oxygen-rich green forest. The majesty of the forest beauty with gardens of alpine vegetation and flowers inspired me to keep climbing to smell and see what new wonders awaited me. I came to think through my senses. I could be still in my mind: listening, seeing, feeling my body, smelling.[135]

With the vigorous workout, Dan reported that during his trek his senses came alive, his muscles became supple, and his mind and emotions grew still. Feasting on new oxygen, he recounted how he started to actually be aware of each molecule in his body. Indeed, Dan's spirit seemed one with the song of the hermit thrush.

I sometimes define healing as a process of primal recovery. Alienation within modern life reflects to a great extent a deprivation of beauty. As we become insensitive to the grandeur of life and its inner rhythms, the sacred beauty of the universe recedes from recognition. Without a vital connection to this grandeur, we become strangers to ourselves, to one another, and to the natural world. There are many ways to experience a connection with life's beauty – gentle touch, kind words, a smile, literature, authentic friendship, lovemaking, sports, artistic expression, film and photojournalism, musical creativity, nature walks, and the like.

As aesthetic sensitivity is lost, nature is replaced with narcissism. We give way to false attraction, and look to consumerism to compensate for feelings of emptiness. Seeking to excite our dulled senses, we turn to chemical stimulants, pornography, crass entertainment, and hedonism. Our homes lose elegance and our workplaces lack soul. In urban industrial sprawls, we travel the topography of traffic and technology and task-driven time.

Sojourns in nature act always as a powerful antidote to self-estrangement. I used to facilitate exercises in sensual awareness with drug recovery groups. Immersed in nature, I asked each person to pick one tree in the forest, and then lie on their back with their head at the base of its trunk. In focusing on a particular tree for several minutes, individuals would become attuned to the extraordinary beauty of nature. Next, I invited the group members to close their eyes and listen attentively to the sounds of the woods – the song of the birds, the buzz of flies, the wind, the rustling leaves. Then, lying face down on the forest floor, we would smell the earth and the ground vegetation, and touch the texture of a tree's bark. Finally, using the sense of taste, we would mindfully chew some edible berries or drink the water of a mountain stream. All these sensual pleasures offered some of the best healing medicine imaginable.

We also enjoyed nocturnal meditations. Lying on the ground, face up, in a circle with our heads to centre, we gazed at the dazzling night sky. I would suggest that we each befriend one star in the Milky Way, and invoke its light to be our personal guide. The majesty of the stars somehow always seemed to suspend the flow of time, and open our souls to pure delight. In the company of friends, we felt ourselves transported to a larger truth, embraced by both heaven and earth.

It is early September as I conclude this chapter. This morning I awoke in the pre-dawn to the sounds of a chirping chickadee. The morning air was still in a scarlet red sky. I rolled over and sank into one more dream. When I reawakened, I noticed that the sun was up, and looked around for my blue swimming trunks. Thin, soft mist covered the smooth glass surface of the lake. Wiping the sleep out of my eyes, I stumbled towards the dock, my bare feet sensitive to the mud and the cool morning dew. Then, curling my toes firmly over the edge of the wharf, I braced myself and sprang forward. A loud splash announced the impact of my body on the water, and in that moment a new day was born. The wet, cold lake was the antithesis of my dry, warm bed. My metabolism ignited in a split second, and I felt a surge of new body heat. Fifteen minutes later, I returned to shore tingling with oxygen, and the morning sunshine served as my towel. I felt my spirit soar. In this sacred awakening, I had become earth and water, breath and fire.

20
Generosity and Gratitude ...
Celebrating Compassion

The day will come when we shall harness for God the energies of love. And on that day, for the second time in the history of the world, the human being will have discovered fire.
　　Teilhard de Chardin

What makes loneliness an anguish
Is not that I have no one to share my burden,
But this: I have only my own burden to bear.
　　Dag Hammarskjöld, *Markings*

Human nature is always grasping, always on the seeking end, looking for what it can get; human nature wants to get and get endlessly. Spiritual nature wants to pour out. ... Be prepared to pour!! Discipline yourself so that you never expect good to come to you, but always expect it to flow out from you.
　　Joel Goldsmith

a wounded riverman

It was the last night of our river adventure. We had been to whitewater school, and then the six of us had flown by seaplane into the wilderness to the headwaters of the Dumoine River. For days we had run rapids and worked our way downstream, and had become totally enchanted by the river and its song. There were fourteen more kilometres to go on our last day to reach the Ottawa River, our journey's end. The early evening sky was deep blue, and the sun was sinking behind a high ridge of pine trees. We'd had an exhilarating day paddling 22 kilometres southbound on the Dumoine, and portaging the long gorge at the Grande Chute. Exhausted, we decided to leave our canoes at the top of the Red Pine Rapids. We would negotiate a kilometre of rather tricky whitewater in the morning when we were fresh.

I had been fetching firewood and was descending a fairly steep slope on my way back to our campsite. A fallen tree lay on the ground in my path. As I stepped over its trunk, the sharp-pointed stub of a broken-off branch pierced the skin on the inside of my right knee, and snapped with the momentum of my downhill descent. Like a dagger, a chunk of wood three centimetres in diameter had become impaled in my leg.

Instinctively, I yanked the stick out of my leg. First aid was ably administered by my rivermates: my leg was properly bandaged and the bleeding arrested. As we supped at a firepit on the river's edge, a fat moon lifted out of the east and flooded our home in the forest with a brilliant light. A wounded riverman, I crawled into my little blue tent by the rapids. In the moonlight I lay down and watched the swiftly moving waters – and felt the pain! I had bits of sleep on and off, and through the night I followed the full moon's journey across the night sky from east to west. As the temperature of the air cooled over the tepid waters of the Dumoine, a morning mist danced in the half light of the dawn.

After 33 hours I reached the Montreal General Hospital, where I was fed antibiotics intravenously to stem an infection. The wound only became worse over the next eight days; eventually, an ultrasound revealed a piece of red pine, the tip of the branch spike, buried deep within my inner thigh. It was surgically removed. As I waited out the healing of my wound in the weeks that followed, a powerful inspiration stirred inside me.

My wounded knee took on symbolic meaning, presenting itself as an image of broken humanity. I recalled that as I held the pain through that night at Red Pine Rapids, I had reflected that life has a rhythm of deep sorrow that we carry in our hearts through the darker passages of time. The moon had offered me its consolation until the dawn and had given me an assurance of light, the promise of a return to wholeness. I welcomed daybreak, which announced the resumption of our homebound voyage and the healing journey that lay ahead. I remembered how the care of my companions had comforted me, a sweet balm to my pain. Compassion indeed heals us at the deepest level. Several weeks later, towards the end of my convalescence, *River of Awareness* was conceived. For, during that short period of forced introversion in the summer of 1997, a multitude of images had poured forth from my unconscious, and the outline of this book wrote itself. The rest of the writing process would take a little longer.

be in love

As a lad, at our summer cottage, I frequently had to walk up Cedar Point Lane in the black of night. I was often terrified, but when I had the company of a friend, we would talk and laugh all the way. The presence of a companion can make all the difference as we journey in darkness. Compassion means not so much fixing another's pain with fast advice and false comfort as being present to an individual's mystery and misery. As we hold the burden of another's pain in our heart, we breathe love into wounded life. A heartfelt presence to someone who is suffering offers the gift of profound peace.

The photograph in the Toronto newspaper pictured a beautiful young African woman with HIV/AIDS. The caption read "I'll die of loneliness before I die of AIDS." It is one thing to suffer, another to suffer alone. Certainly, human affliction is intensified many times over when unattended by love, and experiences of isolation annihilate the quintessential meaning of life. Those whose loneliness is unrelieved invite us to learn the language of love more completely. For is not compassion the true law of life? To be present to those in anguish is to allow our lives to become determined by the needs of others as much as our own. When it is our turn to taste affliction, we, too, will long to trust that we truly matter to others. To be cared for is to know that our suffering is felt by others and included in love; there is no greater consolation to the human spirit than the compassionate presence of another. Conversely, when sensitive understanding and loving-kindness are absent, we experience true desolation. Only compassion, a power that has no limits, miraculously transforms suffering into solace.

law of generosity

Acts of generosity, big or small, always generate miracles of life. Generosity begets generosity and creates a circular flow of compassion and gratitude. Sharing is the true language of interdependence, and life invites us to be generous both in giving and in receiving. When we live out of a spirit of sharing, we come to know the full meaning of loving-kindness. Sharing is not to be thought of simply in material terms, for there is also the generosity of judgment, of patience, of forgiveness, of gentle presence.

Before I left for India in 1973, a group of individuals from an inner-city slum in Montreal passed a hat and put a hundred dollars in my pocket. Four months later, I hired a Bengali carpenter, purchased some bamboo, and constructed a small hut for dying lepers along a stretch of abandoned railway tracks in the Himalayan foothills. In 1995, some 22 years later, I revisited a new generation of lepers who had set up a squatters' village around the bamboo hut for the dying. The lepers were thrilled to show me their individual huts and eager to express their heartfelt gratitude. What was remarkable was to behold the tender care that they bestowed on one another; it was truly one of the most moving moments of my life to witness this vibrant community of love. A small seed sown by the generosity of a few had grown into a tall tree of joy.

When the law of scarcity is foremost in our thoughts, human nature expresses itself in terms of acquisitive desire. This need to acquire is built on a fear of lack. We compete for what we think will run out, what there cannot possibly be enough of: divine favour, parental love, the affections of others, commodities, natural resources. We create categories of the chosen and the unchosen, suffer sibling rivalry and jealous murder, and wage war over land, oil, and water resources. The human propensity to possess, and to protect possession, forms the basis of strife and injustice. Violence grows out of rivalry, and rivalry out of a notion of scarcity. The truth of the matter is that this passion for acquisition robs us of life. As Joseph Campbell puts it,

> But the dragon of our Western tales tries to collect and keep everything to himself. In his secret cave he guards things: heaps of gold and perhaps a captured virgin. He doesn't know what to do with either, so he just guards and keeps. There are people like that, and we call them creeps. There's no life from them, no giving.[136]

The notion of scant supply arises out of a consciousness of separateness, and sets up a me-versus-them duality. A sense of lack and limitation engenders rivalry. Inasmuch as there is an insufficient supply of anything, we perceive others as a threat and begin to compete for what is available. Though the real enemy is not lack, the consciousness of the separate self grasps after the illusion of its own self-protection, and we define boundaries of ownership based on our beliefs of entitlement. Envy and greed abound.

The law of sharing, on the other hand, affirms a view of unlimited potential and creativity. It turns the law of scarcity into a law of abundance, and puts ultimate confidence in the plenitude of the universe and the providence of the divine. Spiritual law teaches that there is enough for everyone. Acts of generosity spur economic creativity to harness the abundance of the universe: goods are not used up; they only circulate, and ultimately multiply through sharing. The few fish and loaves feed the multitudes.

The Judeo-Christian Scriptures contain the appeal to go and sell all we have and give it to the poor. I am fond of two beautiful tales of generosity in the Old and New Testaments. First, from the Book of Kings, is the story of Elijah and the widow:

> After some time, however, the brook ran dry, because no rain had fallen in the land. So the Lord said to him (Elijah): "Move on to Zarephath." As he arrived at the entrance to the city, a widow was gathering sticks there; he called out to her: "Please bring me a small cupful of water to drink." She left to get it, and he called out after her, "Please bring along a bit of bread." "As the Lord, your God, lives," she answered, "I have nothing baked; there is only a handful of flour in my jar and a little oil in my jug. Just now I was collecting a couple of sticks, to go in and prepare something for myself and my son; when we have eaten it, we shall die." "Do not be afraid," Elijah said to her. "Go and do as you propose. But first make me a little cake and bring it to me. Then you can prepare something for yourself and your son. For the Lord says 'The jar of flour shall not go empty, nor the jug of oil run dry, until the day when the Lord sends rain upon the earth'." She left and did as Elijah had said. She was able to eat for a year, and he and her son as well. The jar of flour did not go empty, nor the jug of oil run dry, as the Lord had foretold through Elijah. (1 Kings 17.7-16, New American Bible)

The second story about a poor widow is taken from the Gospel of Mark, and echoes the true meaning of generosity:

> ... and many of the rich put in a great deal. A poor widow came and put in two small coins, the equivalent of a penny. Then Jesus called his disciples and said to them, "I tell you solemnly, this poor widow has put more in than all who have contributed to the treasury; for they all put in money they had over, but she from the little she had has put in everything she possessed, all she had to live on. (Mark 12.42-44)

We should not expect good to come to us but rather to flow out from us. The challenge of love beckons us to pour out, to transform attitudes of grasping into giving. In fact, says Joel

Goldsmith, God is not our supplier, but our supply. When we awaken to the knowledge that our deepest desire is to make another happy, the mind that wants to get and get and get learns a new law of giving.

I recall attending an Aboriginal powwow where this same spiritual principle was echoed. Activities at the powwow included storytelling, drumming, and ritual, and at the end of a long day, an Elder rose to speak. I was deeply moved by his reflection on the practice of that gratitude that finds expression in generosity. His teaching was summed up in three words: returning the gift. What the Elder proposed was that we offer back to life the beneficence that comes our way. That night, as I lay awake in my moonlit tent, I thought about the many blessings life had bestowed on me. I succinctly identified two special gifts: awareness and friendship, and it thus occurred to me that this is what I must give back. The twelfth step of Alcoholics Anonymous encourages us to carry the message of our awakening to others. If we do not share what we learn or receive, it fades away or we lose it. We ignite life in others through passing along the gifts we have received.

the degenerative ego

The wrong departure for humanity begins when we live out of a what's-in-it-for-me ethic, out of a determination to be on our own and not for others. In his treatise on *The Solution of the Ego*, Gerald Heard speaks of the ego as a degenerative process involving greed, fear, and ignorance. This wrong direction happens when we chase pleasure, grab at the goods of life, and become possessive. The net effect of this is "... the complete sundering of that sense of compassion which is the intuitive sense of kinship and union with life."[137] Heard identifies greed as the beginning of our real trouble. In our fear of lack and loss, an attitude of possessiveness takes hold and leads us into the love of gain. But greed causes disintegration and turns to trepidation.

As our sense of separateness grows, our fears are compounded. Such grasping for material benefits, Heard adds, can also be experienced on a higher plane as a rapacity for spiritual gain. He goes on to talk about the love of pleasure, and suggests that the gratifications we crave give rise to addictive behaviours born in the dread of weakness and pain. Lastly, Heard describes the love of fame, and how pretentiousness arises when we fear blame and shame.

The antidote to the love of gain is found in frugality. In this spirit we live out of simple basic need, travel light upon the earth, and learn to trust providence. Beyond self-indulgence, we discover the more sacred uses of the body. According to Heard, the right knowledge of the meaning of life provides the impetus to cast out greed. The love of fame is cancelled by choosing anonymity. As we dismantle the illusions of the false self, we awaken authenticity and a humble spirit. Addictions are counteracted by self-restraint wherein we come to know the body as a vessel, not a nest. As we transcend our need for immediate gratifications, we find what is truly worthwhile and of lasting value. To sum up, our dread of limitation and weakness, our possessiveness and pretentiousness, and our addictiveness all begin to dissolve when we discover the simple way.

I remember once being reproached by a friend who told me to stop my grumbling. I felt a little taken aback, not because I never need correcting, but because, in that particular situation, I was not whining as much as feeling and expressing my sadness. Indeed, there is a time for legitimate complaining: to lament lost love, defiled beauty, compromised truth, wasted talent. There is certainly a time to weep, to feel injury and injustice. The healthy release of sorrow and desolate emotion makes way for gratitude's entry. Our sadness ultimately gives way to gladness, much as the mud gives birth to a beautiful garden.

Indeed, I count it pure grace when I experience gratitude in my heart. The soft refreshing rain, the harvest, our health and happy relationship, everything we have has been received as gift. When I get stuck in my grumbling, and my heart fills with covetous longings, songs of gratitude stop and disenchantment quickly follows. In genuine thanksgiving, I learn to let go of thinking about what I deserve. It is then that I come to know the universe as benevolent, to trust that all is grace.

the wounded healer

Like mud and flowers, the archetype of the wounded healer contains a paradox of meaning: it proposes that our participation in the suffering of others is linked to our own personal woundedness. Compassion is born in the experience of becoming sensitively engaged with our own world of vulnerable feeling. Paradoxically, right in the middle of our suffering and desolation, we hear the call to remedy not only our fragile selves, but also a wounded world. As our personal frailty is accepted and becomes rooted in self-knowledge, our capacity to care for others enlarges. Through finding equanimity inside our own hearts, we awaken a warm compassion that reaches out to bestow itself on others.

I met Ralph in a circle of palliative care volunteers. Later, he shared with me an entry from his personal journal. Ralph's poetic narrative described his own initiation as a healer. The compelling image of an injured tree enabled him to come to terms with his own woundedness:

> The broken crown Beech tree called me with its brilliant yellow leaves smiling to sing to my spirit and calm me. Her crown had broken during the ice storm, but still living, she shone and celebrated her being, her life, her part in the symphony as strongly and loudly as before the breaking. Her spirit paraded her purpose to me. Her purpose, not to grow higher like her brothers and sisters, but still to grow and be a lower part of the forest canopy. She did not see herself as stunted or broken. She ran in creation's race to light with the same speed and intensity as always, as seed,

as bud, as bush. Hers was a purpose to tell this story to my heart. A special gift from Creator, to her and then to me, one afternoon walking on the mountain.[138]

My friend and mentor Tony Walsh was born in 1898. Tony, when he was well beyond his middle years, had embraced enormous challenges in living with the downtrodden. I did not meet Tony until he was 80, at which time he declared that he wanted only two more years to finish his life work. In fact, he was to be my friend for the next fifteen years. During that period, I worked in a hospitality house for the homeless that he had founded in the early 1950s in the inner slums of Montreal. After the first two years of our acquaintance, I kept reminding Tony that he was past his time, but he would smile and say he had just a little bit more work to do. At the age of 89, Tony wrote a long letter describing how the seeding of his call to befriend the poor germinated in the soil of a negative father complex. Here, in part, is that letter:

> It was possibly my mother's concern for me that brought about my father's rejection, though he always came first. He maintained a deep love of, and dependence upon, my mother.

> ... At the growing stage I would get into the usual kind of scrapes that most small boys do. At those times, he would rage at my mother, proclaiming that I was no son of his, and that the nurses soon after I was born mixed his child with another. There was little that I could do to please him, but he never thrashed me. He knew how to use his tongue as though it were a sharpened sword.

> ... Up to a certain age and not knowing how other fathers acted, you just accepted the situation for that was all you knew. But eventually this was to change. It came about when on three occasions he did not keep his word. Soon after the outbreak of the 1914–18 war, he joined the army. He was stationed at a depot at Woolwich near London. Because of his extraordinary skill in dealing with sick and

injured horses, he was in great demand. It was arranged that he would meet me at one of the London railway stations on my way home for holidays. On each occasion, he did not show up. He never expressed regret. It was then that I saw the light.

Then without warning, I got the news of his death. He was injured, possibly through fragments of a bomb, and blood poisoning set in. On a very gray winter's morning, the only mourners were my mother, my sister and myself. We attended his funeral in a very depressing Dickens-like barracks. Within a few weeks, I joined the British army.

Then came the start of thoughts – that part of my role in the future would be with men, supporting those whose fathers had rejected them. I was to find that in many cases they were similar to mine. This direction stemmed from the time I was young and had cared for hurt and suffering animals. I was being prepared to render similar help to humans. So I became a compassionate man, asking nothing in return but to be of service.[139]

In the middle of painful rejection, Tony heard his call to service. A heart that knew so much personal sorrow opened out to the woundings of others. Tony had found the grace of acceptance and chose to be guided by the law of love. The pain of being cast out by his father awakened a deep sympathy within his spirit, and he spent a lifetime welcoming other men similarly rejected. Humility grows in the humus of a broken existence. The humble person meets fragile life with bravery, accepts limitation and powerlessness, and discovers equanimity in obedience to a mystery of suffering. Tony's consciousness and consent and courage transmuted his pain into great spiritual gain both for himself and for others.

spirited meekness

The wounded healer knows a meekness that is strength. Meekness is a virtue possessed by persons who can be strong because they are little. Meekness transcends the fear of failure, and the grace of humility points to gentle strength and spiritual vitality. Though often taken for a fool, the meek person is able to respond creatively to misunderstanding and aggression with kindness. Although the seed falls to the ground and dies, the wounded healer knows that there is hope for a tree to bud again. Job, the Old Testament figure who suffered much affliction, offers a beautiful image of rebirth:

> For there is hope for a tree,
> if it be cut down, that it will sprout again,
> and that its shoots will not cease.
> Though its root grows old in the earth and its stump die in the ground,
> yet at the scent of water,
> it will bud and put forth branches like a young plant.
> (Job 14.7-9, Revised Standard Version)

The enemy of joy is not suffering. In the Sermon on the Mount, Jesus instructed his listeners that happiness belongs to the poor in spirit, to the gentle, to those who mourn, to those who hunger and thirst for what is right, to the merciful, to the pure in heart, to the peacemakers, and to those who are persecuted in the cause of right. Unhappiness reflects our inability to hold personal hardships and the burdens of others in our heart. Through an intimate embrace of our poverty, we become attuned to the tears and toils of all humanity. If we attempt to flee from the impoverished aspects of life and from personal pain, we will lack empathy for the suffering of others.

We see this reflected in the case of Eric. Riding the Montreal subway always depressed Eric. He would gaze at the solemn and sad faces in the crowd, faces full of fatigue and fear, and be filled with gloom. "I hate seeing lonely people with no place to go," he would say. I further recall that Eric did not like to deal with his girlfriend's struggles, and tried to avoid her whenever she wanted to talk about her problems. During his rehabilitation program, Eric began to catch on to the fact that the sorrow out there in the world mirrored the dark places within his own psyche, and that his use of drugs was founded on a strong denial of his own inner poverty. He began to see that he had spent his life running from his own fears and loneliness and pain. One day, months later, Eric acknowledged, "I really don't mind the subway anymore. I know that I can actually bring joy to the people I encounter." As Eric learned to face his own uncomfortable world of feeling, he found a new depth of intimacy with his girlfriend and an ability to participate creatively in her suffering. The principle of compassion had broken into Eric's awareness, a function of facing his own underground world of pain. Survival, for him, was no longer a matter of fleeing sorrow.

call to compassion

For two years I kept company with the homeless in the inner city of Montreal. At that time I was negotiating the terrain of mid-life; these men enabled me to be present to my own woundedness and negotiate my own shadow self. Certainly, to be with those whose afflictions are greater than your own heals ingratitude. I have always felt inspired by the word of the prophet Isaiah as he writes of the Lord's call to compassion, with its promise of light and healing:

> Is not this the fast that I choose:
> to loose the bonds of wickedness,
> to undo the thongs of the yoke,
> to let the oppressed go free,
> and to break every yoke?

> Is it not to share your bread with the hungry,
> and bring the homeless poor into your house;
> when you see the naked, to cover him,
> and not to hide yourself from your own flesh?

> Then shall your light break forth like the dawn,
> and your healing shall spring up speedily....
> (Isaiah 58.6-8, Revised Standard Version)

Tonglen is a Buddhist meditative practice, a practice of mindfulness that enables one to take on the mental and physical suffering of others, and to bestow on them one's own well-being. In a sense, it is a spiritual exchange of peace for pain, imagining the other person as exactly the same as you. When we hold another's hardship deep in our hearts, we send out a "prayer" for happiness and healing, light and love. The Tonglen practice aims to cultivate a spiritual capacity to give our own happiness away in exchange for the suffering of others. Tonglen is opposite to the more typical reaction of a well-meaning friend, who said to me at the time of my river accident, "Man, I'm glad I'm not you!"

Another Buddhist term is Bodhisattva, which refers to an individual who voluntarily participates in suffering, and thereby endeavours to bring joy to a sorrowful world. Beyond sympathy, it is the practical determination to do whatever we can to help alleviate the suffering of others. The *Tibetan Book of Living and Dying* exhorts us to such compassion

> … when experiencing a sight that can open the eyes of your heart to the fact of vast suffering in the world. Let it. Don't waste the love and grief it arouses; in the moment you feel compassion welling up in you, don't brush it aside, don't shrug it off and try quickly to return to 'normal', don't be afraid of your feeling or embarrassed by it, or allow yourself to be distracted from it or let it run aground in apathy. Be vulnerable: use that quick, bright uprush of compassion; focus on it, go deep into your heart and meditate on it, develop it, enhance, and deepen it. By doing this you will realize how blind you have been to suffering, how the pain you are experiencing or seeing now is only a tiny fraction of the pain of the world. All beings everywhere, suffer; let your heart go out to them all.[140]

making the difference

I love anthropologist Loren Eiseley's starfish story. It reminds me that each kind thought and gesture truly matters. A woman asked a boy what he was doing. She saw him repeatedly bending down, picking something up, and tossing it gently into the sea. The boy responded that he was throwing starfish into the ocean so that they would not die in the sun. Looking at miles of beach stretching before her, the woman suggested that the star thrower, despite all his effort, could not make much of a difference The lad listened politely, then stooped to pick up the next starfish, and threw it back into the sea past the breaking waves. Then he looked up, and said, "I made a difference to that one."[141]

Time and time again, I have seen evidence of this truth. I recall one such experience where the difference was very visible. As a hot red sun set over the dusty Indian terrain, Ivana and I leaned over a dying leper who had been found beside some railway tracks five days earlier. His maggot-filled wounds had been washed by another leper, and he had been given some food and medicine. Now he had relapsed and was very weak. Ivana told him he might die. In his native Bengali language, he replied that he believed in God, and he tenderly expressed the gratitude he felt for five days of "beautiful kindness" while he lay dying. As he let go of life, he cherished our presence. I thought to myself that this leper would have no difficulty understanding the invitation to love summed up by Saint John of the Cross: "Friends, let us love one another, because love comes from God. God is love. And where there is no love, let us put love, and then we will find love" (see 1 John 4). I was profoundly touched by this leper whose gentle heart was filled with courage and gratitude.

The task of love is daunting. The work to win love's freedom, the courage to suffer its trials, and the discipline to give what it demands require a continuous inner evocation of being. But love comes from an infinite source, as unable to contain itself as a spring of water can. The river journey of awareness, with its many teachings, leads to the wisdom of happiness. As I begin each new day, I like to remind myself to *be in love*. This is the mantra that steadies my intention. Through awakening a power of compassion, we participate in enchanting each other's lives. As our journey continues, may the spirit of love burn within our hearts.

About the Author

River of Awareness is not an autobiography, but a series of thematic reflections that find reference to Steve's wide range of life experience. After university graduation in the late 1960s, Steve taught at primary and secondary schools in Canada and Australia, and travelled extensively throughout Asia. In 1973–74, he worked in the Darjeeling region of northern India as a paramedic with the sick and destitute dying at Jesu Ashram. Back in Canada, Steve assumed the role of a lay chaplain in campus ministry at Concordia University, afterwards becoming program director of the Spera Foundation, a drug rehabilitation centre. He led prison dialogue groups, and an elder care project in the inner city of Montreal where he lived for seventeen years. Subsequently, he directed the Labre hospitality house for street people.

In 1995, Steve made a second sojourn to the eastern Himalayas, where he facilitated a cross-cultural awareness dialogue, and a peace project to encourage young adult initiatives in community development. Returning to his native Montreal, Steve established the Padua Dialogue, an interdisciplinary wisdom forum exploring the healing arts, the transformational sciences, and the teachings of different spiritual traditions. His other community involvements include several inner-city youth outreach projects, as well as palliative care for the terminally ill.

Throughout the years, Steve has been piloting IASIS, "the awareness project" he founded in the early '80s. IASIS creates opportunities for dialogue in small interactive learning groups – vision quests, healing circles, addiction and spiritual support groups. Wilderness adventure outings are also part of this project. Steve himself is an ardent canoe enthusiast.

The author can be contacted at steve.sims@iasis.ca.

Acknowledgments

There are no words large enough to thank the many wonderful friends who have graced my life and inspired the writing of this book. Through the interplay of our diverse life adventures, I have known a rich texture of intimacy and delight, and the vibrancy of our shared wonder. Indeed we have discovered, encounter by encounter, a greater authenticity of love.

I would like to single out several individuals who have shored up the writing process and steadied my labour. Mark Smith, Ryan Madden, and Andrew Baumberg have made outstanding hands-on editing contributions – your big-hearted support lives on in the pages of this book. I add further tribute to Thérèse Mason and Scott Simons – your gentle and unwavering friendship has encouraged me every word of the way.

My gratitude needs to be measured out to the entire Novalis team. It is nothing short of providence that put an inspired editor like Kevin Burns on my path – thank you for your talented mentorship, for your unbroken faith in a rookie author, and for your adept ability in drawing out my hesitant voice. How much, too, I have appreciated Anne Louise Mahoney as managing editor – your special quality of presence has been pure blessing.

Many friends, with loving impatience, wanted to know why the writing process was taking so long. Thank you for your enthusiastic vigil – your eagerness kept me on task. I hope the arrangement of the 93,000 words herein will be to your liking, and worth the long wait.

Finally, I would like to greet my anonymous readers, and express the happiness it brings me to know that we will meet on the pages of this book and share a common wisdom quest. Though unmet friends, we journey the waters one in spirit.

Endnotes

chapter 1

1   Teilhard de Chardin, *Hymn of the Universe* (London: Fontana Books, 1970), 34.

2   Hermann Hesse, *Siddhartha* (New York: New Directions, 1957), 61.

3   Hesse, *Siddhartha*, 106.

4   Hesse, *Siddhartha*, 119.

5   Avram Davis, *The Way of the Flame* (San Francisco: Harper Collins, 1996), 23–24.

6   Robert Jingen Gunn, *Journeys into Emptiness* (New Jersey: Paulist Press, 2000), 280.

chapter 2

7   Eda LeShan, *Grandparenting in a Changing World* (Newmarket Press, 1993), 173–74.

8   Joseph Campbell, *The Power of Myth* (New York: Doubleday, 1988), 126.

9   Joseph Chilton Pearce, *Magical Child* (New York: Bantam Books, 1980), 90.

10 John R. Van Eenwyk, *Archetypes & Strange Attractors* (Toronto: Inner City Books, 2001), 112.

11 Van Eenwyk, *Archetypes & Strange Attractors*, 16.

12 Sebastian Moore, *The Crucified Is No Stranger* (London: Darton, Longman & Todd, 1977), x.

13 Marie A. Foley, "Christian Meditation and Jung's Understanding of the Ego/Self Relationship" (a talk to meditators, Boston, January 18, 1997), 4.

chapter 3

14 James Baldwin, *The Journal of Rehabilitation in Asia* (Rehabilitation, University of California, 1963), 31.

15 John A. Sanford, *The Kingdom Is Within* (San Francisco: Harper SanFrancisco, 1987), 51.

16 Malcolm Travis, in discussion with the author, August 1997.

17 Placide Gaboury, "Church and Spirituality" (lecture, Loyola College, Montreal, Québec, 1982).

18   Jerome Miller, "The Auroral Hour and the Throe of History" (*Cross Currents*, Spring 1997), 64.

19   Andrew Baumberg, in discussion with the author, July 2000.

20   Thomas Merton, *The Hidden Ground of Love* (San Diego: Harcourt Brace Jovanovich, 1993), 19.

21   James Hollis, *Creating a Life* (Toronto: Inner City Books, 2001), 35–36.

22   John M. Maher and Dennie Briggs, eds., *An Open Life* (New York: Perennial Library, 1990), 28–29.

23   Avram Davis, *The Way of the Flame* (San Francisco: Harper Collins, 1996), 63.

chapter 4

24   Sister Ivana, in discussion with the author, October 1995.

25   Joseph Campbell, *The Power of Myth* (New York: Doubleday, 1988), 124.

26   Stephen and Robin Larsen, "Queste del Saint Graal," quoted in *A Fire in the Mind* (Rochester, VT: Inner Tradition, 1991), 212.

27   Campbell, *The Power of Myth*, 41.

28   Ernest Becker, *The Denial of Death* (New York: The Free Press, 1973), 82.

29   Parker Palmer, *Let Your Life Speak* (San Francisco: Jossey-Bass, 2000), 4.

30   Brian Swimme, *The Universe Is a Green Dragon* (Santa Fe: Bear & Company, 1984), 51.

31   Eknath Easwaran, *God Makes the Rivers to Flow* (Berkeley: Nilgiri Press, 1982), 13–14.

32   Sebastian Moore, *Jesus the Liberator of Desire* (New York: Crossroads, 1989), 91.

33   Victor Frankl, *Man's Search for Meaning* (New York: Pocket Books, 1963), 178.

34   James Hollis, *Swamplands of the Soul* (Toronto: Inner City Books, 1996), 124–25.

35   John M. Maher and Dennie Briggs, eds., *An Open Life* (New York: Perennial Library, 1990), 88.

36   Maher and Briggs, *An Open Life*, 107.

chapter 5

37   Joseph Campbell, *The Power of Myth* (New York: Doubleday, 1988), 115.

38   Stephen and Robin Larsen, *A Fire in the Mind* (Rochester, VT: Inner Tradition, 1991), 257.

39   Campbell, *The Power of Myth*, 99.

chapter 6

40   John R. Van Eenwyk, *Archetypes & Strange Attractors* (Toronto: Inner City Books, 2001), 164.

41   Parker Palmer, *To Know As We Are Known* (San Francisco: HarperSanFrancisco, 1983), 66.

42   Bernard Lonergan, *Method in Theology* (Toronto: University of Toronto Press, 1990), 77.

43   Marilyn Ferguson, *The Aquarian Conspiracy* (Los Angeles: J.P. Tarcher, 1980), 169–70.

chapter 7

44   Sebastian Moore, *The Inner Loneliness* (New York: Crossroads, 1982), 9.

45   Bernard Lonergan, *Method in Theology* (Toronto: University of Toronto Press, 1990), 76.

46   Lonergan, *Method in Theology*, 13.

47   Terry Tekippe, *What Is Lonergan up to in Insight?* (Collegeville, MN: The Liturgical Press, 1996), 80.

48   Robert M. Doran, *Theology and the Dialectics of History* (Toronto: University of Toronto Press, 1990), 161.

49   Doran, *Theology and the Dialectics of History*, 53.

50   Bernard Lonergan, *Insight* (Toronto: University of Toronto Press, 1997), 502.

51   *The Dhammapada*, Juan Mascaró, trans. (London: Penguin Books, 1973), 55.

chapter 8

52 Calvin S. Hall and Vernon J. Nordby, *A Primer on Jungian Psychology* (New York: A Mentor Book, 1973), 49.

53 James Hollis, *Under Saturn's Shadow* (Toronto: Inner City Books, 1994), 23, 25.

54 Sebastian Moore, *The Inner Loneliness* (New York: Crossroads, 1982), 51.

55 Rosemary Haughton, *The Transformation of Man* (Springfield: Templegate, 1967), 17.

56 Haughton, *The Transformation of Man*, 20.

chapter 9

57 Bernard Lonergan, *Insight*, Collected Works/Volume 3 (Toronto: University of Toronto Press, 1997), 215.

58 Jean Belair, "The Contribution of the Nurse to the Human Good" found in *Lonergan Workshop*, Vol. 14 (Boston: 1998), 51.

59 Michael McCarthy, *The Mystery of Evil* (lecture, Center for Lifetime Study, 2001), 10–11.

60 Thich Nhat Hanh, *Being Peace* (Berkeley: Parallax Press, 1987), 23.

chapter 10

61 Ernest Becker, "Paranoia," found in *Angel in Armour* (New York: George Brazillier, 1969), 150.

62 Thérèse Bertherat and Carol Bernstein, *The Body Has Its Reasons* (Avon of Bard, Camelot, 1977), 97.

63 Deepak Chopra, *Quantum Healing* (New York: Bantam Books, 1989), 142.

chapter 11

64 Joseph Campbell, *The Power of Myth* (New York: Doubleday, 1988), 39.

65 Michael McCarthy, *The Mystery of Evil* (lecture: The Center for Lifetime Study, 2001), 12.

66 William Shakespeare, *Macbeth*, Act 5, Scene 5, in *The Arden Shakespeare* (London: Thomson Learning, 2005), 153–54.

67 Ernest Becker, *The Denial of Death* (New York: The Free Press, 1973), 5.

68 Sebastian Moore, "Dying, and Behold, We Live" (Candlemas Lecture, Loyola College, Montreal, Québec, 1987), 16.

69 Gerald Heard, *An Anthology of Devotional Literature* (Michigan: Baker Book House, 1977), 727.

70 Sogyal Rinpoche, *The Tibetan Book of Living and Dying* (San Francisco: HarperSanFrancisco, 1994), 154.

71 John Main, *Death: The Inner Journey* (Montreal: The Benedictine Priory, 1983), 10.

chapter 12

72 André Guindon, *The Sexual Language* (Ottawa: University of Ottawa Press, 1977), 80.

73 *The Psalms: Singing Version* (New York: Paulist Press Deus Books, 1975), 62.

74 Lama Surya Das, *Awakening the Buddha Within* (New York: Broadway Books, 1998), 47.

75 Jerome A. Miller, *The Way of Suffering* (Washington: Georgetown University Press, 1988), 123.

76 Etty Hillesum, *An Interrupted Life* (New York: Washington Square Press, Pocket Books, 1985), 87.

77 Alcoholics Anonymous (June 2001). "Chapter 5: How It Works", *Alcoholics Anonymous* (PDF), 4th edition, Alcoholics Anonymous World Services. ISBN 1893007162. OCLC 32014950.

78 *Francis de Sales*, Joseph F. Power, O.S.F.S., ed. (New York: New City Press, 1993), 57.

chapter 13

79 Thich Nhat Hanh, *Being Peace* (Berkeley: Parallax Press, 1987), 106–08.

80 Terry Tekippe, *What Is Lonergan up to in Insight?* (Collegeville, MN: The Liturgical Press, 1996), 152.

81 Kenneth Melchin, *Living with Other People* (Ottawa: Novalis, 1998), 67–68.

chapter 14

82 Christopher D. Marshall, *Beyond Retribution* (Auckland: Cambridge and Lime Grove House Publishing, 2001), 283.

83 Archbishop Desmond Tutu, opening lecture, Justice, Memory, and Reconciliation International Symposium, February 15, 2000, Toronto.

84 Tutu, opening lecture, Justice, Memory, and Reconciliation International Symposium.

85   Kenneth Melchin and Cheryl Picard, "Mediation and Insight" (Boston: a paper presented at the Lonergan Workshop 2002), 9.

86   Martha C. Nussbaum, *The Therapy of Desire* (Princeton, NJ: Princeton University Press, 1994), 481–82.

chapter 15

87   Parker Palmer, *Let Your Life Speak* (San Francisco: Jossey-Bass, 2000), 98.

88   Henri J.M. Nouwen, *In Memoriam* (Notre Dame: Ave Maria Press, 1980), 26.

89   Joseph Campbell, *The Power of Myth* (New York: Doubleday, 1988), 152.

90   Henri Nouwen, *Seeds of Hope* (New York: Image Books, 1997), 195.

91   Paul Geraghty, homily at the funeral liturgy of Patricia Sims, Montreal, Québec, December 26, 1992).

92   Ernest Becker, *The Denial of Death* (New York: The Free Press, 1973), ix.

93   Gustav Mahler, *Resurrection Symphony* (No. 2 in C Minor).

94   Julian of Norwich, *Julian of Norwich: Showings*, E. Colledge, J. Walsh, J. Leclerq, eds. (Ramsey, NJ: Paulist Press, 1978), 225.

chapter 16

95   Esther Harding, *Journey into Self* (New York: Longmans, Green and Co., 1956), 51.

96   Thomas Merton, *A Thomas Merton Reader* (New York: Harcourt, Brace & World, 1961), 182.

97   Calvin S. Hall and Vernon J. Nordby, *A Primer of Jungian Psychology* (New York: A Mentor Book, 1973), 90.

98   A.D. Sertillanges, O.P., *The Intellectual Life* (Netherlands: Bosch Utrecht, 1948), 92–93.

99   Sogyal Rinpoche, *The Tibetan Book of Living and Dying* (San Francisco: HarperSanFrancisco, 1994), 57.

100 Philip Simmons, *Learning to Fall* (New York: Bantam Books, 2002), 122–23.

101 Dag Hammarskjöld, *Markings* (New York: Alfred A. Knopf, 1964), 85.

102 Carl Jung, *Memories, Dreams, Reflections* (New York: Vintage Books, 1965), 191.

103 Harding, *Journey into Self*, 49.

chapter 17

104 Sebastian Moore, *The Inner Loneliness* (New York: Crossroads, 1982), 11.

105 Brian Swimme, *The Universe Is a Green Dragon* (Santa Fe: Bear & Company, 1984), 57.

106 Moore, *The Inner Loneliness*, 11.

107 Fyodor Dostoevsky, *Crime and Punishment* (New York: Oxford University Press, 1953), 526.

108 A.D. Sertillanges, O.P., *The Intellectual Life* (Netherlands: Bosch Utrecht, 1948), 56.

109 Etty Hillesum, *An Interrupted Life* (New York: Washington Square Press, Pocket Books, 1985), 100.

chapter 18

110 Ram Dass, *Grist for the Mill* (Berkeley: Celestial Arts, 1987), 98–100.

111 Marilyn Ferguson, *The Aquarian Conspiracy* (Los Angeles: J.P. Tarcher, 1980), 76.

112 Rosemary Haughton, *The Transformation of Man* (Springfield, MA: Templegate, 1967), 27.

113 Anthony De Mello, *The Way to Love* (New York: Doubleday, 1992), 87.

114 Brian Swimme, *The Universe Is a Green Dragon* (Santa Fe: Bear & Company, 1984), 147.

115 Stephen R. Covey, *The Seven Habits of Highly Effective People* (New York: A Fireside Book, 1990), 240–41.

116 Dalai Lama, *Beyond Dogma* (Berkeley: North Atlantic Books, 1996), 50.

117 Thomas Merton, *Gandhi on Non-Violence* (New York: New Directions, 1964), 24.

118 Dan Berrigan, *Portraits of Those I Love* (Eugene, OR: Wipf and Stock Publishers, 2007), 19–20. Reprinted by permission of Daniel Berrigan and Wipf and Stock Publishers, www.wipfandstock.com, ISBN 978-1-55635-472-4.

119 Charles Hefling, *Grace, Christ, Redemption, Lonergan* (Boston: Lonergan Workshop, 1997), 6.

120 Hefling, *Grace, Christ, Redemption, Lonergan*, 8.

121 Thomas Merton, *A Thomas Merton Reader* (New York: Harcourt, Brace & World, 1961), 305.

122 Thomas Merton, *Raids on the Unspeakable* (New York: New Directions, 1964), 47.

chapter 19

123 Deepak Chopra, *Quantum Healing* (New York: Bantam Books, 1989), 112, 114.

124 Brian Swimme, *The Canticle to the Cosmos* (Tides Center, 1991), video 1.

125 Swimme, *The Canticle to the Cosmos*, video 1.

126 Fritjof Capra, *The Web of Life* (New York: Anchor Books, 1996), 301.

127 Thich Nhat Hanh, *Peace Is Every Step* (New York: Bantam Books, 1992), 99.

128 Thomas Berry, *Ethics and Ecology* (Montreal: McGill University lecture, April 1994).

129 Swimme, *The Canticle to the Cosmos*, video 4.

130 Capra, *The Web of Life*, 302–03.

131 Teilhard de Chardin, *Hymn of the Universe* (New York: Collins, Fontana Books, 1970), 122.

132 Chief Dan George, *My Heart Soars* (Buffalo: Hancock House Publishers, 1974).

133 Pierre Elliot Trudeau, "Exhaustion and Fulfilment: The Ascetic in a Canoe," in *Wilderness Canada* (1970), edited by Borden Spears. (Originally published in French in *Jeunesse Étudiante Catholique*, November 1944.)

134 Brent George, in discussion with the author, March 2003.

135 Dan Juras, in discussion with the author, July 1997.

chapter 20

136 Joseph Campbell, *The Power of Myth* (New York: Doubleday, 1988), 150.

137 Gerald Heard, *An Anthology of Devotional Literature* (Michigan: Baker Book House, 1977), 727.

138 Ralph Evans, collection of personal reflections, October 1999.

139 Tony Walsh, open letter sent to the author, 1993.

140 Sogyal Rinpoche, *The Tibetan Book of Living and Dying* (San Francisco: HarperSanFrancisco, 1994), 199–200.

141 Loren Eiseley, adapted from "The Star Thrower," found in *The Unexpected Universe* (New York: Harcourt Brace Jovanovich, Inc., 1969), 67–92.